The North American
role in the Spanish
imperial economy
1760–1819

To our wives, Joan and Lourdes, without whom this work would have been immeasurably harder to produce.

The North American role in the Spanish imperial economy 1760–1819

edited by
JACQUES A. BARBIER *and* ALLAN J. KUETHE

MANCHESTER UNIVERSITY PRESS

Published by Manchester University Press
Oxford Road, Manchester M13 9PL
and 51 Washington Street, Dover,
New Hampshire 03820, USA

British Library cataloguing in publication data
The North American role in the Spanish imperial economy, 1760–1819.
  1. Spain—Colonies—Economic conditions. 2. Economic assistance,
  North America—Latin America
  I. Barbier, Jacques A. II. Kuethe, Allan J.
  330.98′001   F1410

Library of Congress cataloging in publication data
Main entry under title:
The North American role in the Spanish imperial economy, 1760–1819.
  Includes bibliographical references and index.
  1. North America—Commerce—Latin America—History—Addresses,
  essays, lectures. 2. Latin America—Commerce—North America—
  History—Addresses, essays, lectures.
  I. Barbier, Jacques A., 1944–   II. Kuethe, Allan J., 1940–
  HF3211.N67   1984   337.708   83-25643

ISBN 0-7190-0964-2

Printed in Great Britain by
Butler & Tanner Ltd, Frome and London

Contents

Acknowledgments

This book grew out of a symposium entitled: 'The North American role in the Spanish imperial economy, 1783–1825'; organized by Jacques A. Barbier as part of the Forty-Fourth International Congress of Americanists held in Manchester, England on September 5–10, 1982. The organizer takes this opportunity to thank the Executive Committee of the Congress and particularly John Fisher of the University of Liverpool for their invaluable help. Similarly, the financial assistance of the Social Sciences and Humanities Research Council of Canada is hereby acknowledged.

The symposium and the contributors to this volume benefited enormously from the participation of Herbert S. Klein of Columbia University as chairman and of John J. McCusker of the University of Maryland as commentator. The critique provided by John Coatsworth of the University of Chicago was also valuable, as were the reactions of the audience. The editors thank them, one and all.

Equal thanks must go to those whose contributions took place behind the scenes: to Lourdes Ramos Kuethe who translated the chapters which were originally submitted in Spanish; to Lynda deForest Craig who strove to keep all authors to uniform conventions; and to Joan Barbier who patiently typed. Their help was vital to the completion of the project.

Introduction

This work constitutes an attempt by several authors to come to a preliminary evaluation of the nature and significance of the North American role in the Spanish imperial economy in the late eighteenth and early nineteenth centuries. It is divided into four parts. The first concentrates upon the impact of North American penetration and example on Spanish colonial policy and Spanish American opinion. The second examines what direct and indirect commercial ties with the Iberian world meant to the North American economy itself. Because of the social and economic diversity of Latin America, the reverse case, the impact of such ties on the Spanish colonies as a whole, could not be readily presented. In the third part, however, we examine the Cuban case, the most striking illustration of Anglo-American Spanish–American symbiosis; while the fourth presents the experiences of two other circum-Caribbean colonies, Venezuela and Louisiana.

Part 1 sets out to establish the framework for subsequent discussion. In the first chapter, Jacques Barbier provides an explanation of the power relationships underlying the reformist legislation of Charles III and the attempts at crisis management of Charles IV. The thrust of the argument is that reform was based upon compromise between the interests of two distinct peninsular economies, compromise which could not readily be sustained in time of war. As reformism was worn away by crisis, the maintenance and implementation of priority policy objectives required outside help. At times the British enemy itself provided the required aid. Most often, however, that assistance came from the newly-independent United States, whose merchants and merchant fleet provided needed supplies and transport. Anglo-American opportunities, it is argued, derived as much from policy priorities as from natural advantages and any possible breakdown of the imperial command structure.

Chapter 2 provides a novel chronology, essential for understanding the period. The thrust of Peggy Liss's argument is that creoles knew more about the economy of the Atlantic world than has often been assumed. For Liss, the American Revolution contributed to the Spanish monarchy's financial problems and intensified creole desires for greater autonomy. The late 1780s and early 1790s were none the less a period of apparent cooperation as Spain launched a campaign of 'Unity and Equality' as a mask for its continued search for peninsular advantage, and as creoles (although increasingly identifying with New World, rather than empire-wide, interests) eagerly seized on the opportunities which reformist legislation provided for attempting to imitate Anglo-American economic growth. Charles IV's war with Great Britain, however, led the Crown to adapt ever more predatory policies, even as they forced the monarchy to open the Empire's doors to renewed North American penetration, with incalculable consequences in view of growing creole alienation and worship of material well-being.

Part 2 provides a statistical overview of the importance of the Spanish American trade to the United States and Canada in the late eighteenth and early nineteenth centuries. Of these, the more important region quantitatively is clearly that made up of what were once the Thirteen Colonies. Indeed, it now seems that the significance of this commerce to the United States has heretofore been underestimated. None the less, the Canadian case, as seen through the St Lawrence River Valley, is qualitatively interesting because of what it shows about mercantilism and dependency.

In Chapter 3 and its extensive appendix, Javier Cuenca provides a study of the United States' balance of payments with Spanish America in the 1790–1819 period. Despite fluctuations in trade volume produced by the vagaries of war and diplomacy, Cuenca finds that 'American' trading performance was extremely dynamic. Further, he implies that the favorable balance of payments in the Indies trade was a significant factor in the overall economic performance of the United States. Net surpluses with Spanish America appear to have covered at least nine-tenths of a sizeable net deficit with the rest of the world in 1790–1811. The war of 1812, of course, had adverse economic consequences. None the less, even considering the entire 1790–1819 period, net surpluses of 15.3 million dollars with the Indies helped to counterbalance an overall deficit with the rest of the world of 36.6 million dollars. For the United States, trade with Spanish America was a timely windfall which at times generated up to one-third of the carrying trade through United States' ports, and up to one-sixth of net customs receipts for the American government. It is ironic that, in the years of the most intensive Spanish American admiration for Anglo-American material progress, that well-being should have been based partly on the United States' profits from trade with its southern neighbors.

Fernand Ouellet's study of Lower Canadian overseas trade in Chapter 4 is significant because of the contrast it offers with the United States' economy. From Ouellet's study, it is evident that Lower Canada imported substantial quantities of products typical of the Iberian Peninsula and Latin America. At the same time, the exports of the St Lawrence River Valley included, at various times, the same items as were shipped from United States' ports. None the less, the wheat, fish and wood products of the region did not compete effectively in Caribbean and Mediterranean markets. The fact that Great Britain owned most of the shipping, and the continued effectiveness of the Navigation Acts, tied the colony to the United Kingdom. The mother country played the same entrepôt role towards Lower Canada as the United States aspired to play towards Latin America. The lesson would seem to be that although overseas trade was crucial to the colony's economic existence, instead of being a factor conducive to diversification and development as in the case of the United States, it produced mere growth.

In the period under consideration, United States' interests were more attracted to Cuba than to other Spanish American zones. The reasons for this preference were varied, ranging from geographical propinquity, through the natural attributes of the island, to the peculiar role it was called upon to play in the Spanish imperial economy. In any event, the primacy given Cuba was such as to justify the in-depth coverage of North American involvement in the insular economy which is provided in Part 3.

James Lewis's study, in chapter 5, of the origins of Anglo-American trade in Cuba, points to the importance of two factors: the wartime inadequacy of Spanish imperial supplies to the Havana market; and the favored position of the Thirteen Colonies, resulting from their domestic production of grains. The net impact of Anglo-American activities was to disrupt Spain's mercantilistic arrangements. Accordingly, North American merchants were expelled after the United States' war of independence. Both Cubans and Anglo-Americans had learned the benefits of reciprocal trade, however, so that the brief experience of 1780-5 proved to be but a rehearsal for the vaster operations destined to follow.

In Chapter 6 Linda Salvucci stresses the cultural flexibility required of those United States' merchants who were determined to operate in the Spanish American market. This implied, according to Salvucci, that they had to be prepared to build upon personal and family ties, engage in combines and monopolies, and operate in devious and corrupt ways.

Jacques A. Barbier's study in Chapter 7 of bills of exchange drawn on Spanish imperial treasuries stresses the degree of Anglo-American purchases of these instruments. For the Spanish empire the development of this trade signalled a fuller entry into the North Atlantic economy. For the United States it was a new source of profit and (presumably) of badly needed hard currency. In any event, in this, as in other respects, Anglo-American interests acted as the mid-wives in the birth of the new Spanish American economy, one more fully integrated into the world economy than before.

Of course, while the development of Anglo-American commercial relations with Cuba was in keeping with the general evolution of the world economy, such congruence does not of itself explain how such ties were established. Indeed, given the mercantilistic rigor underlying Bourbon reform legislation, one might well wonder what device allowed Cuba to develop intimate economic ties with the United States. In Chapter 8 Allan Kuethe finds that the roots of Cuban trading privileges were founded on its planter elite's relations at Court, and their significant military role. The latter, in particular, seems to have been a key element, and dated from the military reorganization carried out after the Peace of Paris of 1763. In return for a commitment to army and militia reform, the Cuban plantocracy received commercial privileges. It retained this advantageous position through the term of José de Gálvez as colonial minister (1776–1787) and on into the reign of Charles IV (1788–1808).

Part 4 presents two brief studies of the impact of Anglo-American trade in two other Spanish colonies: Venezuela and Louisiana. In Chapter 9 Manuel Lucena examines trade relations between the province of Caracas and the United States. In Lucena's view the year 1806 was peculiarly important because it saw the opening of La Guaira to foreign ships and thus the true end of colonial bondage, which was economic rather than political. In the years that followed the United States made deep inroads into Venezuelan trade, even as the roles of Spain and its colonies declined. This phenomenon increased the country's balance of trade deficit, and reoriented its economy away from cacao. Most significantly, it would seem from Lucena's figures that United States' merchants did best when dealing with a war-troubled colonial regime, rather than with an independence-minded one.

In the final chapter Jesús Lorente complements the studies of Cuba and Venezuela with an examination of Louisiana's trade with the United States from the independence of the latter to the annexation of the former. Again, this contribution stresses that Anglo-American opportunities derived from European war and that trade balances were grossly favorable to the United States. None the less, Lorente also concludes that the local economy benefited and that the understanding shown by colonial officials was a necessary precondition for the trade.

Overall, the present work is hardly to be considered as conclusive. None the less, the chapters combine to make several important points. The most critical are that the Anglo-American trade with Latin America was crucial to the economic performance of the fledgling United States, that trading opportunities derived from European wars and that political independence was a vital element in allowing the United States to take advantage of these opportunities and to break out of limitations induced by mercantilism. None of which, of course, negates the importance of Spanish American conditions. The power of local interests, the willingness of colonial officials to be understanding towards them and the Crown's need for commercial and shipping resources were all vital ingredients for North American success. In the final analysis it would seem that the dependent politics, social forms and economic structures of colonies combined with diplomatic circumstances to make Europe's surviving New World dependencies the oysters of the emergent United States' economy.

PART ONE
Penetration and example

CHAPTER ONE

Silver, North American penetration and the Spanish imperial economy, 1760–1800

1

Two distinct coalitions of interests dominated Spanish colonial policy-making in the late eighteenth century: the Court and peninsular cadres on the one hand, the entrepreneurial elites of Cadiz and the Spanish coast on the other. The first had an innate thirst for treasure shipments, the second an inherent need for trade. In the time of Charles III (1759–1788), fiscal and economic reforms combined to satisfy both coalitions. The literature, however, barely notes this balance. Rather, the Crown's need for specie is often taken for granted, whereas its novel economic policies are usually the subject of close scrutiny. In consequence, the politics of reform as they touched the interests of Cadiz and the coast are well understood. Those that relate directly to Madrid interests, save where foreign relations are involved, remain obscure.[1]

For the dominant groups of Cadiz and coastal Spain, the principal thrust of colonial policy had to be the maximization of returns from the Indies trade. Ultimately, policy makers were to pursue objectives favoring the development of the entire Spanish periphery: opening American markets, thereby stimulating metropolitan productive and finishing operations; increasing the output of colonial mining, ranching and agriculture, and so lowering peninsular manufacturing costs and increasing re-export volume; and, lastly, keeping at home the profits drawn from commerce and transportation. As is well known, however, the consulado of Cadiz, representing the traditional middle-men between European manufacturers and Spanish American consumers, fought reform tenaciously. None the less, while the importance of this struggle has been appreciated, its meaning has been misunderstood.

It is now clear that *comercio libre* did not cripple the port of Cadiz, which continued to dominate colonial trade.[2] In addition, there is reason to suspect that the increased trade volume of the late eighteenth century demonstrates less the rise of Spanish production than the continued re-export of European manufactures, a domain in which Cadiz remained dominant.[3] This is not to deny the stimulative effects of the new policies. The opening of colonial markets undoubtedly encouraged the development of manufacturing and agriculture in the peninsular 'outports'. The modest gains of these zones, however, were not at the expense of Cadiz, for the Indies trade had ceased to be a zero-sum game.

The essential moderation of Charles III prevented a decisive break between Cadiz and the monarchy. *Comercio libre* was applied only gradually. From 1765 to 1777 the new policy was extended experimentally only to Caribbean zones marginal to the Cadiz trade. In other areas the register ships (*navios de registro*) and traditional convoy (*flota*) continued to hold sway.[4] In 1778 a general regulation was issued but the crucial Veracruz market was exempted and the immediate impact was blunted by war.[5] Between 1784 and 1789, although *comercio libre* was nominally applied to Veracruz, special tonnage restrictions preserved some of the existing guarantees. Lastly, even after the removal of quantitative limitations, special rules regarding the Veracruz inter-colonial trade continued to restrict competition.[6] The conclusion is clear. Cadiz merchants were given ample time to adjust to the new legislation and the continued dominance of the port shows that it was as able to respond to stimulation as other harbors, drawing enough of the entrepreneurially-minded to sustain its position. By the reign of Charles IV, therefore, all of coastal Spain was united in defense of its exclusive access to colonial markets. Tension between the elite of Cadiz and those of other ports remained because of the former's greater dependence on foreign suppliers but for all of these groups the exclusivity of Spanish trade was the essential issue of colonial policy. The Court's concern with patriation of specie was, for them, a source of mixed feelings; representing a desirable objective in that it kept the state solvent at the expense of someone else but also causing occasional unease because the source of these surpluses was often monopolized items of trade and also because the currency drain could disorganize colonial economies.[7]

Just as Cadiz and the coast were one coalition of interests, the Court and cadres were another. The paramount aims of the latter alliance were the security of the state and the extension of its services (military, naval, judicial, fiscal). To meet these objectives a healthy level of Crown revenues was imperative but most were reluctant to sacrifice Old Regime privileges and structures to fiscal needs. The Spanish Enlightenment, in this as in other respects, proved to be a most conservative affair. The obvious solution was to obtain funds from outside through colonial treasure shipments and taxes on the protected Indies trade. It was understood, of course, that efficient administration was more likely to be effective than predatory policies. Thus, there existed a basis for lasting compromise between bureaucratic and business objectives. The difficulty, however, was that behind the institutional concerns of the cadres lay the economic interests of the court city of Madrid and of much of central Spain. In fact, a disproportionate share of state income was spent in the capital and that expenditure in turn generated an uncommon proportion of the productive activities of the peninsular heartland.[8] This situation ensured that in times of trouble, when difficult choices had to be made, the struggle to determine Crown policy would not be between the administrative cadres and the entrepreneurial elites, but between central and peripheral Spain. The struggle would be between two modes of economic life, and it would be a battle in which one contender ('sólo Madrid es Corte') was supremely well-armed.[9] In any case, when the issue became the solvency of the state, Court and cadres stood as one, invincibly, to protect the ultimate source of their wealth and ease.

Colonial policy was the fruit of peninsular debate. This is not to say, of course, that the Indies population had no role to play in government. Some interests were so situated as to be able to influence Madrid decisions directly, although this was rare. More importantly, colonials could affect the execution of policy at the local level and so modify its impact or compel alterations. This situation was traditional.[10] In Hapsburg times all sectors of American society enjoyed a limited capacity to corrupt or thwart imperial officials, a state of affairs which reached its peak under the first Bourbons.[11] In the second half of the eighteenth century, gradually, the chain of executive command strengthened and the coercive force of the state increased.[12] None the less, these Bourbon Reforms did not completely alter the empire's political culture. Colonial expectations remained as before and the burgeoning fiscal and military corps soon became new avenues of position and influence for the creole elites.[13] Still, stress increased throughout the system as the changes implied both alterations in local power structures and a new balance of force between the various colonial centers.

The latter phenomenon is particularly important for the present study. Indeed, the impact of the Bourbon Reforms varied from place to place. In some instances they served to endow previously backward areas with the socio-economic base and state institutions required to emancipate them from existing colonial centers. Such was the case in the Viceroyalty of New Spain, as Mexican hegemony was replaced by more even-handed relations between the core area and such outlying regions as Havana, Guatemala, the Philippines and the Internal Provinces. This growing multi-polarity, however, had important political consequences. As the reform effort did not emasculate the American elites, the new conditions increased inter-colonial rivalry. Indeed, in a system where the 'superior governments' continued to be swayed by the interests of their capitals, the weakening primacy of Mexico meant that the elites of outlying centers now influenced more powerful tools than heretofore.[14] To the degree possible, this influence was used to shelter the colonies against metropolitan measures, but it was also utilized to reorder fiscal and trade relations within the viceroyalty. In short, policy in these domains may have been set through center-periphery strife in Spain but its execution in the New World depended on the outcome of a complex struggle for control over colonial governments — a struggle pitting three distinct elements against each other: the force of metropolitan orders, the influence of local elites, and the fiscal and geographical realities of the zone.

In my 1980 pilot article, I showed how war increased fiscal pressures to unbearable levels, and demonstrated that from 1800 onwards the monarchy was prepared to sacrifice the trading interests of peripheral Spain to the Madrid region's need for solvency. American treasury became, once again, the lodestone of the peninsula's colonial policy. The decision to adopt this new course came as the outcome of a struggle between Madrid and the coast. Simultaneously, however, another struggle, one involving the execution of the evolving policy decision, had been going on in the colonies.

2

The reign of Charles IV of Spain (1788–1808), was a decisive period in Spanish peninsular life. Succeeding an adulated father, who had presided over reform, expansion and victory, the new monarch ruled over defeat and surrender. At last a deposed cuckold, his leave-taking signaled the start of foreign invasion and fratricidal war, events destined to destroy Spain's Old Regime and its imperial grandeur. In short it was a reign devoid neither of interest nor consequences.[15] Paradoxically, however, despite a growing body of literature, interpretive grasp and factual mastery remain elusive.[16]

In fact, the era of Charles IV is comprehensible only in terms of peninsular–colonial interaction. Because of the weight of colonialism, which nurtured powerful interest groups, colored developmental plans and alone kept Spain a great power, it is difficult to see how true understanding can be sought outside an imperial perspective. 'The lengthening shadow cast by the colonial issue over all aspects of decision-making' was noted by one authority a decade ago, as was the necessity of dealing with the reign of Charles IV within the perspective of 'the impact of the (French) Revolution and its aftermath of war on the most sensitive area of Spanish life, its colonial nexus'.[17] The passage of time has not reduced the value of that insight.

The history of colonial trade policy in the reign of Charles IV falls into easily defined periods. From 1788 until the fall of the Count of Floridablanca in 1792, policy initiatives largely consisted of measures designed to complete the edifice of reform.[18] The most salient measures of these years were, clearly, the extension of *comercio libre* to Venezuela and Mexico and the liberalization of slave trading legislation. The commercial policies which Floridablanca and his associates pushed were clearly mercantilist. They were designed to keep the Indies in a state of economic colonialism, and as such allowed little entry for foreign merchants or ships save where they could not be done without — as with the slave trade.

The palace coup of 1792 which saw the temporary return of the Count of Aranda to power, and prepared the way for the eventual supremacy of Godoy, of itself changed nothing.[19] Reformist elements remained dominant, as the widespread extension of consulados to previously unprivileged cities in the following years amply demonstrates. None the less, the start of war with

revolutionary France in 1793 signaled the start of changes which were ultimately to give North American merchants their chance to penetrate the Spanish
American market legally. Indeed, the well known efforts of the Crown to
resupply its Caribbean strongholds from the United States during this war,
together with slave trade legislation benign to foreigners, combined to bring
United States' ships back into Spanish American harbors in appreciable
numbers.

The true change in imperial policy, however, cannot be dated further back
than the start of war with Great Britain in 1796. This war, given the renewed
strength of the British in the face of the Franco-Spanish alliance, closed off
Spain's trade with the New World. Superficially, the interests of the Spanish
periphery would have been served by a policy of convoys, or of embargo, given
the inability of the Spanish navy to execute the former. In fact, either might
have preserved the colonial market for Spanish merchants, if at the price of
scarcities overseas. In the event, however, the Crown concluded that not all
coastal interests would have been served for a scarcity-driven resurgence of
colonial manufacturing industries could well be feared. Worse, royal officials
also had to be conscious of the fact that a temporary end to sailings would
hurt the economy of Central Spain, which was dependent on taxes on Indies
commerce and receipt of American tax-revenues. Lastly, the Spanish West
Indies and Venezuela could not survive without trade of some sort.

Madrid's response to the crisis came in a series of measures adopted at the
behest of Francisco de Saavedra.[20] Remission of funds to the peninsula by
means of bills of exchange, already general in Venezuela, was extended to the
rest of the empire. For the colonies as a whole a scheme of *comercio neutral*
from European ports was adopted. It was Saavedra's hope that the cheap
foreign goods such ships would bring, would bankrupt colonial manufacturers
and thereby clear the way, once peace was restored, for even greater peninsular
domination of Spanish American markets. The policy clearly hurt Cadiz interests, but held out to other Spanish coastal regions the hope of future gains
to make up for temporary losses. At the same time, as Saavedra would not
countenance granting equal treatment to United States' and European ports,
the chances of Anglo-American Spanish–American reciprocity were limited.

To such centrally-controlled responses to crisis, was added the possibility
of local options being exercised in Venezuela and the Spanish West Indies.
The obvious need of these zones for continuing trade to sustain their export-
based economies and maintain their naval and military forces imposed a degree
of flexibility. And, in any event, the influence of local elites was such as to
induce the local colonial administration to bend to their wishes in such a capital
matter. The result was that from 1797 onwards, Caribbean markets were
thrown open to Anglo-Americans simply because the Crown could offer no
alternative and consequently had to respect local policy-making.

On the whole, it can be said that up to 1799 the Spanish administration
carried out an orderly retreat to prepared positions. The retreat was

necessitated by military weakness. It was made tolerable by the belief that the temporary entry of foreign vessels into Indies ports would be inevitably followed by a tremendous increase in Spanish trade once peace was restored, and by the hope that the most dangerous foreigners, Anglo-Americans, would be restricted to a limited Caribbean zone. Cadiz was sacrificed, but the industrializing periphery somewhat saved. Most importantly, damage to the interest of central Spain was limited.

In 1799, however, the Spanish Ministry of Finance temporarily lost control of policy-formation as the consulado of Cadiz secured the abolition of *comercio neutral* on April 20, 1799, and managed to impose a rigid posture for some months thereafter.[21] The consulado achieved its success by gaining the ear of Minister of State Mariano Luis Urquijo, but it proved to be an evanescent victory.[22]

The fiscal needs of the monarchy no more allowed it to do without the service of foreign ships (see Chapter 7 below) than did the security problems of certain of its colonies, notably Cuba and Venezuela. In these colonies, the local governments delayed or sabotaged compliance with the order of April 20, 1799, and the Crown eventually accepted their attitudes. Protests from the consulado of Cadiz were stifled. More to the point, by placing the sale of government bills of exchange in the hands of the *Dirección General del Giro* of its General Treasury, Madrid ultimately signaled a momentous policy choice. Agents of that office proceeded to authorize trading expeditions by Anglo-Americans on the grounds that this was necessary to facilitate their exchange transactions.[23] To guarantee to central Spain the government revenues required by its command economy North American merchants and British manufacturers were to be given broad access to the trade of the empire. From 1801 onwards, fiscal priorities completely dominated trade policy-making. The balance between center and periphery had inevitably broken down and Anglo-Americans had become the informal partners of Madrid interests in their exploitation of the Spanish Indies.

3

The basic thesis presented here is that over the course of the reign of Charles III an alliance developed in matters of colonial policy between the interests of central and peripheral Spain. Economic growth in the colonies was to fuel the rise of Crown revenues to dizzying heights. The income was to pay for the elaboration of the state apparatus (and the resultant amplification of career opportunities), the confidence of rentiers, the commercial greatness of Madrid-related institutions, and in general for the viability of the economy of the region dependent upon the *corte y sitios reales*. At the same time the periphery's agricultural exporters and new manufacturers were to enjoy the benefit of the expanding colonial market and commercial interests were to profit from the marketing and re-export of the Indies' agricultural products. Lastly, even the old monopoly center, Cadiz, could prosper under the new dispensation, as it adapted to the profits to be made in marketing and re-exporting the increased production of Spanish America and as it learned how to adjust, through fraudulent and semi-legal means, to the reigning mercantilism.

In the colonies, in the meanwhile, the changes wrought by Bourbon policy were producing adaptive reactions in all colonial centers. These reactions, of course, were still in progress at the time of the death of Charles III. Indeed, further adaptations were to be impelled in the years following the culmination of the Bourbon Reforms during the first years of his son's reign. None the less, by the mid 1790s the role of colonial centers had been re-defined, a new set of relationships between government and economic interests had been established in each, so that the interests of colonial elites had become, or were becoming, homogenized once more with those of the Crown and metropole.

A new stasis, however, was not to be. Fiscal problems, foreshadowed by the American War, beginning during the struggle with revolutionary France, breaking over the government with the start of renewed strife with Great Britain, ultimately forced the peninsular alliance asunder and led the imperial government down a path which defrauded the ambitions of the periphery and of the colonies.[24]

Once finances were allowed to dominate all official thinking about colonial policy, those colonies which did not produce revenues were forced to begin to devise their own solutions to their economic problems. Worse, even in those colonies which did produce revenues economic life was integrated into that of its trading partners in peripheral Spain. The wartime disruption of trade with the peninsula seriously disrupted economic life and in many areas whole sectors were brought to the brink of ruin. They were to take their vengeance in 1808. Further, the need for money was now so great and the capacity to transport it on Spanish ships so limited that the Crown resorted to throwing even Mexico open to British and North American trade as a device for the patriation of funds. Although the evidence remains inconclusive, it may well be that this desperation ruined Mexican-oriented industries causing the dislocation which provided the cannonfodder for the Hidalgo rising of 1810.

In conclusion, this explicative scheme is one which places the interests of cities at the forefront of political strife in late colonial Spain and Spanish America. Within the cities, creole and peninsular economic elites met with the fiscal, judicial and military cadres to work out arrangements of mutual benefit. In this they were not entirely free for they had to take into account the power of the spokesmen of other centers, not the least of which was the king. Such a scheme, I believe, accounts better for observed behaviour than analyses which depend more upon class or small groups to provide the explicative framework.

CHAPTER TWO

Creoles, the North American example, and the Spanish American economy, 1760–1810

A close look at the existing literature works its own revision of some accepted ideas of inter-American relationships between 1760 and 1810. It is clear that creoles had more concurrent information, including economic, on Anglo-America before, during and after the Revolution of 1776 than has been assumed. There were in Spanish America more people wise in the economic way of the Atlantic world than generally thought, and those same people were often influential in the course of internal affairs in the late eighteenth and early nineteenth centuries and in events and decisions leading to the movement for separation from Spain. My *Atlantic Empires: The Network of Trade and Revolution, 1713–1826* (Baltimore, Johns Hopkins University Press, 1983) considers the broader international context of these relationships. Here I will focus on creole attitudes and activities, current bibliography, the state of some key questions, and offer some suggestions for avenues to explore.

1

The Bourbon reform program in Spanish America began in earnest with the Seven Years' War. It was given urgency by the British capture and occupation of Havana and by two consequences of the British presence: the highly visible prosperity that port then enjoyed and the increased economic and commercial contacts that necessarily resulted between Cubans and Anglo-Americans. Men from the Thirteen Colonies had been instrumental in taking Havana for Britain.[1] As Franklin W. Knight has explained, the Cuban elite then began its great development of sugar and the Cuban economy its ties to what would become the United States.[2] Allan J. Kuethe (Chapter 8 below) tells us more about that elite.

Mexicans felt the effects of Havana's capture in ways not yet sorted out. James A. Lewis (Chapter 5 below) speaks of Cuba's turning to North America for wheat. Was there a connection between this trade and, first, Puebla's inability to supply Havana, and, secondly, Michoacan's encroaching upon

Puebla's wheat market? Further, did this situation bear on the anti-Spanish, pro-British outbursts reported to be occurring in Puebla? There in 1766, as Nancy Farriss mentioned, a creole priest was denounced to the Inquisition for publicly declaring, 'we would be better off with the English than the gachupines'.[3] And that year also rumors reached the government of a conspiracy afoot there, involving disgruntled aristocrats, merchants and clergy seeking commercial and economic advantages they thought would come through an alliance with Britain.[4] Francisco Javier Clavijero, in his *Descripción de la ciudad de la Puebla de los Angeles o Angelopolis*, addressed the problem of depression in his home region, and in other tracts the more general problem of Mexican commerce.[5] These writings indicate that some early prime interests of Clavijero were regional, economic and commercial. This is not so surprising when, as Edith Couturier has pointed out, his father, Blas, had contracts to provision garrisons and ships.[6] Can we connect all this to the accentuation among creoles of certain feelings toward England and its North American colonists: admiration for economic and commercial abilities, some desire for commercial relations, and dismay at Spanish American competitive disadvantage whose root cause they believed to be imperial policies?

Not only did British North American ties with Cuba endure after 1763, as the essays by Lewis and Kuethe affirm, but creoles in Venezuela and down the Atlantic coast came to have contact with Yankees, as shown by Manuel Lucena Salmoral (Chapter 9 below). In 1774 Aaron Lopez of Newport sent 30 ships to the Falklands-Malvinas for whale oil.[7] In view of recent events, it is interesting to note that while England removed its garrison from those islands in that year, its subjects — especially its North American colonists — and, afterwards, seamen from the new United States, continued to go on using them as a whaling, sealhunting and refitting base up to and beyond the confrontation of such people in 1831 with the governor sent out from independent Buenos Aires.[8]

Throughout Spanish America in the 1760s and 1770s creole landowners, mineowners, merchants, clergy and people in the professions and the bureaucracies were aware of new books on English colonial government, economy and trade, and acquired some of them, as Mexican Inquisition papers reveal. And, for example, the Chilean, José Antonio Rojas, shipped home from Spain in the early 1770s crates of books, including new, anonymous, works on Britain's America and sets of Raynal, 'this divine man', who devoted much space to the institutions, economy, and society of the Thirteen Colonies.[9] In addition, Luis Miguel Enciso Recio has stated in introducing his compilation of *'La Gaceta de Madrid' y 'El Mercurio Histórico y Político, 1776–1781'*, that those gazettes had wider circulation in America than in Europe. They reported on Anglo-American complaints from 1765, riots in Boston against the Stamp Act, appeals for permission to manufacture, and denunciations of the Navigation Acts. Among other observations, the *Mercurio* commented that the Stamp Act had as a most salutary effect the non-importation movement, which stimulated production of manufactures in the colonies and did no harm to agriculture: 'Industry and frugality reign today in all the [British mainland] colonies with an emulation so patriotic' that everyone tries to make more textiles and clothing.[10] Contact with British wares and tenets of political economy and with Anglo-American premises and products was also ongoing, and mounting, by way of Spain.

2

The American Revolution of 1776, we are learning, had a good deal of impact on creoles and on the economies of their regions. That impact was economic, commercial and ideological, and it had political and social ramifications. First, Spain's aid to the Continental Congress — arms, military stores and credit — arrived chiefly through New Orleans and Havana, often, ostensibly for purposes of security, intermeshed with private commercial transactions. James Lewis has explained the workings of a loan by *habaneros* which abetted victory at Yorktown.[11] His paper here adds depth and breadth to that account. We know that an international, even multinational, commercial and financial web involved the master spider, Robert Morris of Philadelphia, other leaders of the American Revolution, Spaniards, Frenchmen and some future leaders of Spanish American independence movements, notably Francisco de Miranda (who was in Cuba in these years and in correspondence with Simón Bolívar's brother, Juan Vicente).[12]

After 1776, in Franklin Knight's words, the United States became Cuba's largest trading partner. James Lewis writes of the impact on Cuba. Forrest McDonald offers the other side: 'Havana was such a good market for American wheat that many felt it had saved the United States' economy during the hardest war years'.[13] And, as Javier Cuenca shows (Chapter 3 below) this was merely the start of Latin America's crucial role for the United States' economy. North American ships also participated in Cuba's trade with Campeche, carrying to that island, called by Alexander von Humboldt 'the crossroads of empire' and certainly a major imperial emporium, salt meat from Venezuela and Buenos Aires. Knight, Lewis and Kuethe make clear that the years of the American Revolution, 1779–1783, also mark the initial impulse to Cuban economic expansion, that wealthy and well-placed creoles there were not reluctant to engage in trade, to innovate, or to push technical development and that they had a special relationship with both Spain and the United States.

A Spanish official, Ramón Posada, the *fiscal* for the treasury in the Mexican audiencia, joined José de Gálvez's special envoy, Francisco de Saavedra, in warning of the harmful impact of the American Revolution on the imperial economy of Spanish America. Their solution was greater liberty of overseas commerce and of trade within and among Spanish American regions. Thus, Saavedra criticized the cutting out of Mexican planters and mule-owners by official restrictions on internal trade in grains, and opposed hindrances to interregional trade of wheat. Posada concurred and added that such restraints enriched 'a neighbor powerful at its birth', allowing *los bostoneses* to exchange grain at Havana for over three million pesos in silver.[14]

Venezuelans and their intendants welcomed United States' wheat and flour; they did not, as did Mexicans, suffer from North American competition. Rather, they exchanged with Anglo-Americans cacao, hides, indigo, and, less happily, specie. It is no coincidence that by 1777 one *caraqueno*, José Ignacio Moreno, a priest, professor and man of means (he owned haciendas, slaves, scientific instruments, a library and a journeyman press), greatly admired some principles of the revolution to the north. His commonplace book has been found. It contains copies of the proclamations made in 1774 and 1775 by the Continental Congress in Philadelphia. They included economic complaints of British threat to American commerce and American need for markets. Moreno's country house adjoined that of the Bolívars.[15]

Spanish authorities commenting on the growth of creole unrest in these years and its causes found that prominent among them was the British American example. Thus in 1778 the Captain General in Havana, Navarro, informed the Mexican viceroy, Bucareli, that in Veracruz people were speaking of following North American precedent. Bucareli replied that he was aware of the threat.[16] Saavedra reported much the same thing from Mexico, that Spain's tender treatment of Anglo-American rebels as well as the inundation of new foreign books were important factors in 'making a species of revolution in creoles' modes of thinking'.[17] We should put within this context Humboldt's remark that after the Peace of Versailles creoles preferred to say 'I am not a Spaniard; I am an American'.[18]

Ella Dunbar Temple has published a facsimile edition of *La Gaceta de Lima* for 1776. It contains several discussions of the course of the war and its high cost to Britain. One piece explained the opposition to a parliamentary bill to defray war costs on the basis that such imposts weighed on commerce and caused artisans to emigrate. The author also wrote of 'the American party'.[19] That year the Bourbon reforms were extended to Peru. Thus, they were introduced in South America during a time when the onset of war against Britain caused a drain on the Spanish treasury, bringing inflation and a greater squeeze on the colonies. By 1781 that confluence of circumstances contributed in Peru to the revolt of Túpac Amaru and in New Granada and Venezuela to the rebellion of the *Comuneros*. To essentially economic grievances indirectly connected to the American Revolution, must be added the more direct impact of what José de Abalos, intendant of Venezuela, described as 'the sad and lamentable rising in the United States of North America'.[20] Abalos warned that the Revolution of 1776 was subverting creoles in his jurisdiction, and a senior military official in Peru reported that a number of *limenos* and *cuzquenos*, opposed to higher taxes and influenced by the North American example, supported Tupac Amaru.[21] From New Granada the viceroy,

Manuel Antonio Florez, informed José de Gálvez that 'news of the independence of the English colonies of the north goes from mouth to mouth among everyone in the uprising'.[22] John Leddy Phelan concluded that creoles drew up the *capitulaciones de Zipaquirá*. These protests included seven articles concerning commerce. They called for free trade and simplified duties, with the proceds to be spent at home, and they suggested deep discontent among merchants and planters with new Bourbon measures. Their authors wanted effective home rule even if in the King's name.[23] Francisco de Miranda later wrote that this document had combined with events northwards to influence him greatly in 1781 (he was then in Havana):

When I realized on receiving the *capitulaciones de Zipaquirá* how simple and inexperienced the [Spanish] Americans were and on the other hand how astute and perfidious the Spanish agents had proved, I thought it best to suffer for a time in patience until the Anglo-American colonies achieved their independence, which was bound to be ... the infallible preliminary to our own.[24]

The American Revolution contributed to Spain's double bind: the confluence of the costs and the dislocations of war and reform. These, in combination with the triumph and the prosperity of the new republic, intensified among creoles a desire for greater autonomy and promoted a new awareness of America as a unique, distinct, and universally esteemed entity.

3

By the 1780s the Industrial Revolution had become a factor in world trade. A large part of the cargoes reaching Spain and Spanish America on United States' ships were re-exported English textiles. American flour was another. Latin Americans in Cuba, Buenos Aires, Venezuela and Santo Domingo received these shipments by way of Spain or directly, legally and otherwise. There was American commerce too at New Orleans and along the borderlands. Smuggling flourished as never before. While the bulk of United States' trade was with the Caribbean and Gulf areas, contraband, carried by whalers, seal hunters, and China traders, was reaching the west coast of South America. Pelts and specie for the China trade were gathered along Spanish American coasts.[25]

Spanish American economic growth in many regions spurred the desire for export opportunities and cheap labor. In New Granada more labor was sought for mining gold, in Cuba and Peru for sugar, in Venezuela for cacao, and in La Plata and Chile for the hide industry and domestic service.[26] We still need information on the slave trade, particularly on the nature and scope of North American participation. We do know that with peace in 1783 creoles welcomed a surge of all sorts of imports. Then within two years markets for products were glutted, export difficult and specie dissipated. The experience of boom and bust caused mutual recriminations among peninsular-associated

and other merchants, numerous propertied creoles, and governing authorities.[27] In this period, too, Miranda began plotting in London, joined by
other Spanish American dissidents.

Internal growth and antiquated marketing structures fueled the impulse
of leading creoles to take charge of regional economies, and the government
then showed a disposition to cooperate. While Spain's immediate postwar
policy was a continuation of prewar goals, the official tone altered, for the
government was more defensive and needier, and it calculatingly emphasized
cooperation between Spain and creoles in American defense, internal development and imperial exchange. Thus, ministers hoping to use American raw
materials in peninsular manufactures presented this process as one of mutual
benefit to Spaniards and creoles. They also took pains to show restraint in
American taxation and to bind the colonies through appeals to self-interest.
Americans were exhorted to build up their regions for the benefit of the organic
nation and its peoples on both sides of the Atlantic. As José de Gálvez wrote
to Saavedra, then intendant of Caracas, in 1785: Americans should be made
to feel they 'have influence in their own happiness'.[28] Here was the genesis
of what, in 1787, was articulated as a policy of unity and equality.

Jacques Barbier has seen that policy as 'designed to reassure vested interests
[in America], while continuing to readjust the imperial balance even further
in the Peninsula's favor'.[29] By 1787, as Stanley and Barbara Stein have
outlined, it was clear that though Spain's trade with America had mounted
so had contraband and that Spain could not supply the colonies with its own
manufactures.[30] Two aspects of the old system, freer trade and the shipping
of American specie to Spain, then gained new importance. In 1789 the Crown
extended 'free' trade to Veracruz and Caracas and established an open slave
trade to the Spanish colonies.[31] Throughout the 1780s and 1790s creoles
received cooperation from the authorities in founding new economic or
patriotic societies (the interchangeable use of those adjectives is instructive)
and consulados and gazettes as well. Spanish Americans responded affirm-
atively but increasingly their emphasis was American, not imperial, and their
model for development was the United States.

The difficult but heady times from 1789 to 1793 presented the possibilities
of greater wealth and position to some ambitious, risk-taking Americans of
talent and property. From La Plata hides and wheat continued to be profitably
exported, often by slavers. Pre-eminent in this business was the audacious
Tomas Antonio Romero who outtraded the old monopolists, had close
relations with viceroys and dealt directly with Boston. He used the new freedom
of trade to traffic in blacks as a front for contraband.[32] In Mexico the
viceroy, the Conde de Revillagigedo, reported that 'free' trade had resulted
in brisk contrabanding involving Mexican merchants and that the new
American republic was presenting creoles with both a highly visible model of
prosperity and much competition. That nation, he went on, had better
roads and ships, and it profited from a harder-working populace devoted to

frugality and endowed with better farming equipment and more economic sense[33]

In 1788 José Alzate's *Gazeta de Literatura*, sponsored by the viceroy in line with court policy, aired the developing vogue for political economy and made admiring references to Benjamin Franklin and the scientific awareness of Anglo-Americans. One article by José Mariano Mocino, a creole member of Malespina's scientific expedition, concluded that New Spain was at the mercy of foreign industry and urged reform. Alzate himself proposed Mexicans have their own fleet in order 'to activate commerce'.[34]

More radical was the creole corregidor of Zipaquirá, the site of the *Comunero*'s treaty with colonial authorities. He was Pedro Fermín de Vargas, a contributor to the new *Papel Periódico* and an associate of the botanical expedition headed by José Celestino Mutis. In 1790 Vargas urged regional reforms and that the United States be visited to learn about bettering agriculture and commerce and increasing population. He also wrote a tract, a *Dialogo entre Lord North y un filósofo*, in which the philosopher saw free trade as the key to achieving international harmony and domestic well-being. He lamented to Lord North the war between England and its colonies. England should have freed them, he said, then made alliances with their inhabitants and he recommended all European nations with dominions in America follow that procedure. Vargas' message was independence, his exemplar was the United States. In 1791 he fled to Philadelphia on the proceeds from selling his large library.[35] His friend, Antonio Nariño, whose career is better known, bought it. Nariño's models were North American and French, his thrust political and constitutional. Even so, in 1797 Nariño, too, in a plan he presented to New Granadan authorities, stressed the primacy of economic development.[36]

Most of all, the French revolutionary era witnessed a heightened creole sense of popular entitlement and a renewed tendency to view monarchy as properly constitutional. But these years also, as Nariño's opinions indicate, reaffirmed for creoles the desirability of emulating the United States, not France. As Miranda later instructed Pedro Gual: 'Two great examples lie before our eyes, the American and the French revolutions. Let us discreetly imitate the first; let us carefully avoid the disastrous effects of the second'.[37]

The royal emphasis on unity and equality fed sentiments of *criollismo* imbued with a new activism and the post-revolutionary progress of the United States provided a pattern for development. Americanism and, within it, regional patriotism, mounted. Thus a founder of one literary society felt it his duty in 1793 to inform the government in Lima that such conclaves were arousing too much patriotic enthusiasm. Conversations, he reported, constantly returned to admiration of the new American republic: 'In fact, nothing else is discussed by the educated and the unlettered in gatherings and conversations'.[38]

When Spain went to war with France, from 1793 to 1795, a result was more trade (both licit and contraband) between the United States and Spanish America, especially New Orleans, the Floridas, and Santo Domingo. (The Mississipi was opened in 1795). Again facing expenses of war, Spain turned with renewed enthusiasm to economically-oriented creole self-help programs and to draconian measures designed to extricate immediate revenues from America. One effect was to sensitize colonials to the ambiguous nature of their situation. Still, the new economic societies, consulados and gazettes provided creoles with forums to air their dissatisfactions and develop opinions. Thus in Guatemala the American-born *oidor*, Jacobo de Villaurrutia, who was a founder of the economic society and its periodical, proposed more trade with the United States as a means of securing necessary imports and foreign sales.[39]

In Havana the founder of its *Sociedad de Amigos del Pais*, Francisco de Arango y Parreño, sought with a good deal of success to establish regular trade with the United States. Like other planters and merchants, he understood that both Cubans and the Crown could profit through more open trade — the Crown through greater revenues, Cubans by acquiring more slaves, selling more tropical products, notably sugar, and turning Havana into an imperial emporium.[40] In Buenos Aires the new secretary of the consulado, Manuel Belgrano, fired by a vision of imperial partnership, compiled economic reports and drew up the well-known *representación* to the Crown of 1793, certain as he was that his personal and patriotic intentions were in harmony with those of 'an enlightened minister like [Diego] Gardoqui, who has lived in the United States'.[41]

4

Jacques Barbier has outlined Spanish policies behind the orders of 1797 which opened imperial trade to neutral carriers. The new directive was impelled by war with Britain. It came, to some extent, after the war primarily benefited North Americans. Saavedra, an architect of these policies, pursued them quite consciously. He looked forward to cheap imports killing colonial industry so that with peace Spain could dominate American markets, but the time never came. In addition, neutral trade was also designed to enable Spain to finance its war, for by that year the Crown was issuing to its better-connected creditors bills of exchange on American treasuries. Foreign ships were vital for carrying necessary supplies, for ensuring capital flow and to enable the bill of exchange trade to attract investors.[42]

From 1797 great shipments of North American flour came to Havana where large, legitimate regular cargoes had come most recently by way of Spain. United States' ships supplied the bulk of Caribbean food imports and did business with Venezuelan ports, Cartagena, the Rio de la Plata and the Pacific coast. In 1798 the Mexican press reported most ships into Veracruz were North American.[43] The situation after 1793 recurred: market gluts of imports once again dampened expectations and products for export piled up. Creole reaction this time, however, was intensified by other sources of tension. In Caracas, wholesalers, who wanted United States' ships to carry out cacao and to bring in flour, other provisions, and naval stores, but who also demanded a stop to their import of British textiles, argued in the consulado with planters who saw no advantage in regulating the flow of dry goods.[44] In New Spain merchants associated with United States' shippers profited and Veracruz supplanted Mexico City as the commercial capital of the viceroyalty. In Guatemala Villaurrutia continued to side with planters in a quest for freer commerce and particularly for opening legitimate trade with the United States, implicit was the galling example of Cuba's closer and more open relationship with North America and its consequent prosperity.[45]

In Chile the secretary of the consulado, José de Cos Iriberri, complained in 1798 of exports backing up and of the economy stagnating and ultimately falling under the control of British and North American merchants. He proposed a Chilean-run trading company, the protection of domestic agriculture and embryonic industries and that Chilean residents be given the right to determine the country's economic policies free of Lima, Buenos Aires and Cádiz.[46] Cos was a Spaniard residing in Chile. Such cases, of course, demonstrate that we should know more about commercial alliances than we do and lead us to suspect that borders between creoles and certain *peninsulares* were vague.

Some enterprising and adventurous creoles turned to more speculative trade. The Guatemalan merchant, Juan Bautista Irisarri, sold indigo in Philadelphia, then sent a frigate from there laden with clothing for Chile. His son would settle in the latter country and become a force in its commerce and public life.[47] In Buenos Aires Tomás Antonio Romero, who had out-traded the old monopolists since the 1780s, continued to deal with Boston and Newport and to use trade in blacks as a front for contraband. He and other *porteños* also patronized local shipyards, ordered vessels from New England and became part of an international commercial network, engaged in legitimate and contraband exchange, which included North Americans.[48] In Cartagena Ignacio de Pombo headed a highly successful, many-branched, export–import firm. He founded the city's economic society, sat on its consulado, scanned gazettes from all over Spanish America and from Philadelphia and Charleston, and he underwrote scientific projects for developing the resources of New Granada. Pombo spoke of the United States with great admiration, as a nation which, by simple and just means and by farming and trade, had rapidly achieved power and greatness, wealth and public felicity. He wanted commercial alliances with that paragon 'in order to brake the despotism of the English'.[49] Did he do business with North Americans and find the British on Trinidad and Jamaica strong competitors? Investigations of the trading networks of Romero, Irisarri, Pombo, and probably of other creole entrepreneurs and of the Murphys in Veracruz would tell us a good deal more about Spanish American history within an international context.

In 1800 legitimate Spanish American exchange with the United States reached a new high. In the first decade of the nineteenth century, with Spain mostly at war with England, that trade continued to prosper. Even so, imports were often either scarce or overabundant and exports equally sporadic at a time when Spanish American output of agricultural products rose. Planters and merchants repeatedly complained of their products piling up and rotting on the docks and they saw as causes insufficient carriers, lack of markets (and marketing), and, in some regions, growing United States' competition. In 1791 New Spain had exported six times as much cotton as had the United States. By 1805 Mexicans recognized that the United States had taken a substantial lead. Mexican exports of cotton, wheat and sugar, as well as mining, suffered in the early 1800s from a combination of Anglo-American competition, Havana's rise at the expense of Veracruz, British blockade, the use of the cotton gin in the United States, Spain's policies, specie drain and debility. Not surprisingly, a large sugar and cotton grower would lead the movement deposing the viceroy. In addition more open foreign trade and the effects of other royal policies after 1800 contributed to depressing further much of the inter-regional trade in Spanish American products.[50]

It was in this atmosphere that the economic and, increasingly, political arrangements of the United States became more appealing to creoles. And propaganda seeped in advocating both, strongly and effectively. Miranda abetted the distribution in America of the *Carta a los americanos españoles* of the former Jesuit, Pablo Viscardo. That tract owed a good deal to Thomas Paine's *Common Sense* and it was soon circulating among creoles in Venezuela and Mexico. Viscardo scoffed at Spain's claim to have fostered unity and equality. He extended to both hemispheres Paine's observation that nature had separated America from Europe by immense seas and he pressed for independence: the English colonies of America 'have ceded us the palm'. The liberty they now enjoy so gloriously 'covers with shame our indolence'. His vision of a new free era ended on a economic crescendo: 'What an agreeable spectacle the coasts of America will present, covered with men of all nations exchanging their products for ours. They will come too to settle and enrich us with their hard work ... America will be a great family of brothers'.[51]

Viscardo's *Carta* contained no isolated message. In those same years, creole spokesmen and gazettes revealed an increasing sophistication about Spanish American relations with both the imperial economy and the United States. Thus, in Buenos Aires in 1802, the new *Telégrafo Mercantil* noted the interdependence of producers and merchants and urged exporting in *porteño*-owned ships and promoting finishing industries. The United States, it suggested, should be emulated in its exporting of wheat and flour, and master tanners should be brought from there to abet Argentine industry.[52] In Chile Manuel de Salas, in 1804 a leading member of the consulado, was among those requesting more authority to direct the development of their region and to distinguish between varieties of free trade. Those *chilenos* protested United

States' contraband and criticized most severely the type of commercial liberty Spain imposed. Salas complained that Chile had too much trade. And, in 1805, his letter to Belgrano attested to creole understanding of the decline of royal policy into *realpolitik*: 'The hope of reform having disappeared', he wrote, 'there has come to substitute for it the execution of a fiscal project'.[53]

A catalyst in the development of creole attitudes toward North America and toward the imperial system was Alexander von Humboldt. On his travels through Spanish America Humboldt conversed with like-minded creoles, people who were imbued with a world view including many assumptions derived from enlightened precepts and from the principles of political economy. Humboldt himself viewed the United States as an American prodigy and its growth in population, agriculture and industry as an example of unfettered progress. He also warned the Spanish government that creoles were greatly taken with its example.[54] His stay in Mexico is well known. Less noted is his visit to Pombo in Cartagena, to the Marqués de Selva Alegre in Quito and his conversations with the savant, Hipólito Unanue, in Lima. Interestingly, Unanue in turn corresponded with Dr Samuel Mitchell of New York who, in his preface to DePons' account of Venezuela evidenced his scale of values in stating, 'to many it may be a recommendation that the author writers more like a man of business than a man of science'.[55]

Two interrelated measures afoot in 1804 and 1805 exposed Spain's preoccupation with siphoning American wealth, showed Spain's program of unity and equality to be a sham and soured patriotic creoles on the imperial connection. They were: the *consolidación* or sequestration decree, well-documented and chiefly applied in Mexico and the silver transfer scheme, also centered on New Spain, the numerous pieces of which are still not fitted into a full picture. The *Caja de Consolidación*, acting as a form of central bank, was, at least, the funnel for both programs.[56] Their connections need exploring. In addition, we need to know more about the flow out of Mexico of the funds collected through the sequestration program. Did they become part of the silver transfer to France, and possibly to Britian, by way of the United States? What is the full history of the relationship between government debt from the 1770s and 1780s and the silver transfer? What roles did creoles play in this international, indeed multinational, scheme?

Linda Salvucci has told us more (Chapter 7 below) about the activities of some of the merchants involved in the Mexican transfer, and she and Lucena about the dealings of this group in Venezuela. As DePons noted, and scholars have begun to detail, in the early 1800s Venezuela was the hub of intense activity within an international network. Glimpses of its workings have been provided by Barbier, Harold Bierck and Humberto Tandrón. Involved centrally were John Craig, the Philadelphia merchant, and the Olivers of Baltimore. They brought in wheat, flour, textiles and slaves, within some sort of monopoly arrangement with the government, sometimes in ships under other flags.[57]

In the same period, Mexicans complained bitterly of the recall of certain church mortgages by the *Caja de Consolidación* and they knew that the silver thereby secured was being funneled out of the country through a multinational arrangement made by the Spanish government. It is quite possible that this multinational scheme affected Cartagena where in 1806 and 1807 an English warship took on specie. There Ignacio Pombo, in an *informe* to the consulado meant for the viceroy, reacted to the unholy alliance of Spanish officials and monopolists, Napoleonic bankers and British politicians and merchants, by appealing to the United States as a prototype for New Granada and suggesting a commercial alliance with it.[58]

We do know that trade between Latin America and the United States peaked from 1806 until Jefferson's embargo took effect in late 1808.[59] In 1806 the Chilean consulado complained that North American captains had an 'enormous propensity to contraband'.[60] Buenos Aires dominated much of the trade of the Río de la Plata, Chile and Peru, and its entrepreneurs dealt with North American merchants and used ships and captains from the United States. At least one entrepreneur had dealings with John Stoughton, then liberally issuing letter-patent in his capacity as a Spanish consul in the United States.[61] It was in 1806, possibly at the urging of some anti-French *norte-americanos*, that Sir Home Popham of the British navy invaded Buenos Aires, and in 1807 the English also took Montevideo. During the occupation, however, while more United States' vessels came into port, British traders and imports triumphed. None the less, it was the United States form of government that *portenos* smarting under conquest first thought to emulate.[62]

5

By 1808, creole grievances were substantial and United States' economic progress and political arrangements had become inseparable in creole minds. Even so, in some areas creoles also feared United States' competition in exports overseas and American territorial designs, an expansionism they saw as not unmixed with economic and commercial interest. Fray Servando Teresa de Mier, an ideologue of independence, for example, voiced these mixed sentiments in 1807. So did other creoles, including members of the cabildo of Veracruz. In the summer of 1808 that cabildo also spoke out for developing interior trade, manufacture and self-sufficiency: 'This is the only way to attain our independence'.[63] Its members, as did many creoles throughout Spanish America, viewed politics and economics as inseparable, as had exponents of political economy from the middle of the eighteenth century on, and they saw independence as involving both. Members of the Caracas consulado, which by 1810 was a center of pro-independence sentiment, were furious in 1805 at Spain's granting John Craig's son-in-law, Francisco Caballero Sarmiento, a monopoly on overseas trade and so the control of the country's economy.[64] In Bogotá, a *junta* spokesman, Ignacio de Herrera, urged the abolition of monopolies and protection of New Granadan commerce and industry. His colleague and mentor, Camilo Torres, advocated the United States as a model for government and he blamed Spain for Spanish America's poor position within the world economy, for, as he said, American gold being 'buried in Indostan'.[65] And in 1810 when Torres explained the reasons for the junta's call for a constitutional electoral assembly it came down to the failure of the Bourbon reforms to bring economic well-being. Spain's commercial monopoly, he recounted, had been breached only by contraband and had isolated the Spanish dependencies economically and regionally until the eighteenth century, when Spain had had to diversify colonial economies in order to expand its own trade. Economic barriers in European markets and Spain's incapacity to supply its colonies with manufactures had doomed the reforms, making it necessary for Americans now 'to resume the rights of sovereignty'.[66] Cubans, on the other hand, prospering and opposed to abolition of the slave trade, still preferred the old imperial tie.

By 1810, political economy more than anything else was the Bible of creole *juntistas*. If the United States was then viewed ambivalently and later in the century came to be seen as a Caliban of materialism, it was that very quality of material advance that enchanted creole leaders in the late colonial period. They saw the imperial system as bankrupt and material prosperity as indissolubly mixed with constitutionalism, republican ideals and patriotism, and as leading to social well-being. Our understanding of the causes and nature of Spanish American revolutions needs revising, as does our grasp of the ramifications of relations of creoles with both Spain and North America in the last half-century before those movements.

PART TWO
Statistical overview

CHAPTER THREE

The United States balance of payments with Spanish America and the Philippine Islands, 1790–1819: estimates and analysis of principal components

From the rise of the United States as a major international carrier in the 1790s to the formulation of the Monroe doctrine in the early 1820s, trade with the Spanish Empire played multifaceted and often vital roles. For the United States, this trade was regarded as a valuable source of badly needed specie to cover deficits with the Far East and elsewhere.[1] For the Spanish American colonies, trade with the northern neighbor helped erode the mother country's commercial monopoly and served as a catalyst for the eventual breakdown of the empire. For Spain itself, the United States was the largest carrier of Spanish and foreign commodities during two naval wars with England (1796–1802, 1804–08) and a major supplier of produce to the peninsula during the French occupation (1808–13).

Historians have long stressed the significance of United States' *exports* to colonial Spanish America,[2] but, in the absence of official *import values* for much of the period[3] and other data, the scope of analysis has remained far narrower than that of related fields. The early trade and shipping of the United States had been traced and analyzed with considerable sophistication since the appearance of Douglass North's improvements of previous estimates of the balance of payments.[4] North's thesis on the crucial role of the foreign sector as an engine of growth in 1793–1808 aroused considerable controversy.[5] Yet recent assessments have conceded the importance of re-exports and carrying earnings for north-eastern sub-sectors of merchants and industrialists.[6] By comparison, research of this kind on the late Spanish empire remains in its infancy, despite John Coatsworth's analysis of United States' exports to Spanish America[7] and recent attempts to quantify the trade with the mother country up to 1820.[8] In the specific area of United States' trade with Spanish America, conceivable issues now range far beyond the actual course of this commerce and its mediations with contemporary events. They extend, at the very least, to the relative importance for the respective partners of the commodity flows, the carrying services provided and the financial claims and specie movements thus generated. Yet no series exist but for the first of the following principal components of the United States' balance of payments with this part of the world: the current values of exports, the current values of imports, the costs of freight and insurance, the shares of these costs that accrued as earnings of foreign exchange to the parties involved, the merchants' profits and the capital and specie flows.

This paper draws from contemporary sources and statistical elaboration to estimate, for the period 1790–1819, the principal components of the United States' balance of payments with Spanish America and the Philippines. The various stages of the process embody five methodological innovations in the wider field of historical studies of the United States' balance of payments prior to 1821. First, import values at United States' ports (inclusive of cost, insurance and freight) are calculated for each fiscal year covered by the official sources, from almost exhaustive samples of commodity weights and volumes valued at wholesale monthly prices net of rates of customs duties.[9] Second, cargo tonnage for each commodity is estimated with stowage factors used by contemporaries to calculate freight charges.[10] Third, freight rates per ton are adjusted for nautical mileage as well as for annual fluctuations.[11] Fourth, average rates of insurance on Spanish American and Philippine routes are derived, for all but two years, from brokers' accounts and commercial newspapers of Philadelphia and Boston.[12] And fifth, a lower bound for mercantile profits is set at rates paid to ship captains for the sale and purchase of cargoes.[13] With a number of qualifications, the net balances with these areas will be compared with those estimated by Douglass North for the United States with the rest of the world in the same period. The compilation of volume, price and tax data also yields a number of useful by-products: import and export values at constant prices, the net barter terms of trade (export prices over import prices) and two series of customs revenue (gross and net of draw-backs returned upon re-export) on total imports from Spanish America and the Philippines. The new figures are analyzed in the text and the rather elaborate matters of method and computation will be discussed in detail in the Appendix.

It would be illusory to expect accuracy in the estimation of balance of payments components in the pre-statistical era; even today, direct reckoning of freight earnings poses insurmountable problems in most countries.[14] It cannot be stressed sufficiently that the present series are at best rough approximations to trends and cycles with varying degrees of reliability. For this reason, the analysis will focus on clearly differentiated periods of three to five years, and the specific weaknesses of the estimates will be mentioned, and alternative results supplied if possible, wherever they are felt to bear significantly on the conclusions. Though many of the new series will probably stand with few significant corrections,[15] those based on estimates of freight rates and insurable values,[16] and in particular the allocation of carrying earnings and mercantile profits,[17] may have to be substantially modified as new evidence becomes available.

Yet even the weaker statistical results, when cautiously interpreted, seem defensible in the present state of research. According to three leading historians of international trade, series of freight rates for United States' shipping routes in this period do not exist.[18] The estimates adopted in this paper are admittedly subject to question and so is, to a lesser extent perhaps, the derivation of insurance costs. But the tonnage figures and the insurance rates are grounded on contemporary sources and the magnitudes of total carrying costs are consistent with contemporary and twentieth-century estimates.[19] Some of the financial credits against the Spanish empire, however conservative, are subject to significant compound error. But the estimates of net money flows or indebtedness may be viewed as *minimum* contributions to the United States' financial position because sizeable earnings from smuggling,[20] from trade not carried through United States' ports[21] and from ship sales[22] have not been estimated for lack of adequate evidence. It is hoped that historians will respond constructively by directing research to these and to other areas that bear directly on the allocation of earnings of foreign exchange to the parties involved.[23] To facilitate future revisions, both sources and procedures have been described in detail.

1

In analyzing the commodity trade of the United States with the Spanish 'Indies' in the period 1790–1819 it is useful to bear in mind the changing international and legal circumstances that mediated its fortunes. The origins of this trade go back to the American Revolution itself, but the outbreak of naval warfare between Spain and England in 1796, and the resumption of hostilities that followed the peace years 1802–04, forced Spain to open wide the ports of Spanish America to neutral ships. This was done by decree in November 1797 and, following a pre-mature revokation of this act in April 1799, through special licenses and contracts. The period 1808–12 saw dramatic turns in the framework of Atlantic trade, including the occupation of the Spanish Peninsula by French troops from late 1807 onwards, a shift in European diplomacy whereby England sided with Spain against Napoleon in 1808, the deterioration of relations between the United States and England that culminated in Jefferson's embargo on United States' exports from December 1807 to March 1809 and the outbreak of secession and revolt in Spanish America in 1810. In 1812 England and the United States went to war while Spain continued to cling to a formal monopoly of her colonial trade. After 1815 the United States endeavoured with moderate success to maintain a share of Latin American trade against overwhelming competition from Britain. Every one of these events affected United States' trade with the Indies, but only a detailed statistical record can trace the strength of the ebb and flow and the structural transformations.

Deflated values at ports of origin,[24] displayed in fig. 1, confirm the

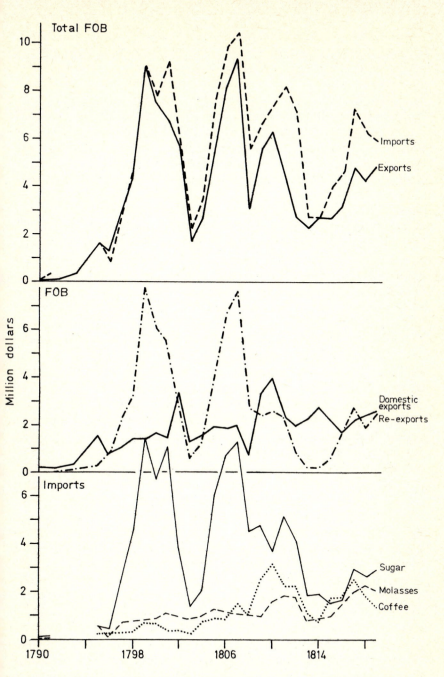

Fig. 1 United States: Value of trade with Spanish America and the Phillipines at constant prices of 1791, 1790–1819. See *Appendix*, sections A, B, C and G: most figures are given in Table 12.

spectacular growth and transformation of United States' trade with the Indies during the mother country's two naval wars with England. Both imports and total exports had already sprung from virtual insignificance in 1790–91 to over 1.5 million dollars at the close of Spain's hostilities with revolutionary France (1793–95). But the first naval war (1796–1802) saw nearly ten-fold increases in both fronts over the 1790–96 averages, and at the end of the second war (1804–08) similar heights were attained and perhaps even surpassed. By far the most impressive growth in the southward trade took place in the area of re-exports, the value of which appears to have soared to unprecedented heights, by 1806–07 at least, in both absolute and relative terms.[25]

By contrast, during the peace years of 1802–04 all branches of United States' trade with the Indies came to a virtual standstill as the value of Spanish colonial trade, which had collapsed under the weight of naval blockade, regained prewar levels.[26] This setback, which paralleled developments in the equivalent branch of British trade but coincided with a considerable expansion in British exports to Spain, reveals the latent strength of British competition in the shadow of Spain's continuing ability to assert her commercial monopoly in the Indies.[27]

British competition in Spanish America came into its own in 1808–11 while Spain saw its territory occupied and its political control over the Indies challenged. The strength of Britain's drive may be measured, however imperfectly, by a more than three-fold increase in its official exports to the 'Foreign West Indies and South America' in 1808, followed by further gains in both exports and imports only partially abated by 1811.[28] Significantly, British exports to the United States, a major source of re-exports to the Indies, reportedly declined by 56 per cent in the year ending January 5, 1809.[29] Britain's success owed much to Jefferson's export embargo of 1808, which enabled English merchants to open new lines of supply to the Spanish colonies.[30] But these inroads were also facilitated by warm local acquiescence and by Spain's pro-British policy following the enthronment of José Bonaparte.[31] The resulting setback to the re-export trade of the United States in 1808 (see fig. 1) was probably compounded, in the following two years, by Spain's short-lived reappearance as a now modest carrier of foreign goods to the empire once the ocean had been made safe by alliance with Britain.[32] The continued poor performance of United States re-exports to the Indies, down to the onset of war with England and beyond, suggests that the carrying trade had been dealt a severe blow. By contrast, domestic exports soared in 1809–10 and held significant gains in 1811 over the previous decade. Imports likewise suffered a smaller setback than re-exports in 1808 and regained half of the lost ground in the following three years.

War with England drastically curbed trade with the Indies, but the patterns that emerged with the return of peace closely resemble those already established in the preceding period. Predictably, cessation of imports from England and naval blockades of major United States' ports brought re-exports to the Indies to a virtual standstill and cut imports by more than half at the height of hostilities in 1813–14 (see fig. 1). Such strength as remained on the import side, and the moderate gains of domestic exports in the same years, owed much to the active participation of foreign vessels, which brought 77 per cent of the current value of imports in 1813–14 compared with 12 per cent in 1808–11 and 15 per cent in the entire period 1790–1819.[33] By September 1815, however, the volume of imports was again rising and gathering momentum and United States' ships had regained their customary share.[34] Thereafter imports peaked in 1817 and remained within the range established in 1808–11 and domestic exports settled on a mild upward trend at post-1809–10 levels. Exports of foreign goods rebounded with the return of peace; but subsequent volumes mirrored those of 1808–11, and even the moderate annual fluctuations betray continued sensitivity to English competition in the Indies: re-exports fell in 1818 as British shipments to the 'foreign West Indies and South America' reached a postwar peak and rose again in the following year.[35]

2

To contemporaries beguiled to monetary illusion the trade volumes involved must have appeared stabler and far greater than they were, for most prices fluctuated wildly and stood far above the 1791 levels through much of the period. Import prices were governed, for the most part, by those of sugar, molasses and coffee, the average value of which accounted for 49, 19 and 16 per cent of the total respectively.[36] A weighted index of import prices at ports of arrival, displayed in fig. 2 (upper panel), conveys the impact of changing supply conditions imposed by the ebb and flow of international warfare. During the wars between England and Spain, sugar and other colonial crops were diverted to United States' markets with consequent falls in prices. And the reverse held true as supplies dwindled with the return of peace and stocks were sold or re-exported (see lower-middle panel). When seen from the peak of 1796, the index of import prices shows a mildly downward trend to a trough in 1808–12 when sugar prices fell while those of now plentiful coffee dived and molasses remained relatively cheap. The opposite swings in volumes and prices of coffee, a crop with long periods of gestation, suggest lagged response by producers to inelastic demand in the classic cobweb pattern (see figs. 1 and 2, lower and lower-middle panels). The last coffee cycle significantly contributed to relatively high import prices after the Anglo-American war. The indices of export prices, particularly that for re-exports, are less reliable for lack of comprehensive breakdowns by commodities.[37] But the trends they convey also seem highly plausible (see fig. 2, upper-middle panel): the prices of domestic exports (largely agricultural goods with low elasticities of supply and demand) were by far the most volatile, while those of re-exports soared in 1808–15 as tense relations with England culminated in war. An index of

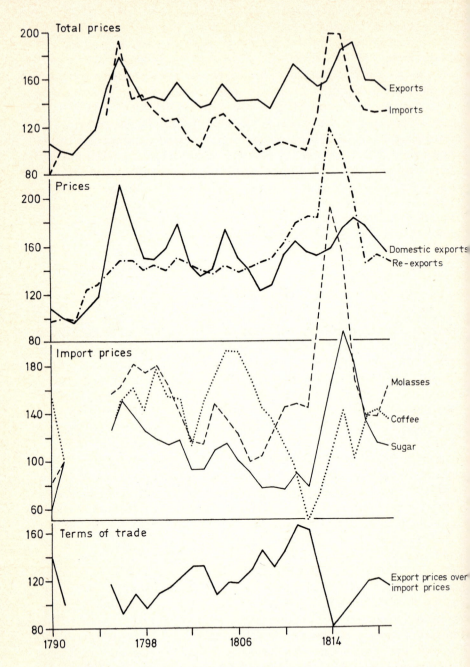

Fig. 2 United States: prices of exports and imports to and from Spanish America and the Phillipines, 1790–1819 — principal components and terms of trade (1791 = 100). See *Appendix*, section G: most figures are given in Table 12.

total export prices, weighted by the domestic and foreign shares, shows gains of nearly 80 per cent in the mid 1790s and remains above the 140 per cent mark in most subsequent years (see upper panel).

The differential rates of change in export and import prices, relative to 1791, yield favourable terms of trade for the United States in most years, with an unsteadily rising trend after 1798 to an absolute peak in 1811 (see fig. 2, lower panel). Only in the period 1812–15 is this trend reversed, with the ratio turning against the United States in the last two years of war despite phenomenal prices for the few foreign goods then re-exported. If the index of terms of trade is reckoned at the average prices of 1790 and 1791, the favorable trend emerges in 1801 and the gains peak at 45 per cent. With full allowance for possible distortions in the re-export index, it seems likely that United States' merchants at home ports often received much higher prices for domestic staples than they paid for Spanish American and Philippine goods in relation to the early 1790s.

3

The prices of imported commodities at ports of arrival incorporate charges for freight and insurance. Freight costs appear to have been greater on the average despite relatively short voyages to and from Cuba, where much of the trade under study was concentrated.[38] But, judging from the estimates presented in tables 1, 8 and 11, the costs of insurance on both imports and exports widely exceeded those of freight in the war years 1797–1801 and 1814. These apparent reversals, and in particular the cycles involved, reflect complex interactions between the bulk of the shipped goods, the demand and supply forces affecting freight rates, the trade values at current prices and the changing exposure to risk imposed by international conditions.

Fluctuations in tonnage and related variables are best illustrated with reference to the return cargoes, the composition of which is amply documented in the official sources. Weights and volumes of each commodity have been converted into cargo tons with stowage factors used by contemporaries to calculate freight charges.[39] The resulting series of total import tonnage fluctuates with that of import values at constant prices (see fig. 3, lower panel), but the correlation is weakened by frequent shifts in composition between bulky commodities with different values per cargo ton. This is particularly true of the two war periods when large volumes of sugar were diverted to the United States while shipments of molasses remained at moderate levels (see lower panel). Since these commodities accounted for 82 per cent of total import tonnage and sugar was nearly three times as valuable relative to bulk in 1791[40] total values per ton at constant prices rise significantly in 1797–1801 and again in 1805–07. As will be noted, however, the implicit reductions in freight costs per value are offset by rising ratios of freight rates over import prices, and the same holds true for the milder opposite trends of the late 1810s.

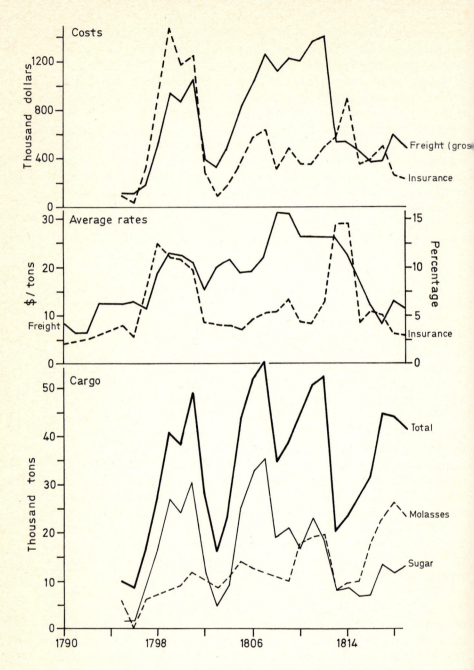

Fig. 3 United States: freight and insurance costs on imports from Spanish America and the Phillipines, 1790–1819 — principal components. See *Appendix*, section B: most figures are given in Tables 1, 7 and 8.

Far more significant than shifts in commodity composition were fluctuations in the rates at which the actual tons were priced. Series of freight rates on United States' ocean routes do not seem to exist for this period,[41] but the index derived by Douglas North from British and North American evidence is largely consistent with contemporary trends and cycles in related economic variables. The series displayed in fig. 3 (upper-middle panel) combines an official estimate in dollars per ton, adjusted for nautical mileage on several routes to Spanish America and the Philippines, with North's estimates of annual variations.[42] In the 1790s, sharply growing demand for the services of the United States' merchant fleet conceivably drove freight rates to unprecedented heights. Despite record registrations of ships in 1789–92,[43] the subsequent bursts of expansion in the carrying trade severely strained an industry subject to rising costs of lumber, naval stores, labour and metals.[44] Trade with the Indies expanded at a much faster rate than the total in 1797–1801,[45] and the accompanying shift to the long haul, as Chile and the River Plate became more frequent destinations, further increased demand for shipping in this area.[46] From 1801 onwards, cost factors bearing on the supply of shipping services at times reinforced, and eventually offset, those operating on the demand side. Fluctuations in the costs of shipbuilding strikingly mirror, albeit with lower intensity, the freight-rate cycles of 1801–05, 1808–10 and 1815–19.[47] Judging from the index of domestic prices displayed in fig. 2, the changing costs of victuals for the crews often magnified variations in those of shipbuilding, and the other major component of variable costs, the nominal wages paid to able-bodied seamen,[48] also increased dramatically after 1793[49] and held most of the gains until 1816.[50] The record freight rates for 1808–13 are poorly documented[51] and the peak levels of 1808–09 hardly conform to known conditions of slackening demand and abysmally low shipbuilding activity at mildly rising costs in these years.[52] One hypothesis is that poor capacity utilization due to the embargo coupled with unusually high wages for seamen in 1809[53] may have raised total carrying costs per ton to a considerable degree. From 1809 to 1812, the recovery of trade would have restored efficiency and certainly led to brisk shipbuilding activity at rising costs.[54] Low wartime demand and sharply falling costs after 1815 account for the better documented collapse of freight rates in the deflationary environment of the last 6 years.

The products of cargo tons and freight rates yield rough estimates of freight costs on imports for most years (see fig. 3). Fluctuations in tonnage, by far the best documented, were relatively much larger in 1795–1807 and consequently they shaped the course of freight costs in this crucial period despite opposite cycles in rates from 1802 to 1805.[55] The evidence for record freight rates in 1808–13 is particularly weak, but even if they had *fallen* to 20 dollars per ton, tonnage levels comparable to those in the previous peaks would have held costs at close to one million dollars per year in 1810–12.[56] Freight costs collapsed with tonnage in 1812 and were held down during the subsequent recovery by sharply falling rates.

While freight costs soared and dived, their shares in current import values remained relatively stable through the ebb and flow of warfare. Such trends as emerge through the main cycles (see fig. 3, upper panel) incorporate changing ratios of freight rates over import prices. In the period 1797–1801, rising rates and falling prices (see figs. 3 and 2) substantially raised costs per value to an average of 8.1 per cent. Rates and prices moved together in 1802–04 and parted again in 1805–07 but the ratios further increased at first and held most of the gains in 1805–07. Rising rates alone would have driven freight costs to 17.2 per cent of value in 1808–11, and soaring prices in 1813–15 and sinking rates after 1813 account for subsequent falls in costs per value to the documented levels of 1790–96.

The rates of insurance displayed in fig. 3 (middle panel) have been derived, for the period 1797–1804, from actual quotations for 219 voyages to and from Spanish-American and Philippine ports, and for all other years but 1790 and 1794, from narrow ranges of premiums on the same routes as published in weekly newspapers of Philadelphia and Boston.[57] The first naval war between England and Spain drove average rates on these routes from less than 5 per cent in 1795–96 to over 10 per cent in 1798–1800. Most documented rates in the latter years range from 10 to 15 per cent, but premiums of 20 and 25 per cent were at times quoted on Veracruz, Cuba and La Guaira. The rates for 1805–12 seem strikingly low at a time of repeated British attempts to restrict the West India trade of the United States.[58] Part of the explanation may lie in increasingly competitive conditions as companies grew in number[59] and associations of shipowners expanded their insurance operations.[60] It is also worth noting that the standard policies explicitly excluded coverage for loss or damage incurred in 'any illicit or prohibited trade'. War with England did drive rates to unprecedented heights, and lower exposure to risk with the return of peace accounts for the subsequent decline.

The total sums insured will probably remain unknown for lack of comprehensive records, and the present estimates of insurance costs from 'at sea' trade values are at best rough approximations. One significant source of error is the probable inclusion, in some cases at least, of freight costs and other charges in the principal sums underwritten at ports of departure.[61] To allow for such charges, the reference values of both imports and exports have been reckoned at a premium over those of the cargoes ready for loading.[62] Less disturbing is the fact that merchants did not always insure their consignments, particularly during peacetime.[63] Risks borne by the owners were probably incorporated into the prices of cargoes at ports of arrival, and such undervaluation as may remain would tend to be offset by unaccounted premiums on vessels. Errors also stem from varying rates and values within each fiscal year not covered by evidence of actual settlements. But again such variations would tend to offset one another so long as the rates appear to have remained stable through several months. The products of modified trade values and rates place average costs of insurance at 6.1 and

7.1 per cent of imports and exports at United States ports respectively (see tables 1 and 8).

The present estimates of freight and insurance costs, unlike those of import values,[64] cannot be checked with contemporary calculations. The most that can be said is that the total magnitudes are consistent with official and twentieth century estimates for the overall trade of the United States in the same period. A report to the Senate dated December 20, 1819 placed the value of imports at ports of arrival, inclusive of customs taxes, at more than 35 per cent over import values at European ports.[65] The tax component of the former reference value in 1819 can be estimated at 21.6 per cent by division of gross customs revenue[66] by the current value of imports in that year.[67] Subtraction of this percentage from the official estimate puts carrying costs across the Atlantic at roughly 14 per cent of imports — a conceivable excess over the present estimate of 9.3 per cent in the same year[68] for shorter routes.[69] Stern's estimate of over 20 per cent[70] and North's own range of 15 to 20 per cent for goods subject to ad valorem duties[71] are likewise consistent with the results arrived at in the present work for the period as a whole (see table 1).

4

The current value of imports upon arrival in the receiving country, referred to as a CIF value (cost + insurance + freight), is customarily deducted from the FOB value of exports upon departure (free-on-board) to obtain the balance of merchandise trade in a given year.[72] Table 2 depicts annual fluctuations in these and other balances and throws much light on their principal determinants. The balances on CIF imports (exports FOB — imports CIF: column 4) were unfavorable to the United States in most years, to the tune of over 40 million dollars in the aggregate. The annual deficits on this account, already considerable during the two naval wars and in 1808–11, doubled to an average of 3 million dollars by 1812–15 and remained above 2 million in 1816–19. If the balances are reckoned on FOB import values (column 3), which exclude the estimates of carrying costs, the first four deficits turn into an overall credit of 156 thousand dollars per year. These reversals suggest that the negative balances at United States' ports in 1797–1811 were almost fully accounted for by freight and insurance costs.

The trade deficits of 1812–19 require further analysis because they do not disappear upon deduction of carrying costs (see table 2, columns 4 and 3). The estimates summarized in table 2 point to structural transformations that go back to the rise of British competition in the Indies during Jefferson's export embargo of 1808. During the embargo, export values at constant prices had declined by two-thirds and those of imports by only half. In the following three years re-exports stagnated while most gains in domestic exports were cancelled by those in imports. So long as the terms of trade were even more favorable to the United States in 1808–11 than before (see column 2), the now

Table 1   United States: total Imports from Spanish America and the Philippines, 1790–1819 and principal cost components (*thousands of dollars at current prices*)

Fiscal years	Total imports CIF[a]			Total freight costs[b] (gross)			Total	insurance[a]		Total imports FOB (1−2−3)	
	X̄	1	Shares re-exported[c]	X̄	2	% of 1	X̄	3	% of 1	X̄	4
1790		88			5			2			81
1791		354			10			8			336
1795		2419			126			92			2201
1796	1180	1861		63	113	5%	37	48	3%	1079	1700
1797		4719			192			349			4178
1798		8281			523			958			6799
1799		14514			945			1498			12071
1800		11788			873			1174			9740
1801	10666	14028	47%	718	1059	7%	1047	1259	10%	8900	11710
1802		7039			446			285			6307
1803		2809			338			101			2370
1804	5026	5229	45%	432	512	8%	193	193	4%	4400	4523
1805		11230			822			364			10043
1806		13359			1021			585			11753
1807	12621	13273	56%	1037	1267	8%	528	634	4%	11056	11372
1808		6895			1121			315			5458
1809		8601			1233			491			6877
1810		9477			1216			366			7895
1811	8813	10281	34%	1235	1372	14%	386	371	4%	7192	8538
		146245			13194	9%		9093	6%		123952
	7697			694			479			6524	
1812		9007			1417			487			7103
1813		4530			541			581			3409
1814		6769			543			905			5321
1815	7241	8657	7%	743	470	10%	583	358	8%	5915	7828
1816		7768			381			406			6981
1817		10556			387			508			9661
1818		9140			594			278			8268
1819	9014	8592	15%	463	492	5%	357	238	4%	8193	7862
		65019			4825	7%		3761	6%		56433
	8127			603			470			7054	
		211264			18019	9%		12854	6%		180385
	7825			667			476			6681	

a Breakdowns by United States' and foreign ships are given in table 8.
b Breakdowns by United States' and foreign ships are given in table 7.
c Based on very rough estimates of re-exports of Spanish–American and Philippine goods to the rest of the rest of the world: see notes 99 and 103.

Sources and procedures: see Appendix, sections A and B.

Table 2 United States: balance of trade with Spanish America and the Philippines, 1790–1819 — principal determinants (*thousands of dollars*)

Fiscal years	Exports FOB − Imports FOB (*deflated values*)		Terms of trade 1791=100		Exports FOB − Imports FOB (*current values*)		Exports FOB − Imports CIF (*current values*)		
	X̄	1	X̄	2	X̄	3	X̄	4	Σ
1790		+39		131		+67		+60	
1791		−246		100		−246		−264	
1795		−39		117		+302		+84	
1796	−17	+177	116	116	+180	+598	+79	+437	+317
1797		+142		109		+592		+51	
1798		−153		97		−427		−1909	
1799		−79		109		+958		−1485	
1800		−343		114		+873		−1175	
1801	−585	−2494	110	123	+153	−1232	−1614	−3550	−8068
1802		−78		131		+1816		+1084	
1803		−580		132		−26		−465	
1804	−530	−933	124	109	+304	−877	−321	−1583	−964
1805		−2138		118		−1553		−2740	
1806		−1530		117		−225		−1831	
1807	−1588	−1095	121	129	−7	+1758	−1571	−143	−4714
1808		−2478		145		−1079		−2516	
1809		−1196		131		+547		−1177	
1810		−1106		145		+1827		+245	
1811	−2092	−3587	146	165	+172	−608	−1450	−2351	−5799
		−17717				+3065		−19228	
	−932		123		+161		−1012		
1812		−4492		161		−2890		−4794	
1813		−506		123		+14		−1107	
1814		−7		80		−1058		−2506	
1815	−1614	−1451	114	94	−1768	−3139	−3094	−3968	−12375
1816		−1529		104		−1028		−1815	
1817		−2500		119		−2118		−3013	
1818		−2118		121		−1657		−2529	
1819	−1827	−1161	114	114	−1368	−670	−2189	−1400	−8757
		−13764				−12546		−21132	
	−1720		114		−1568		−2641		
		−31481				−9481		−40360	
	−1166		121		−351		−1495		

Sources: calculated from tables 1, 3, and 12.

larger deficits in the balance of trade volumes (column 1) could be converted into a small net gain in the current balance on imports FOB (column 3). But the terms of trade turned against the United States in the last two years of war with Britain and thereafter they remained a mere 14 per cent over the 1791 level. From 1812 onwards, therefore, mildly favorable terms of trade no longer sufficed to offset sizeable deficits in the balance of trade volumes.

The impact of these complex forces on the balance of payments with the Indies is not readily apparent from the trade balances, because the large differences between CIF and FOB values include freight and insurance costs that must be allocated among the parties to whom they accrued as earnings of foreign exchange; moreover, mercantile profits were probably a major source of foreign exchange in the war years at least. If the trade balances are reckoned on the best documented series (official exports FOB — estimates of imports CIF), all such earnings that accrued to United States' citizens must be credited to the United States, for those made on imports are included as debits in the CIF values at ports of arrival. This exercise is fully spelled out in the Appendix (section E) and the results are summarized in table 3 (columns 1 through 7).

The net balances given in column 7 may be interpreted, with a number of important remarks and qualifications, as *minimum* estimates of net money flows or indebtedness between the United States and the Indies.[73] The credits and debits on commodity account (columns 1 and 2) seem fully justifiable so long as probable errors in the underlying series of exports and imports tend to offset one another.[74] So are the next largest credits from freight costs in United States ships (column 3), because sizeable earnings on the carrying trade between Spanish American ports have not been estimated for lack of adequate evidence. Perhaps for this reason, the shares of the present freight earnings in Douglass North's estimates for the trade of the United States with the rest of the world (see column 3) are so much smaller than the proportions of exports and imports in the respective totals[75] (see columns 1 and 2). Only small errors are likely to stem from the lesser balances on foreign-port charges (column 4). The allocation of insurance earnings to the United States rests on rough but reasonable assumptions about the changing participation of Spanish, Spanish American and British underwriters. To introduce a conservative bias in the insurance account (column 5) no allowance as been made for significant sources of foreign exchange in this area. The credits from mercantile profits (column 6) have been set, deliberately, at minimum conceivable levels with only small allowances for favorable business conditions during wartime. The adopted rates do not allow for the spoils of smuggling, and they average a mere 3.4 per cent of imports plus exports compared with a minimum of 10 per cent estimated by James Shepherd and Gary Walton for the West India trade in 1768–72. Finally, no allowance has been made for the proceeds of ship sales and for other potentially favorable items on capital account.[76]

With these qualifications, the picture conveyed by table 3 would confirm the central conclusion already advanced from more reliable estimates: once net credits on carrying earnings and mercantile profits are taken into account (columns 3 through 6) the war with England does appear as a major turning point for the entire period. Prior to 1808, net credits of 32.1 million dollars would have turned merchandise deficits of 13.4 million into net financial claims against the Indies of perhaps 18.6 million or 1.2 million per year (data in column 7). In 1808–11 the annual claims would have risen slightly to 1.4 million as growing strength in domestic exports, substantial improvement in the terms of trade and, perhaps, record freight rates helped cushion deficits in a carrying trade to the Indies severely curtailed by British competition.[77] From 1812 onwards the FOB value of imports persistently exceeded that of exports,[78] and freight rates sank after 1813,[79] so that the net balances would have swung in favor of the Indies (see column 7). Over the entire period 1790–1819, however, the United States would have accumulated net financial claims of over 15 million dollars.

The significance of these claims and liabilities is hard to ascertain for lack of strictly comparable series for the trade of the United States with the rest of the world. Douglass North's estimates of total freight earnings were derived with different procedures,[80] and either reckoning of insurance earnings and mercantile profits rests, inevitably, on informed speculation. Nevertheless, the strength of the official records of merchandise trade and other similarities of method and documentation[81] warrant tentative comparisons of the overall balances with those with the Indies. The export and import values adopted by North turn by far the largest credits and debits to the United States, with negative balances on CIF imports in most years.[82] The same is true of commodity trade with the Indies despite wide fluctuations in the shares of exports and imports in the respective totals (see table 3, columns 1 and 2). Freight earnings alone barely offset the overall trade deficit[83] and probably covered two thirds of that with the Indies at least (see columns 1, 2 and 3).[84] The largest discrepancies arise in the insurance and profits accounts. North assumed that total deficits in the import trade with Britain exceeded total net surpluses on the export side.[85] By contrast, the present estimates of insurance earnings and minimum mercantile profits turn sizeable credits against the Indies (see columns 5 and 6). If only the foregoing components are taken into account, the net balances with the Indies add up to more than a fourth of total net gains in 1790–1811 and to less than a tenth of total losses in 1812–19 (see columns 7 and 8). The most significant contributions to the international position of the United States would have been made during the apogee of the carrying trade when net surpluses with the Indies furnish more than a third of total credits (1797–1801) and held reduce total deficits in the same proportion (1805–07).

The net balances with the Indies appear in a still different light when compared with North's estimates of total international indebtedness. The latter

Table 3   United States: Balance of payments before specie flows with Spanish America and the Philippines, 1790–1819. Estimates of principal components and comparisons with North's total balances with the rest of the world (*thousands of dollars at current prices*)

Fiscal years	Exports FOB[a] Σ	1	% of U.S. total	Imports CIF[a] Σ	2	% of U.S. total	Freight earnings[b] (gross) Σ	3	% of U.S. total[c]
1790		+148			−88			+13	
1791		+90			−354			+15	
1795		+2503			−2419			+392	
1796	+5039	+2298	3%	−4722	−1861	2%	+629	+209	1%
1797		+4770			−4719			+425	
1798		+6372			−8281			+1086	
1799		+13029			−14514			+1944	
1800		+10613			−11788			+1761	
1801	+45262	+10478	12%	−53330	−14028	12%	+6977	+1761	5%
1802		+8123			−7039			+1090	
1803		+2344			−2809			+461	
1804	+14113	+3646	7%	−15077	−5229	6%	+2267	+716	3%
1805		+8490			−11230			+1458	
1806		+11528			−13359			+1986	
1807	+33148	+13130	11%	−37862	−13273	9%	+5939	+2495	5%
1808		+4379			−6895			+1633	
1809		+7424			−8601			+2194	
1810		+9722			−9477			+2471	
1811	+29455	+7930	15%	−35254	−10281	13%	+8648	+2350	5%
		+127017	10%		−146245	9%		+24460	4%
1812		+4213			−9007			+1944	
1813		+3423			−4530			+376	
1814		+4263			−6769			+515	
1815	+16588	+4689	13%	−28963	−8657	15%	+3521	+686	5%
1816		+5953			−7768			+583	
1817		+7543			−10556			+636	
1818		+6611			−9140			+1014	
1819	+27299	+7192	8%	−36056	−8592	8%	+3194	+961	4%
		+43887	10%		−65019	10%		+6715	4%
		+170904	10%		−211264	10%		+31175	4%

a The trade balances on imports CIF are given in table 2. Breakdowns of exports by domestic and foreign goods are given in table 10.
b Exclusive of freight earnings on trade not carried through United States' ports (cf. note c below).
c North's estimates of gross freight earnings *include* those on trade not carried through United States' ports.
d The balances of foreign port charges have been estimated with similar methods to those used by North. See p. 66.
e North's estimates of insurance earnings appear to encompass mercantile profits but make no distinction between the two components.

Balances of foreign port charges[d]		Insurance[e] earnings		Credits from mercantile profits[f]		With the Indies (1+2+3+4+5+6)		Net balances — with rest of the world (Indies included)		
Σ 4		Σ 5		Σ 6		Σ 7		On same components Σ 8	−Interest +Default[g] Σ 9	Total[h] Σ 10
	−1		+4		+5		+81			
	−1		+6		+8		−236			
	−13		+140		+154		+757			
−26	−11	+223	+73	+297	+130	+1440	+838	−9900	−25900	−26100
	−38		+464		+397		+1299			
	−95		+1114		+575		+771			
	−182		+1775		+1108		+3160			
	−173		+1622		+904		+2939			
−699	−211	+6550	+1575	+3935	+951	+8695	+526	+24200	−1800	+1600
	−80		+488		+473		+3055			
	−31		+134		+114		+213			
−169	−58	+854	+232	+803	+216	+2791	−477	+33500	+19800	+10800
	−151		+459		+788		−186			
	−222		+783		+1065		+1781			
−652	−279	+2156	+914	+2995	+1142	+5724	+4129	−11300	−24300	−21500
	−244		+262		+457		−408			
	−176		+561		+459		+1861			
	−250		+492		+604		+3562			
−983	−313	+1708	+393	+2105	+585	+5679	+664	+55500	+33800	+37300
	−2529		+11491		+10135		+24329	+92000	+1600	+2100
	−312		+422		+375		−2365			
	+82		+585		+90		+25			
	+40		+815		+139		−998			
−267	−77	+2133	+311	+918	+314	−6072	−2734	−16800	−31000	−26200
	−77		+401		+370		−538			
	−85		+485		+514		−1463			
	−139		+281		+473		−900			
−419	−118	+1426	+259	+1878	+521	−2678	+223	−91500	−15800[g]	−12500
	−686		+3559		+2796		−8750	−108300	−46800	−38700
	−3215		+15050		+12931		+15584	−16300	−45200	−36600

f Minimum estimates: see Appendix, section E, pp. 66–7.
g Default adds up to a total credit of $100 million in 1816–19.
h Includes annual credits on ship sales and debits on payments to Barbary pirates (1795–96) and the purchase of Louisiana (1803).

Sources and procedures: *Column 1:* table 10, column 7. *Column 2:* table 1, column 1. *Columns 3 through 6:* see Appendix, section E. *Columns 8, 9, and 10:* calculated from Douglass North, *'The United States' balance of payments, 1790–1860'*, p. 600, Table A–4 (North's figures for 1792–94 not included).

include, in addition to the balance of payments components aggregated in column 8, large interest payments on the public and private debt held abroad, largely in England, and a number of lesser items on current and capital account. Outflows for debt service nearly cancel the 90 million dollars surplus accumulated in 1790–1811[86] and add a further 38.5 million to net losses in 1812–19. Even discounting 100 million reportedly written off by default in 1816–19,[87] the interest account raises the overall net deficit to 45.2 million (see columns 8 and 9). Other debits stem from the purchase of Louisiana (11.2 million dollars in 1803) and from payments to Barbary pirates (1.2 million in 1795–96).[88] North also estimated, from evidence for the years 1814–19, annual credits on ship sales abroad to a total of 21 million. The balances of total international indebtedness (column 10)[89] show little change by 1811 with respect to 1789[90] and turn a total debit of 38.7 million dollars in 1812–19.

Judging from North's overall balances and bearing in mind that the present estimates exclude potentially favorable items, net surpluses with the Indies appear to have covered at least nine-tenths of a sizeable net deficit with the rest of the world in 1790–1811, while subsequent losses to the Indies would have accounted, at most, for less than a fourth of the total deficit in the last eight years (see columns 7 and 10). Over the entire period, the annual balances with the Indies would have turned a net credit of at least 15.3 million dollars, in contrast with an overall net debit of 36.6 million in the same 27 years. The size of other credits against the Indies not included in column 7 must remain a matter of speculation. The carrying trade between Spanish American and Philippine ports conceivably increased net freight earnings by 20 per cent or 5.4 million dollars.[91] Had ship sales in the Indies stood in the same proportion as exports and imports with this area in the respective totals, they would have added a further 2.1 million. The estimates of minimum mercantile profits given in column 6 do not allow for the spoils of smuggling; even if they were doubled from 12.9 to 25.8 million dollars, they would remain one third below those estimated by Shepherd and Walton for the West India trade in 1768–72.[92] Without the net balances with the Indies, the international indebtedness incurred by the United States in this period might well have more than doubled.

The foregoing comparisons are subject to significant compound error but the general picture they convey is by no means implausible. Timothy Pitkin, calling in 1816 for 'good understanding and free commercial intercourse' with the Spanish West Indies and American possessions, noted that

'It is from this quarter that the United States obtain large quantities of the precious metals, by which they are enabled to carry on a trade with China and the East-Indies, as well as to pay the balances due, in Europe and elsewhere'.[93]

Evidence on specie flows in this period has not been found[94] but there can be little doubt that sizeable claims against the Indies in the neutrality years, and the resulting inflows of precious metals, helped finance far higher levels of imports and re-exports than would otherwise have been possible without severe strain on the country's debtor position.[95] By the time Pitkin made his case, the net balances of payments with the Indies appear to have turned against the United States and a large proportion of the inflows of specie from this area may have come indirectly through the mother country: research now in progress suggests that, while trade flows with Spain were far smaller than those with the Indies, they turned much larger financial surpluses to the United States.

5

For the United States, trade with the Indies was a timely windfall and a partial redress in a period when, in Douglass North's estimation, international indebtedness would grow to the point of default. To be sure, the carrying trade appears to have played a residual role, the boundaries of which would have been set by recurrent revivals in Spanish colonial trade and, in the last decade, by British competition. Growth in home exports may also have been dampened, in the mid 1790s, by lagging response in the supply of foodstuffs due to long gestation periods and to high costs of domestic transport[96]; and in subsequent decades by saturated demand in the largely self-sufficient markets of Mexico and South America.[97] In these and in other fields, however, there were compensations and outright benefits denied to most European nations. Re-exports to the Indies alone averaged 14 per cent of the total and often surpassed a fifth at the height of the Napoleonic wars.[98] Together with exports of Spanish—American goods to the rest of the world, they probably reached a fourth, at times well over a third, of total re-exports through United States' ports.[99] To the extent that the foreign sector was a strong and dynamic influence on the economy of the north-east,[100] the commercial, agricultural and shipbuilding activity made possible by these exports and imports, together with substantial improvement in the terms of trade in the busiest years, significantly contributed to local prosperity and, perhaps, to national income as well.[101] Without the financial claims and the earnings of foreign exchange associated with this trade, the international indebtedness incurred by the United States in this period might have more than doubled.[102] Gross government revenue on imports from the Indies often came close to a fifth of total customs receipts from merchandise (see table 4, column 1). Even allowing for substantial drawbacks returned upon re-export to the rest of the world (column 2), net customs revenue may have approached a sixth of the total in 1797—1801 and again in 1808—15 (column 3).[103] The benefits from trade with the Indies thus ranged from contributions to domestic income and employment, in farming and shipbuilding as well as in carrying services, to the buttressing of international solvency and a strong government so vital to a young economy on its journey to maturity.

Table 4   United States: Customs revenue on merchandise imports from Spanish America and the Philippines, 1795–1819 (*thousands of dollars*)

Fiscal years	Gross revenue $\bar{X}$	1	% of U.S. Total	Drawbacks returned upon re-export (*estimates*) $\bar{X}$	2	% of U.S. Total	Net revenue (1 − 2) $\bar{X}$	3	% of U.S. Total
1795		417			21			396	
1796	333	249	3%	74	127	2%	259	122	3%
1797		886			339			547	
1798		1892			927			966	
1799		4216			2033			2184	
1800		2990			1355			1635	
1801	2728	3655	19%	1298	1836	24%	1430	1819	16%
1802		1682			754			928	
1803		724			233			491	
1804	1151	1048	7%	508	536	11%	644	512	5%
1805		2234			1280			954	
1806		2849			1446			1403	
1807	2750	3166	11%	1547	1916	16%	1203	1251	7%
1808		1827			32			1795	
1809		2326			1398			928	
1810		2458			1297			1162	
1811	2311	2634	19%	793	445	29%	1518	2189	16%
1812		4637			648			3989	
1813		2085			183			1902	
1814		1930			11			1919	
1815	2538	1500	16%	227	68	24%	2310	1432	15%
1816		1590			234			1355	
1817		2393			428			1965	
1818		2067			268			1799	
1819	2006	1975	8%	309	307	8%	1697	1668	8%
		53430	12%		18122	17%		35311	11%

Sources and procedures: see Appendix, section F.

APPENDIX
Sources and procedures

The official trade statistics of the United States are among the most reliable national records of this kind for the period 1790–1819.[104] The export figures are based, in most cases, on actual valuations at market prices by the collectors of the customs and less frequently on written statements submitted under oath by the masters of vessels, who themselves had no incentive to misrepresent the facts.[105] Import quantities were likewise ascertained, and in some cases valued as well, by the customs officers.[106]

For all their virtues, however, the official records are far from comprehensive and pose problems of interpretation yet to be fully elucidated. The most serious difficulty stems from the absence of contemporary valuations for imports subject to specific duties, which accounted for more than a third of total import values in the period 1790–1819.[107] Douglass North, in his pathbreaking revision of earlier studies of the United States' balance of payments in this period, resorted to import data given in a report of the Secretary of the Treasury in 1835. This report incorporated eight annual import values for 1795–1801 and 1815, published independently by Timothy Pitkin in 1816 and by Adam Seybert in 1818, and furnished new valuations, without stating the methods employed, for the remaining years.[108] In accepting these total import values as a point of departure, rather than the official weights and volumes by commodities to be used in the present paper, North introduced a further element of speculation as to the share of freight costs that accrued to United States citizens as earnings from abroad.[109] And, improving upon a long tradition in historical studies of the British balance of payments, he estimated freight volumes from official data of registered tonnage.[110] The resulting reconstruction of the United States balance of payments, though very valuable indeed, is now susceptible of improvement in these and in other areas.

The official breakdowns of trade with Spanish America and the Philippines in 1790–1819, and other printed and manuscript sources bearing on the United States balance of payments with these areas, lend themselves to considerable elaboration for analytical purposes. This appendix spells out the strengths and weaknesses of the sources and the methods employed.

A   Imports

The official import figures require extensive elaboration but yield by far the most detailed and comprehensive series. Import data are available by geographical origins for all fiscal years (October–September) except 1792–94, but only *quantities* are given for goods subject to specific duties and only *total values* for those paying ad valorem.[111] Annual values for the former group have been derived from an almost comprehensive sample of import quantities[112] and modified wholesale prices. The prices used for valuation were

Table 5   United States: total imports from Spanish America and the Philippines: geographical origins and commodity composition, 1790–1819 (*current CIF values in thousands of dollars*)

Fiscal years	Spanish West Indies and other American colonies 1		Floridas and Louisiana 2		Honduras, Campeche, and Mosquito shore 3		Philippine Islands 4	
1790	52		21		15		0	
1791	319		28		7		0	
1795	1500		498		368		53	
1796	1644	74%	217	16%	1	8%	0	1%
1797	4573		145		1		0	
1798	8104		175		2		0	
1799	13937		530		16		30	
1800	10676		874		68		168	
1801	12631	94%	1002	5%	57	0%	338	1%
1802	5824		938		14		262	
1803	1876		884		2		47	
1804	4662	82%	382	15%	7	0%	178	3%
1805	10862		20		28		320	
1806	12797		45		29		488	
1807	13156	97%	29	0%	88	0%	0	2%
1808	6818		43		34		0	
1809	8434		159		8		0	
1810	9337		123		17		0	
1811	10074	98%	111	1%	95	0%	0	
1812	8871		105		31		0	
1813	4441		84		5		0	
1814	5966		797		6		0	
1815	7649	93%	925	7%	24	0%	59	0%
1816	7617		123		4		26	
1817	10376		125		55		0	
1818	8702		182		103		153	
1819	8225	97%	88	1%	125	1%	154	1%
	199123	94%	8653	4%	1210	1%	2276	1%

Sources and procedures: see Appendix, section A.

X̄ Sugar	5		X̄ Molasses	6		X̄ Coffee	7		X̄ Cocoa	8		X̄ Other	9		X̄ Total	10
	47			5			3			1			32			88
	109			41			7			84			113			354
	551			723			85			8			1052			2419
306	517	26%	385	773	88%	59	142	5%	23	0	2%	406	429	35%	1180	1861
	3226			935			200			53			305			4719
	5519			1077			225			935			525			8281
	9959			1198			999			1366			992			14514
	7521			1207			788			789			1483			11788
7117	9359	67%	1157	1367	11%	504	309	5%	868	1198	8%	1020	1795	10%	10666	14028
	3375			937			237			783			1707			7039
	1153			812			101			5			738			2809
2228	2156	44%	998	1244	20%	460	1041	9%	273	30	5%	1068	758	21%	5026	5229
	6724			1560			1501			931			514			11230
	7627			1271			1395			1695			1371			13359
7247	7389	57%	1263	958	10%	1756	2371	14%	1307	1295	10%	1048	1260	9%	12621	13273
	3366			922			1422			430			755			6895
	3597			1010			3304			166			524			8601
	2689			2087			3489			163			1049			9477
3540	4509	40%	1581	2305	18%	2526	1888	29%	238	194	3%	928	1385	11%	8813	10281
	3192			2324			1061			43			2387			9007
	2051			1452			663			4			360			4530
	3013			2489			626			0			641			6769
2811	2990	39%	2130	2255	29%	1177	2357	16%	12	0	.2%	1111	1055	15%	7241	8657
	2751			2441			1679			34			863			7768
	3677			2575			3344			68			892			10556
	2957			3066			2413			89			615			9140
3136	3159	35%	2666	2584	30%	2373	2057	26%	93	181	1%	745	611	8%	9014	8592
	103183	49%		39618	19%		33707	16%		10545	5%		24211	12%		211264
3822			1467			1248			391			897			7825	

those of Philadelphia, which are available in print as monthly relatives[113] and closely match the official classification of imported goods.[114] Each relative-price matrix was first converted into October–September averages in dollars and cents.[115] The resulting wholesale prices for each fiscal year were then reduced by deduction of official annual rates of specific duty on each commodity so as to approximate as closely as possible the actual values upon arrival at United States' ports.[116] No price reduction was made for commissions of wholesale merchants, which appear to have ranged from 2.5 to 5 per cent,[117] because the resulting overvaluation is probably offset by the incompleteness of the sample[118] and by the absence of official data for duty-free imports.[119]

The products of commodity quantities subject to specific duties times modified wholesale prices yield 27-year series of current import values CIF by commodities and geographical areas. Breakdowns by United States' and foreign ships are also available for all but 5 years. These were estimated from the official shares in 1803–04 (1791–92, 1795–96) and in 1798, 1800 (1799).

Comparable series of goods paying ad valorem duties, for which no quantities are extant, had to be estimated separately. The official figures for these imports are customs valuations at ports of departure (FOB) compounded in most cases by 10 per cent[120] — a procedure that placed them far below their CIF values at United States' ports.[121] To obtain proxies for true CIF values, each official sub-series has been reduced by the respective proportion added at the customs and the resulting FOB values augmented with independent estimates of freight and insurance costs.[122] Resulting errors are slight because the FOB values of goods subject to ad valorem duties amount, on the average, to a mere 3 per cent of the estimated totals of imports FOB. The most useful series of total import values (for goods subject to specific *and* ad valorem duties) are presented in tables 5, 8 and 12.

The present estimates of import values compare well with contemporary calculations, presented in table 6. The point of reference is Pitkin's well known import figures for 1795–1801,[123] also published by Seybert in 1818[124] and eventually adopted in the 1837 report used by North in 1960.[125] Pitkin's figures closely approximate the estimated 7-year total at United States' ports (CIF) and most of the annual values. The large discrepancy of 1799 may be due to the omission, in Pitkin's source, of 32.4 million pounds of Havana brown sugar from the Spanish West Indies, or to a wrong valuation of a similar entry of loaf sugar at Havana brown prices. It is also worth noting that the account of 1799 has an irregular layout for this period, with goods which arrived in United States' and foreign ships lumped together. If the figures for 1799 are excluded, the overall discrepancy in Pitkin's import figures with the present estimates of CIF values is smaller than 4 per cent. These results suggest that North's total import figures, for 1795–1801 at least, are probably true CIF values and not 'at sea' valuations as he was led to conclude from the evidence he used.[126]

Table 6   United States: Total imports from Spanish America and the Philippine Islands, 1795–1801 (*current values in thousands of dollars*)

Fiscal years	Pitkin's totals 1	Estimated totals		% Differences	
		CIF 2	FOB 3	col. 2/col. 1	col. 3/col. 1
1795	2402	2419	2201	+ 0.7	− 8.4
1796	1962	1861	1700	− 5.1	− 13.4
1797	4523	4719	4178	+ 4.3	− 7.6
1798	8390	8281	6799	− 1.3	− 19.0
1799	11704	14514	12071	+ 24.0[a]	+ 3.1
1800	12494	11788	9740	− 5.7	− 22.0
1801	15043	14028	11710	− 6.7	− 22.2
	56518	57610	48399	+ 1.9	− 14.4

a see text.
Sources: *Column 1:* Calculated from seven sub-totals by geographical areas in Timothy Pitkin, *A statistical view of the commerce of the United States* (Hartford: 1816), 214–217. *Columns 2 and 3:* table 1.

B   Freight and insurance costs on imports

Indirect estimations of freight costs in historical studies of the balance of payments have relied, as points of departure, on either registered tonnage data adjusted for shipping activity and valued in dollars per ton, or freight factors (freight costs per unit as a percentage of value per unit) for a sample of commodities.[127] The first approach, used by North for the period 1790–1819, has been found impracticable because the official statistics of registered tonnage seldom give breakdowns for Spanish America and the Philippines. Even if such breakdowns could be retrieved, there is now considerable evidence that registered tons are poor indicators of a ship's carrying capacity and were not used by contemporaries to calculate freight costs.[128] Moreover, it would have to be assumed that ships arriving from Spanish America or the Philippines were always fully loaded and never carried commodities from other nations or their colonies. The second method is potentially more reliable as it draws on individual weights and volumes, but it had to be rejected for lack of evidence of freight factors for a sufficient number of commodities in this period.[129]

The approach adopted here combines features of both methods: freight tonnage has been estimated directly from commodity weights and volumes and has been valued in dollars per ton at rates adjusted for both distance travelled and annual fluctuations. The main steps are summarized in table 7.

Direct estimation of freight volumes from commodity data requires accurate knowledge of contemporary practices. Since the known freight rate is expressed

Table 7   Estimation of freight costs in United States imports from Spanish America and the Philippines, 1790–1819

	Average freight rates (dollars per ton) $\left[\dfrac{5+10}{2+7}\right]$		Total imports in U.S. ships					
			Goods subject to					
			Specific duties		Ad valorem duties			
			Cargo tons (00)	Freight costs $000	Freight costs $000		Total freight costs (gross) (3+4) $000	Foreign port charges (25% of 5) $000
Fiscal years	X	1	X 2	3	4	X	5	6
1790		7.9	4	3	0		4	1
1791		6.5	9	6	0		7	2
1792		6.5						
1793		12.4						
1794		12.4						
1795		12.4		68	84	1	85	21
1796	10.2	13.0	35	58	75	1	43 75	19
1797		11.5		147	168	1	170	42
1798		18.8		234	440	4	444	111
1799		22.8		358	816	7	823	206
1800		22.5		341	768	7	774	193
1801	19.4	21.2	303	437	926	12	630 939	235
1802		15.5		238	367	11	378	94
1803		19.9		109	213	7	220	55
1804	19.1	21.9	170	163	351	5	318 357	89
1805		18.8		372	696	5	702	175
1806		19.3		478	922	25	948	237
1807	20.2	22.4	456	518	1161	22	944 1182	296
1808		31.3		321	1010	30	1039	260
1809		31.3		296	925	14	939	235
1810		26.5		403	1071	23	1094	274
1811	28.9	26.5	376	484	1286	20	1094 1305	326
1812		26.5		494	1310	13	1324	331
1813		26.5		23	57	1	58	15
1814		22.9		76	146	5	152	38
1815	23.1	16.4	204	222	369	12	479 381	95
1816		11.8		280	332	7	340	85
1817		8.5		418	355	6	361	90
1818		13.2		428	564	10	574	143
1819	11.3	11.6	384	409	473	8	439 481	120
	17.2		274	7388			561 15156	3788

Sources and procedures: see Appendix, section B, and section E for columns 6 and 11.

	Total imports in foreign ships					
	Goods subject to					
	Specific duties		Ad valorem duties	Total freight costs (gross) (8 + 9)		Foreign-port charges (20% of 10)
$\bar{X}$	Cargo tons (00)	Freight costs $000	Freight costs $000	$\bar{X}$	$000	$000
	7	8	9		10	11
	2	2	0		2	0
	5	3	0		3	1
	33	41	0		41	8
17	29	37	0	21	38	8
	19	22	0		22	4
	42	79	1		79	16
	53	121	1		122	24
	43	98	1		99	20
42	55	118	3	88	120	24
	41	65	3		68	14
	57	116	2		118	24
55	67	153	3	144	155	31
	63	120	1		121	24
	36	71	3		73	15
45	37	82	3	93	85	17
	26	79	3		82	17
	93	291	3		294	59
	44	118	4		121	24
47	24	63	3	141	66	13
	34	90	4		94	19
	179	477	5		483	97
	158	389	3		391	78
106	51	80	9	264	89	18
	35	41	1		42	8
	29	25	2		26	5
	15	20	0		20	4
22	9	10	1	25	11	2
47	1279			106	2865	573

in dollars per ton, the official weights and volumes of imports subject to specific duties must be converted to a common unit. This unit, moreover, must be representative of the actual tonnage reckoned for valuation purposes at the time. Recent findings by John McCusker have ascertained that freight rates were collected on the basis of the cargo ton and that cargo tons were reckoned, in the well established trades at least, from standardized stowage factors for each commodity (weights or volumes per cargo ton). The same author has compiled a list of such factors used in New York in 1771–72.[130] Stowage factors are known to have changed over time, effectively altering the costs of freight,[131] but comparisons with mid-nineteenth-century data show little variation in the ton equivalents of sugar and molasses, which together accounted in most years for over 85 per cent of the total tonnage imported from Spanish America and the Philippines.[132] McCusker's list has accordingly been adopted for the conversion of import weights and volumes in four separate routes from these areas.[133] Two aggregates of the resulting series of cargo tonnage are presented in columns 2 and 7.

The valuation of the tonnage figures rests, inevitably, on weaker evidence. The point of departure was a contemporary estimate that put the freight from the United States to France in 1821 at an average of 20 dollars per ton.[134] To allow for distance travelled from the areas of the Spanish empire covered by the official trade records, freight rates for each route were estimated with reference to the nautical mileage between Philadelphia and Bordeaux.[135] Ships bound for the Far East from Salem and Boston usually sailed, respectively, around the southern tips of Africa and America, and most skippers chose the former route for the return voyage with a number of stops along the way.[136] It is also known that Salem merchants were the first to establish a direct and prosperous trade with the Philippines.[137] Accordingly, freight rates on imports form this area were derived from the nautical mileage between Manila and Salem via Cape Town (84.39 dollars/ton in 1821). The rates for 'Floridas and Louisiana' are based on the distance from New Orleans to New York[138] (1790–1803: 10.36 dollars/ton) and on the average mileage from Pensacola and St Augustine to the same port (1804–19: 7.49 dollars/ton). The rates for 'Honduras, Campeche and Mosquitoe Shore' were derived from the average distance to Baltimore[139] from Veracruz and Cartagena (10.13 dollars/ton).

The remaining adjustments of the reference freight rate for distance travelled posed additional problems because the official trade records do not distinguish between the Spanish West Indies and 'other [Spanish] American colonies' after 1802. In all documented years up to 1802, the Spanish West Indies accounted for over 90 per cent of the combined tonnage of imports subject to specific duties. From 1798 to 1802, however, the value of goods paying ad valorem, for which no quantities were given, turned strongly in favor of 'other American colonies'. These are the years when large numbers of United States' ships are known to have arrived in Chile, the La Plata region and

La Guaira.[140] The share of total tonnage shipped from these areas is only roughly conveyed by extant data from the Philadelphia Custom House records: in four years covering the period 1798–1809, the number of United States' ships which arrived in Philadelphia from Spanish America other than Cuba and Puerto Rico averaged 25.7 per cent of the total.[141] The actual proportions were probably greater because ships stopping at Havana on the way north may have been recorded at Philadelphia as arrivals from Cuba.[142] The best that can be done on such evidence is to weight the average distances to Boston and Philadelphia[143] from the Spanish West Indies and other American colonies with the official shares of import tonnage (1790–97) and with the four documented proportions of numbers of ships bound for Philadelphia. The average proportions in 1798, 1801 and 1807 were assigned to all war years and that in 1809 to peace years, for the decade 1810–19, the 1809 proportions were averaged with the official shares of import values in 1821.[144] The distance from the Spanish West Indies to Boston/Philadelphia was reckoned as the nautical mileage from Havana, and that from other American colonies as the weighted average from Valparaiso (25 per cent), Buenos Aires (40 per cent) and La Guaira (35 per cent).[145] In view of the small weights assigned to these routes compared to that from Havana, conceivable variations in the estimated proportions have little bearing on the overall results. The shares of the estimated distances in that from New York to Bordeaux at 20 dollars/ton yield annual freight rates from the Spanish West Indies *and* other Spanish American colonies to an average of 12.87 dollars/ton in the period 1790–1819.

Only one further adjustment of the freight rates, that for fluctuations through time, is warranted by the available evidence. The allowances made for nautical mileage are only rough approximations to relative shipping costs. Deviations from the known rate to Bordeaux should be less than proportional to distance because the shorter (or longer) the voyage the greater (or smaller) the fixed costs per unit of loading, unloading and administration. Moreover, shorter voyages may have involved longer idle periods, thus further raising overhead unit costs. In the absence of data on the production and cost functions involved, however, the weight of these and other such factors cannot be estimated with any semblance of precision. Far more important are the sharp fluctuations in freight rates known to have occurred in this inflationary period. The only available index is that estimated by Douglass North for 1790–1819 on routes centred in Britain.[146] Since the reference freight rate from the United States to Bordeaux was quoted from 1821 data, North's index has been converted to a base 1818 = 100 to reflate the estimated rates for the Spanish empire.[147] The resulting series, summarized in table 7 (column 1) as annual averages weighted by tonnage, roughly account for both distances travelled and varying rates through time.

The three ingredients so far discussed can at last be combined for the calculation of freight costs. The products of cargo tons and rates estimated for each route, weighted with the freight rate index and added up, yield 7 series of gross freight costs for goods subject to specific duties. These series have been aggregated by United States and foreign ships (columns 3 and 8) to illustrate the estimation of insurance costs and the allocation of freight earnings and foreign port charges, to be discussed below and in Section E. The proportions of gross freight costs in total import values were used in turn to estimate costs on goods paying ad valorem (columns 4 and 9) for which no official quantities are extant. All proportions were halved to account for the fact that the goods in question, which were largely manufactures, probably had much greater values per cargo ton than goods subject to specific duties. Resulting errors are slight because the official FOB values of goods paying ad valorem amount, on the average, to a mere 3 per cent of total import values.

The estimation of insurance costs also incorporates, for reasons that will become apparent in Section E, the distinction between United States and foreign ships (see table 8). The annual rates of marine insurance (column 1) are based, for the period 1797–1804, on actual quotations for 219 voyages to and/or from Spanish American and Philippine ports, compiled from insurance policies and subscription accounts with several brokers of Philadelphia.[148] The subscription accounts do not distinguish between cargo and vessel insurance, but, judging from the policies consulted and from the printed sources mentioned below, one-way rates on cargoes were slightly over half those on the carrying vessels making the round trip. Accordingly, all unspecified quotations for round trips were halved and entered only once to avoid double counting. The annual rates were calculated, for each fiscal year (October– September), as simple averages of all available data on the plausible assumption that the extant quotations closely reflect the geographical distribution of this trade: nearly half of the documented voyages involve Cuban ports and the others are almost evenly spread between La Guaira, New Orleans (up to 1803), the River Plate and other Spanish colonial harbours. Rates for all but three of the remaining years were derived from current ranges for one-way voyages ('single risks') as published in contemporary weekly newspapers of Philadelphia and Boston for major ports and areas of the world including Spanish America.[149] Since the ranges are small and tend to remain stable for several months, the annual rates were calculated as simple averages from the mid-points of the first quarterly quotations within each fiscal year. Rates given for individual ports (1805–12) were averaged with the weights used for the estimation of freight rates from the Spanish West Indies and other Spanish American Colonies.[150] For reasons mentioned in the text, the adopted insurance rates were multiplied, as percentages, by the known import values CIF (at ports of arrival) net of gross freight costs (see columns 4 and 7).

Table 8 Estimation of gross insurance costs in United States trade with Spanish America and the Philippines, 1790–1819 (*thousands of dollars at current prices*)

Fiscal years	Average rates of insurance % X̄	Average rates of insurance % 1	Imports (goods paying specific and ad valorem duties) — In U.S. ships — Total value (CIF) X̄	In U.S. ships — Total value (CIF) 2	In U.S. ships — Freight costs (gross) 3	In U.S. ships — Insurance costs 1×(2−3)÷100 4	In foreign ships — Total value (CIF) X̄	In foreign ships — Total value (CIF) 5	In foreign ships — Freight costs (gross) 6	In foreign ships — Insurance costs 1×(5−6)÷100 7	Exports — Total official value (FOB) 8	Exports — Insurance costs 1×[8+(1×8÷100)]÷X̄ (X̄)	Exports — Insurance costs 1×[8+(1×8÷100)]÷X̄ 9
1790		2.2		61ᵃ	4	1		27ᵃ	2	1	148		3
1791		2.3		244ᵃ	7	6		110ᵃ	3	2	90		2
1792		2.5									149		4
1793		3.0									324		10
1794		3.5									1095		40
1795		4.0		1686ᵃ	85	64		733ᵃ	41	28	2503		104
1796	2.9	2.7	819	1284ᵃ	75	33	362	577ᵃ	38	15	2298	33	65
1797		7.7		4160	170	307		559	22	41	4770		396
1798		12.4		7124	444	825		1157	79	133	6372		886
1799		11.0		12776ᵃ	823	1319		1738ᵃ	122	178	13029		1599
1800		10.8		10609	774	1058		1178	99	116	10613		1266
1801	10.3	9.7	9415	12408	939	1113	1250	1619	120	145	10478	1053	1117
1802		4.3		6126	378	249		913	68	37	8123		367
1803		4.1		1709	220	61		1101	118	40	2344		100
1804	4.2	4.1	3850	3715	357	138	1176	1514	155	56	3646	208	156
1805		3.5		9552	702	310		1678	121	55	8490		308
1806		4.7		12344	948	540		1015	73	45	11528		572
1807	4.5	5.3	11443	12433	1182	594	1178	840	85	40	13130	537	730
1808		5.4		6327	1039	289		568	82	27	4379		252
1809		6.7		6738	939	386		1863	294	104	7424		527
1810		4.4		8480	1094	328		997	121	39	9722		450
1811	5.2	4.2	7771	9541	1305	343	1042	740	66	28	7930	393	344
1812		6.4		8431	1324	456		576	94	31	4213		287
1813		14.6		554	58	72		3976	483	509	3423		572
1814		14.6		2000	152	268		4769	391	637	4263		712
1815	10.0	4.4	4546	7199	381	298	2695	1458	89	60	4689	446	214
1816		5.5		6949	340	363		820	42	43	5953		345
1817		5.0		9717	361	467		839	26	40	7543		396
1818	4.1	3.2	8449	8764	574	266	565	376	20	12	6611	295	222
1819		2.9		8366	481	231		225	11	6	7192		218
	5.8		6641	179297	15156	10385	1184	31966	2865	2468	172472	409	12264

a. Breakdowns of imports CIF by United States' and foreign ships in these five years estimated as explained in Section A.
Sources and procedures: see Appendix, sections A (import values), B (rates of insurance and freight costs), and C (export values).

C   **Exports**

Export values at ports of departure were ascertained, as has been noted, by the customs collectors in most cases, and the official totals by receiving regions are extant and seem on the whole reliable with one significant qualification. The outgoing cargoes, particularly those bound for England and Gibraltar, were not always delivered at the stated ports of destination, so that exports to other areas are relatively under-represented.[151] The same is probably true of exports to the Indies, for some of the vessels that cleared at the United States' customs for the 'West Indies generally' may well have touched at Spanish–American ports.[152]

The extant *commodity breakdowns* by destination end in 1799 and are far from comprehensive. Such partial figures as can be estimated from official and secondary sources are summarized in table 9. The sub-series of exports to the Indies for 1790–99 have been derived from two separate samples of commodity weights and volumes,[153] multiplied by full wholesale prices in the case of domestic goods and by CIF import prices (net of customs duties returned as drawbacks) in the case of re-exports.[154] The sample coverage for this period is severely restricted to an average of 38 per cent of the official total[155] by the presence of large entries for non-enumerated goods in 1796–99 (column 9). If the values of these goods are added to the estimates from the sample, the overall coverage in the four years increases to 90 per cent of the official totals. The figures of domestic exports for 1800–16 are valuations of weights and volumes exported to the Spanish West Indies, supplied by Pitkin, at full wholesale prices.[156] The relatively wide sample coverage for 1790–96 and for 1812–15, the periods when the proportions of domestic goods were relatively high (see table 10, column 5), suggests that non-enumerated goods were for the most part re-exports.

The official export values by geographical origin and destination, compiled from the annual summaries and presented in table 10, make up for the paucity of commodity breakdowns. The one major drawback of these figures is that no distinction was made between domestic and foreign goods prior to 1803. Values for both groups in 1790–99 have been estimated from the two samples of commodities referred to in the foregoing paragraph. Proportions were first taken of sample domestic goods in the total sample values *plus* non-enumerated goods, which, as has been noted, appear to consist predominantly of re-exports. The annual values obtained by applying these proportions to total official exports were adopted as proxies for total domestic exports, and re-exports were derived by subtraction. Values of domestic and foreign exports for 1800–02[157] were in turn estimated from the corresponding shares in 1797–99 (for 1800–01: also naval war years) and in 1796 (for 1802: a year marked, like 1796, by recovery in Spanish exports and re-exports to the Indies, this second time at the expense of foreign competition).[158] The resulting estimates are admittedly rough, but the magnitudes are fully consistent with

Table 9 United States: exports to Spanish America and the Philippines[a] (estimates by commodities and official totals), 1790–1816 (current FOB values in thousands of dollars)

Fiscal years	Flour (x̄) 1	Pork & beef (x̄) 2	Rice (x̄) 3	Fish (x̄) 4	Tobacco (x̄) 5	Wines & spirits[b] (x̄) 6	Other[c] (x̄) 7	Sample totals (% of 10) 8	Goods not enumerated (% of 10) 9	Official totals (x̄) 10
1790	68	11	9	3	3	1	8	103		148
1791	21	4	23	0	1	0	14	64		90
1792	43	19	10	2	5	1	7	86		149
1793	150	18	9	3	3	20	8	210		324
1794	519	82	41	28	14	71	57	811		1095
1795	739	105	32	35	12	100	191	1214		2503
1796	909	114	60	8	26	116	108	1341		2298
x̄ / %	*350*	*50*	*26*	*11*	*9*	*44*	*56*	*58%*	*727 / 32%*	*943*
1797	772	176	48	84	17	365	139	1602	1932	4770
1798	1094	194	111	204	11	665	204	2483	3191	6372
1799	1099	185	189	103	109	1683	361	3730	8785	13029
1800	978	188	224	64	50		8	1511		10613
1801	1026	195	225	96	10		11	1563		10478
x̄ / %	*994*	*188*	*159*	*110*	*39*	*904*	*145*	*15%*	*58%*	*9052*
1802	520	165	92	148	0		5	929		8123
1803	240	30	20	14	15		6	324		2344
1804	704	181	60	28	186		53	1211		3646
x̄ / %	*488*	*125*	*57*	*63*	*67*		*21*	*17%*		*4704*
1805	1382	321	185	67	44		14	2013		8490
1806	851	418	129	82	21		16	1516		11528
1807	1193	180	87	63	40		11	1575		13130
x̄ / %	*1142*	*306*	*134*	*71*	*35*		*14*	*15%*		*11049*
1808	260	44	18	12	0		1	335		4379
1809	926	216	150	206	122		188	1808		7424
1810	1222	328	140	86	102		20	1897		9722
1811	1303	229	299	156	55		10	2052		7930
x̄ / %	*928*	*204*	*152*	*115*	*70*		*55*	*21%*		*7364*
1812	1082	125	114	139			17	1477		4213
1813	1466	172	194	54			186	2072		3423
1814	662	120	199	44			1011	2035		4623
1815	1219	115	299	47			40	1720		4689
x̄ / %	*1107*	*133*	*201*	*71*			*313*	*44%*		*4147*
1816	977	173	189	82	82		5	1427		5953
x̄ / %								*24%*		
Total / x̄	21425 / 794	4108 / 152	3156 / 117	1858 / 69			2699 / 100	37109 / 24%		151486 / 5611

a Spanish West Indies only from 1800 onwards. b Foreign distilled. c See note 159.
Sources and procedures: see Appendix, section C.

Table 10 United States: official exports to Spanish America and the Philippines: destinations and composition, 1790–1819 (current FOB values in thousands of dollars)

Fiscal years	Spanish West Indies and other American colonies	Floridas and Louisiana	Honduras, Campeche, and Mosquito Shore	Philippine Islands	Domestic goods x̄	Foreign goods x̄	Total (1+2+3+4 = 5+6)
	1	2	3	4	5	6	7
1790			0	0	144[a]	4[a]	148
1791	65	25	0	0	90[a]	0[a]	90
1792	112	37	0	0	147[a]	2[a]	149
1793	159	164	0	0	293[a]	31[a]	324
1794	873	223	0	0	996[a]	99[a]	1095
1795	1389	1114	0	0	2254[a]	249[a]	2503
1796	1821	477	0	0	1313[a]	985[a]	2298
x̄					748	196	943
%	68%	32%			79%	21%	
1797	3596	1044	130	0	1598[a]	3172[a]	4770
1798	5081	1074	218	0	1938[a]	4434[a]	6372
1799	8993	3504	531	0	1924[a]	11105[a]	13029
1800	8271	2036	292	14	2397[a]	8216[a]	10613
1801	8970	1408	100	0	2367	8111[a]	10478
x̄					2045	7008	9052
%	77%	20%	3%		23%	77%	
1802	6016	2076	32	0	4641[a]	3482[a]	8123
1803	878	1405	61	0	1652	692	2344
1804	2903	409	334	0	2053	1592	3646
x̄					2782	1922	4704
%	69%	28%	3%		59%	41%	
1805	7691	135	622	43	3138	5352	8490
1806	10867	152	472	37	2616	8913	11528
1807	12341	81	684	24	2659	10472	13130
x̄					2804	8246	11049
%	93%	1%	5%		25%	75%	
1808	4177	43	160	0	699	3681	4379
1809	6686	722	11	5	4038	3386	7424
1810	6787	2583	124	228	5861	3861	9722
1811	7580	204	146	0	3861	4069	7930
x̄					3615	3749	7364
%	86%	12%	1%		49%	51%	
1812	3972	104	77	60	2827	1386	4213
1813	2993	405	24	0	3238	184	3423
1814	2020	2232	11	0	4213	50	4263
1815	3699	849	86	55	3733	967	4689
x̄					3503	644	4147
%	76%	22%	1%		84%	16%	
1816	5781	107	63	3	2873	3080	5953
1817	7084	156	303	0	3834	3709	7543
1818	5912	166	533	0	3796	2815	6611
1819	6500	199	494	0	3774	3419	7192
x̄					3569	3256	6825
%	93%	2%	5%		52%	48%	
	143217	23134	5508	469	74967	97508	172472

a Breakdowns estimated as explained in the text.
Sources: compiled and calculated from United States Congress, *American State Papers*, Class 4, *Commerce and Navigation*, 2 vols., Gales and Seaton, Washington D.C., 1832 (1789–1815) and 1834 (1815–1823), *passim*.

the expansion of the carrying trade known to have occurred after 1796 and with its subsequent contraction in the last two years of the truce of Amiens (1803–04: official data in table 10, column 6).

D Freight and insurance costs on exports

Since the official export figures were valued at United States' ports, they do not include freight and insurance. Both of these costs, however, incorporate significant components of the balance of payments and have therefore been estimated. Gross insurance costs on exports were derived from the ocean rates presented in section B (see table 8). The insurance rates (column 1) were applied, as was done for imports and for the same reasons, to 'at sea' export values, in this case exports FOB plus gross insurance costs at ports of departure (see column 9). The estimation of freight costs also parallels that for imports as explained in section B, but the tonnage figures are less reliable for lack of comprehensive breakdowns by commodities. For domestic exports up to 1816, cargo tons estimated from a reasonably large sample of quantities and volumes[159] were compounded with ratios of official over sample values at constant prices.[160] This procedure rests upon the plausible assumption that the average tonnage of domestic goods not included in the sample did not differ significantly from that of the known quantities. Tons for 1817–19 were derived from the share of estimated tons in official domestic exports at constant prices in 1816. Re-export tons up to 1799 were estimated from a much smaller sample of enumerated quantities and volumes[161] in the same manner, with the only difference that the excess tonnage over that in the sample was reduced to 60 per cent.[162] The plausible assumption in this case is that re-exports to the Indies were composed largely of manufactures with smaller than average weights and volumes relative to value. Re-export tons from 1800 onwards, a period for which no weights or volumes have been found, were derived from the share of estimated tons in official re-export values at constant prices in 1798–99. The resulting series of export tonnage were multiplied by the freight rates derived in section B to obtain costs in current dollars. The series of total export tonnage and freight costs are presented in table 11 (columns 1 and 3).

E Allocation of credits and debits in the United States' balance of payments

By far the largest credits and debits in the United States' balance of payments stem, respectively, from the export and import values at current prices. Since the best documented trade series are those valued at United States' ports, the merchandise balance has been reckoned as exports FOB at ports of departure minus imports CIF inclusive of freight and insurance at ports of arrival (see table 3, columns 1 and 2). One implication of this procedure is that all earnings from freight, insurance and mercantile profits that accrued to United States'

Table 11 Estimates and derived allocation of gross freight costs in United States' exports to Spanish America and the Philippines, 1790–1819

Fiscal years	U.S. total exports to Spain & Spanish Empire							Net credits to U.S. shippers	
	Estimated cargo tons		Estimated gross freight costs		Spanish tonnage entering U.S. Ports (00)	Credits to Spanish shippers [5×(0.75)×4)]÷2 $000	% of U.S. tonnage in (total Spanish) tonnage employed in U.S. foreign trade %	Total (4−6)×7÷100 $000	Against the Indies 8×3÷4 $000
	To the Indies (00) $\bar{X}$	Total to Spain + Spanish Empire (00)	To the Indies $000 $\bar{X}$	Total to Spain + Spanish Empire $000					
	1	2	3	4	5	6	7	8	9
1790	21	523	16	776	74	82	59.5	413	9
1791	22	244	14	364	43	49	60.6	191	8
1792	33	422	22	646	27	31	63.2	389	13
1793	68	398	84	886	31	52	73.6	614	58
1794	138	578	170	1365	22	39	86.7	1149	143
1795	279	608	345	1328	20	33	91.4	1184	307
1796	122	193	158	367	24	35	93.8	312	134
$\bar{X}$	98		116						96
1797	253	385	290	631	6	7	88.9	555	255
1798	401	564	754	1228	5	9	85.7	1045	642
1799	581	783	1325	2037	11	22	85.5	1723	1121
1800	523	820	1179	2227	14	29	84.8	1863	987
1801	471	674	1000	1677	25	46	84.5	1378	822
$\bar{X}$	446		910						765
1802	584	828	904	1411	86	110	85.4	1111	712
1803	198	425	394	1017	155	279	84.1	621	241
1804	244	509	534	1309	163	315	88.6	881	359
$\bar{X}$	342		611						437
1805	452	723	848	1640	25	43	91.5	1461	756
1806	588	798	1135	1772	6	11	92.0	1621	1038
1807	654	946	1464	2467	7	13	90.2	2213	1313
$\bar{X}$	565		1149						1036
1808	211	316	662	1076	9	24	91.8	966	594
1809	513	713	1606	2394	124	313	89.9	1871	1255
1810	644	1035	1709	3250	193	455	93.7	2619	1377
1811	452	799	1198	2565	114	274	97.7	2238	1045
$\bar{X}$	455		1294						1068
1812	299	746	794	2553	184	473	95.9	1995	620
1813	272	806	720	2820	464	1219	77.9	1247	318
1814	381	390	871	902	201	349	67.9	376	363
1815	325	435	533	828	153	219	77.7	473	305
$\bar{X}$	319		729						401
1816	310	487	367	679	98	103	77.9	449	243
1817	450	511	382	459	62	41	79.1	330	275
1818	435	508	574	719	50	53	82.8	552	440
1819	479	547	554	671	31	28	90.5	581	480
$\bar{X}$	418		469						359
	10403	17713	20608	42064	2427	4756		32419	16233
$\bar{X}$	347		687						541

Sources and procedures: see Appendix, sections D and E. The sources of columns 5 and 7 are given in notes 163 and 165.

citizens must be credited to the United States, for all such earnings as were made on imports are included as debits in the CIF values at ports of arrival.

Credits from carrying services have been allocated to the United States from the estimates of freight and insurance costs, most of which are grounded, however imperfectly, on contemporary evidence. At a number of junctures, however, it has been necessary to speculate on the shares that accrued to other nations as earnings of foreign exchange. This is particularly true of the allocation of freight earnings on exports, the groundwork for which has been laid in the preceding section (see table 11, columns 1 and 3). The main difficulty is that the official export figures, unlike their import counterparts, do not group commodities by United States' and foreign ships, so that credits from total freight costs had to be estimated, indirectly, from the known cargo capacities of Spanish, foreign and domestic vessels engaged in the total trade of the United States. The point of departure was an official series of *Spanish* tonnage arrived at United States' ports in calendar years (column 5).[163] Some Spanish captains may have sold their entire cargoes at United States' ports and taken full loads of United States' merchandise for the return voyages. More likely, vessels bound for the Indies or Spain also carried Spanish or Spanish American commodities in transit and were not always fully loaded. Accordingly, it was assumed that United States' goods made up 75 per cent of the cargo capacity of departing Spanish ships. Resulting errors are small in most years because the cargo capacities involved amount, on the average, to less than a sixth of the total tonnage exported. The freight earnings per ton on goods carried in Spanish bottoms have not been ascertained, but they probably approximated those on total shipments from the United States to Spain and the Indies. To obtain proxies for total average earnings, tonnage and freight costs on United States' exports *to Spain* were derived from sample quantities and rates per ton as already explained in sections B and D, and both series were added to the respective sub-totals to the Indies (see columns 2 and 4).[164] Total credits to Spanish shippers (column 6) were reckoned as the estimated shares of cargo capacity allotted to United States' exports (75 per cent of column 5) times the ratios of total freight costs (column 4) over total export tons (column 2). Total credit to United States' shippers (column 8) were estimated as the differences between total and Spanish freight earnings (column 4 − column 6) weighted by the shares of the United States in the total (net of Spanish) tonnage engaged in foreign trade (column 7).[165] Finally, the net claims of United States' shippers against the Indies (column 9) were derived from the shares of freight costs on exports to the Indies in the totals to Spain and its empire (columns 2 and 4). Column 9 is subject to significant compound error, but it is worth noting that the total would be a mere 7 per cent larger if freight earnings on exports to the Indies (column 3) had simply been multiplied by the share of United States' ships in total import tonnage (data in table 7, columns 2 and 7).

The credits from carrying earnings in the balance of payments have been grouped by freight and insurance in table 3. Freight costs on exports were allocated to the United States as explained in the preceding paragraph (column 9 in table 11). The credits from insurance on exports were reckoned as total costs (table 8, column 9) minus half the shares of re-exports in total export values,[166] to allow for substantial foreign participation in this area: as is well known, Britain's insurers dominated operations on her export trade and Lloyd's appointed agents in the principal ports of the world. Payments for wreckage or spoilage of goods have not been deducted from the insurance credits on exports: so long as domestic ships predominated in this area of trade, most such payments must have been settled between United States' citizens. On the import side, freight costs in United States' ships (table 7, column 5) were credited in full to the United States. Not so the insurance on the respective cargoes (table 8, column 4), for Spanish underwriters had agents in the Indies and colonial companies prospered before they were struck by bankruptcy in the 1800s.[167] Moreover, British insurers probably set a firm foothold in the Indies after 1807 as did British merchants. Accordingly, insurance earnings on imports in United States' ships were credited at 65 per cent of total costs before 1800 and only 40 per cent after 1807. In 1800–07 the proportion was raised to 80 per cent in favor of United States' companies and associations of ship owners, which are known to have expanded their marine insurance operations with the rise of the carrying trade.[168] To introduce a conservative bias in the insurance account, no allowance was made for other sources of foreign exchange earnings. Settlements for loss or damage in United States' ships possibly turned significant credits against foreign insurers, and United States' citizens may well have insured foreign vessels at a profit.

Foreign port charges probably turned net debits to the United States in all years when the tonnage carried in home ships exceeded that in foreign vessels. Charges at United States' ports have been reckoned, after a nineteenth-century estimate,[169] at 20 per cent of gross freight costs in foreign vessels (table 7, column 10). Charges at Spanish American ports, which seemed exorbitant to a creditable agent from Connecticut who resided in Havana in the winter of 1805–06,[170] at 25 per cent of gross freight costs in United States' ships (table 7, column 6). The net balances on foreign port charges are given in table 3 (column 3).

Mercantile profits were probably a major source of foreign exchange for the United States, but only the minimum magnitudes involved can be estimated in the present state of research on prices in Spanish–American ports. Richard Pares, in one of his admirable studies of late colonial trade with the West Indies, found but a few unrepresentative accounts of profits and losses on southward cargoes.[171] United States' merchants received frequent reports from their agents in Havana at the turn of the nineteenth century and beyond, but such correspondence as has been consulted[172] gives no indication of overall rates of return.[173] Partial estimates by Stephen Girard's brokers in 1808–11 were highly sensitive to local market conditions, and they ranged from 'very profitable' on sales of dried beef from Buenos Aires and Rio de Janeiro[174] to at least 100 per cent net on German linens brought in United States' ships.[175] One conceivable proxy for minimum total profits are the commissions of resident factors.[176] It has been ascertained that Stephen Girard's agents in Havana willingly lowered their rates in June 1809, upon request from their employer, to 3 per cent on sales and 2 per cent on returns.[177] These agents' commissions, however, are deductions from total revenue rather than profit shares actually received as earnings of foreign exchange by United States' merchants, who were required by Spanish law, in Cuba at least, to employ local agents.[178] The best that can be done is to set a lower bound upon rates of 5 and 2.5 per cent normally paid to captains of United States' ships, prior to the American Revolution, for the sale and purchase of cargoes in the West Indies.[179] These rates presumably remained stable in subsequent decades, for those charged by resident factors on both sales and purchases in the West Indies stood at 5 per cent in the 1760s[180] and had not changed by the turn of the century.[181] The actual rates of return were probably much larger: Shepherd and Walton, drawing on contemporary evidence, estimated profits in the West Indian trade at a minimum of 10 per cent in 1768–72.[182] And Spanish America was still regarded as a major source of foreign exchange in the mid 1810s despite the trade deficits with the Indies in these years.[183]

Nevertheless, the rates of 5 and 2.5 per cent probably paid to ship captains, for sales and purchases respectively, have been adopted as proxies for minimum profit rates, with moderate premiums in certain years for unusually favorable business conditions. In the early years of naval warfare between England and Spain, importable goods must have become scarce in the Indies and exportable commodities abundant, thus enhancing the profit opportunities of United States' merchants. With the return of peace, competition from Spain and eventually from Britain certainly produced the opposite effects. One of many examples is furnished by Stephen Girard's agents in Havana, who, late in 1808, expressed concern over the rising prices of sugar and other staples as news of imminent Spanish and British arrivals reached the port.[184] Accordingly, profit rates have been set, in all years of naval war, at 1 per cent above those probably paid to ship captains. Following Albert Imlah's example in his estimation of the British balance of payments, re-exports were included in the trade values subject to profit markups.[185] Rates of 5 to 6 per cent were applied to estimates of export values in United States' ships[186] at ports of departure, and rates of 2.5 to 3.5 per cent to the values of imports in United States' ships at ports of arrival. The resulting estimates of minimum total profits have been given in table 3 (column 6).

F   Customs revenues

Customs revenues on imports from the Indies are easily derived from official import quantities, rates of taxation and drawbacks returned upon re-export of the principal imports. Gross revenues on goods subject to specific duties were reckoned as the aggregate of import weights and volumes for each commodity times the corresponding tax rates — all of which had already been compiled for the estimation of import values at United States' ports.[187] Gross revenues on goods paying ad valorem were calculated from official import values and tax rates given for non-itemized groups of these goods. To obtain proxies for the shares of gross revenue returned upon re-export to the rest of the world, ratios of drawback payable over duties received were calculated, for a sample of seven major commodities and goods paying ad valorem imported from the Indies[188] from parallel official series for the years 1795–1814.[189] The products of these ratios and gross revenue for each commodity were adopted as estimates of drawbacks for the period 1795–1814. Drawbacks for the remaining five years were derived in the same manner from annual values of debentures issued on total re-exports as percentages of total import revenue on merchandise.[190] Series of gross and net customs revenue, together with shares in the respective totals for the United States as a whole, have been presented in table 4.[191]

G   Import and export prices and terms of trade

The deflation procedures also draw from materials used in the estimation of import and export values. The price index for imports, presented in table 12 (column 1), is an arithmetic average of two separate indices for goods subject to specific and ad valorem duties, each weighted by the proportions of the respective group in total import values in each year. The index for the first group was obtained by division of current imports over the respective constant values calculated at 1791 prices. The index for goods paying ad valorem, which were largely manufactures,[192] is a geometric average of prices of 40 industrial raw and semi-finished commodities imported into Philadelphia.[193] Since goods subject to specific duties averaged 96.6 per cent of total imports, the deflated import figures (column 2) are very close to actual constant values. The indices for exports are less reliable owing to the absence of comprehensive breakdowns by commodities.[194] Two separate indices from samples of domestic (1790–1816) and foreign (1790–99) goods were first obtained, as before, by division of current over constant values, and each index was weighted by the proportions of the sample totals in the respective breakdowns of official exports in each year.[195] The remaining weights[196] were assigned to two secondary indices derived, once more, from Philadelphia prices. The secondary index for domestic exports is a geometric average of wholesale prices of 69 domestic commodities[197] and that for re-exports combines prices of

Table 12 United States: deflated trade values and terms of trade with Spanish America and the Philippines, 1790–1819 (*thousands of dollars; 1791 = 100*)

| Fiscal years | Total imports FOB | | Exports FOB | | | | | | Terms of trade (PEx/PIm) | |
| | | | Domestic goods | | Foreign goods | | Total | | | |
	Price index $\bar{x}$ 1	Deflated values $\bar{x}$ 2	Price index $\bar{x}$ 3	Deflated values $\bar{x}$ 4	Price index $\bar{x}$ 5	Deflated values $\bar{x}$ 6	Price index $\bar{x}$ 7	Deflated values $\bar{x}$ 8	On domestic exports (3÷1)×100 $\bar{x}$ 9	On total exports (7÷1)×100 $\bar{x}$ 10
1790	81	100	107	135	98	4	106	139	132	131
1791	100	336	100	90	100	0	100	90	100	100
1792			97	152	98	2	97	154		154
1793			106	276	124	25	108	301		
1794			117	854	129	77	118	931		
1795	132	1668	156	1449	139	180	154	1629	118	117
1796	153	1111	211	623	148	665	178	1288	138	116
$\bar{x}$	116	804	128	511 (79%)	119	136 (21%)	123	647	122	116
1797	144	2901	177	904	148	2139	157	3043	123	109
1798	147	4625	150	1294	140	3178	142	4472	102	97
1799	133	9076	149	1295	144	7702	145	8997	112	109
1800	125	7792	157	1528	139	5921	142	7449	126	114
1801	127	9220	178	1329	150	5397	156	6726	140	123
$\bar{x}$	135	6723	162	1270 (21%)	144	4867 (79%)	148	6137	121	110
1802	110	5734	143	3245	144	2411	144	5656	130	131
1803	103	2301	135	1224	139	497	136	1721	131	132
1804	127	3562	140	1466	137	1163	139	2629	110	109
$\bar{x}$	113	3866	139	1978 (59%)	140	1357 (41%)	140	3335	124	124
1805	131	7667	173	1811	144	3718	154	5529	132	118
1806	121	9713	151	1731	138	6452	141	8183	125	117
1807	109	10433	144	1888	141	7450	141	9338	129	129
$\bar{x}$	120	9271	155	1810 (24%)	141	5873 (76%)	145	7683	129	121
1808	98	5570	122	573	146	2519	142	3092	124	145
1809	103	6677	126	3203	149	2278	135	5481	122	131
1810	107	7379	152	3855	160	2418	155	6273	142	145
1811	104	8210	164	2356	179	2267	172	4623	158	165
$\bar{x}$	103	6959	141	2497 (51%)	158	2370 (49%)	151	4867	136	146
1812	100	7103	153	1852	183	759	161	2611	153	161
1813	124	2749	151	2142	183	101	153	2243	122	123
1814	197	2701	157	2675	258	19	158	2694	80	80
1815	196	3994	175	2138	236	405	184	2543	89	94
$\bar{x}$	154	4137	159	2202 (87%)	215	321 (13%)	164	2523	111	114
1816	150	4654	182	1583	200	1542	190	3125	121	104
1817	133	7264	176	2178	143	2586	158	4764	132	119
1818	131	6311	163	2329	151	1864	158	4193	124	121
1819	132	5956	153	2467	147	2328	150	4795	116	114
$\bar{x}$	136	6046	168	2139 (51%)	160	2080 (49%)	164	4219	123	114
	127	144807	149	48645	151	66067	146	114712	123	121
$\bar{x}$		5363		1621		2202		3824		

Sources and procedures: see Appendix, section G. The current values of imports are given in table 1, column 4, and those of exports in table 10, columns 5, 6 and 7.

59 imported commodities (1790−1819),[198] total imports from Spain (1790−91 and 1796−1819),[199] 6 textile fabrics (1797−1808),[200] and wines and spirits (1800−02 and 1805−08).[201] The weighted indices and deflated values of exports are presented in columns 3 through 8. Finally, two series of terms of trade on domestic and total exports were calculated from the relevant indices of export and import prices (columns 9 and 10).

Colonial economy and international economy: the trade of the St Lawrence River Valley with Spain, Portugal and their Atlantic possessions, 1760–1850

Historians have been conscious for some time of the problems inherent in defining the connection between the economy of the St Lawrence River Valley and that of the world at large. As early as 1940 Harold Innis in his study of the international fisheries, *The cod fisheries*, indirectly unveiled the trans-Atlantic dimension of the local economy even though he had defined the Laurentian economy as continental, tied to the French or British empires exclusively by the fur trade.[1] A few years later, J.B. Brebner, a partisan of the continental thesis which placed the accent on the north-south orientation of the North American economy, was more explicit in his book, *The North Atlantic Triangle*.[2] But he did not go so far as to reveal the mechanisms or evaluate the scale of integration of the colony's economic life into the trans-Atlantic or international economy.

In 1965, based on the numerous statistical series which I gathered for my *Histoire économique et sociale du Québec, 1760–1850*,[3] I analyzed the context of international rivalry within which the external trade of Quebec and Canada developed, demonstrating in particular the competition for the British market between the St Lawrence Valley, the United States, and Northern and continental Europe. As to the more specific issue of the continental or international character of the economy of the St Lawrence Valley, I arrived at conclusions which, although preliminary, remain valid in the present perspective. Concerning the relationship between domestic and English prices, I wrote:

One could go even further and maintain that, insofar as the British economy is the motor or reflection of an international conjuncture, Quebec prices react to the movement of the international economy ...[4]

Indeed, it was difficult not to see through the twenty odd agricultural price series whose curves I traced, the striking similarities which existed between the Quebec and British curves, and between these and the American and French ones.[5]

But behind prices, of course, there was trade, and with trade an aggregate of commercial and financial relationships which went well beyond imperial frontiers and mercantilist norms. Thus, I had to add that

Sensitive from the first to the short and long-term oscillations of the British economy, Canada came in time to react to the movement of the American economy. It is through the mediation of these two foci of activity, and more through the first than through the second, that the St Lawrence Valley was drawn into the fluctuations of the international economy.[6]

In an article in 1967 P. Paquet and J.-P. Wallot considered the question anew, placing the emphasis on what they termed 'a global indicator of international economic activity, the number and tonnage of ships entering or leaving the port of Quebec' during these twenty years.[7] The quantitative data which they published in that article are extremely important to their thesis that the early nineteenth century saw an economic restructuring of the zone, and are equally useful as a complement to my own series which are spread over nearly a century. But because their statistical series only cover two decades and are undifferentiated, they are not adequate to shed light on the phenomenon in all of its breadth. Indeed, far from appearing at the end of the eighteenth century, as they maintain, the international character of the colonial economy of the St Lawrence Valley was already evident even before 1760 and was incessantly reinforced thereafter.

The fishermen of metropolitan France frequented the fishing banks of Newfoundland and sent their catch to all of the West Indies, to Spain, to Portugal and elsewhere. The merchants of Louisbourg, besides maintaining close business ties with those of New France, profitably traded with a zone encompassing the regions mentioned above and New England.[8] Indeed, over the course of years, the French fortress guarding the North Atalantic had become, to a certain degree, an economic outpost of New England. At that level, regulations and prohibitions had little effect on the orientation of trade, as the contrabanding of furs to New England in the same period attested.

Thus, even in the short term, the colony's trade towards other countries and other empires hardly seems modest, despite what has been alleged. Begun in the French period, that commerce was so rooted in the economic structure that it continued even after the British took possession of the St Lawrence Valley. It then spread to Spain, Portugal, to their colonies (before and after independence), and even to countries like China, Russia, Sweden, France and particularly the United States. Contraband was important. To accurately measure the scale of these relations, however, one must concentrate on the official statistics on direct and indirect foreign trade.

1 The structure of the colonial economy and of its external trade

The economic structure created in the St Lawrence Valley during the French period was the result of conditions which, on the whole, responded to the imperatives of the mercantilist system, which aimed to regulate the colony's commercial relations with the metropole, other parts of the empire and foreign dominions. Those parts of New France which could not readily fit into this economic order, like Acadia and Louisbourg, for practical purposes divorced themselves almost completely, willingly or otherwise, from the St Lawrence Valley.[9] Thus, the colony became a source of raw materials, primarily for the metropole and secondarily for the French West Indies. It goes without saying, that it was difficult for manufacturing to develop in suitable fashion so that attempts to stimulate the forest industry, to encourage naval construction and to establish the Saint-Maurice ironworks on a sound footing had only mediocre results. Besides, as long as France could obtain its wood more cheaply in Northern Europe than in its colony, it was not prepared to use tariff advantages to stimulate the expansion of production in that domain. External trade, despite the continental character of the economy and the weight of the agricultural sector, played a crucial role in the life of this poor and scanty colony population.

After 1760, despite a softening of the mercantilist system, this economic structure remained in place down to 1849, as did the doctrines which justified it. So as to properly situate the role of external trade as an engine for economic growth, and as a base for the study of the relations which this economy could maintain with areas outside of the British empire, I prepared four statistical tables describing the incoming and outgoing high seas trade of Quebec, Montreal, Gaspé and New Carlisle (see Appendix: tables 29, 31, 32 and 33). From this data, there can be no doubt that maritime trade volumes, like commerce by land with the United States, increased in a more or less continuous fashion until 1850; and that, in the long term, it grew more rapidly than the population of the St Lawrence Valley, despite the fact that the latter increased by a factor of twenty-six.

In the long term, this enormous growth in port activity coincided with technological change which manifested itself in a rapid increase in the size of ships, even as the number of crewmen rose much more slowly during the century. From 1760 to 1770 the mean tonnage of ships arriving in or leaving the ports of Quebec and Montreal towards the high seas was 85 tons and the mean size of the crew was 7.8 men. From 1840 to 1850, those averages rose to 357 tons and 13.2 men (see table 14). One should note, however, that during the last years of the American Revolution the situation was somewhat confused, since, from 1771 to 1783, the number of crew temporarily doubled while ship size increased by only 43 per cent. Half of these seamen were, no doubt, charged with the handling of the 2,635 cannons which were carried on these ships from 1776 to 1782. This situation did not recur during the

Table 13   The population of the St Lawrence Valley

	Quebec	Upper Canada[b]	Total
1760	70,000[a]		70,000
1784	130,415[a]	5,000[a]	135,415
1825	373,199[a]	157,923	531,122
1832	515,528[a]	236,702	752,230
1851	890,261	952,004	1,842,265

a Estimate.
b Upper Canada was officially created as a separate political unit in 1791, and was reunited anew with Quebec (Lower Canada) in 1840, before becoming the Province of Ontario in 1867.

Source: Recensement du Canada, 1871, vol. IV; F. Ouellet, 'L'accroissement naturel de la population catholique québécoise avant 1850: aperçus historiographiques et quantitatifs' (Forthcoming in *l'Actualité économique*).

war of 1812, perhaps because of a labor shortage. In any event, the technological change was not limited to high seas ships frequenting Quebec harbors. The same phenomenon characterized construction in Quebec naval shipyards between 1788 and 1850, as the size of the ships to be sold in England and the West Indies (and not to transport local products to market as in the case of the Atlantic seaboard colonies) grew in the same fashion. In 1800 these new vessels averaged 155.9 tons, while in the 1840s the mean rose to 403.3.

This technological revolution,[10] with its gradual onset, contrasts with another change whose character was far more brutal: the trade revolution which began in the middle of the first decade of the nineteenth century and paved the way for the alteration of commercial activities from the fur trade to the lumber trade. This restructuring was, therefore, an event of capital importance since the existing economic forms had grown during the seventeenth century and survived such cataclysmic events as the British conquest of 1760 and the American Revolution. This early nineteenth century break affected an economy which depended on two relatively independent sectors, furs and agriculture, and on three sectors of subsidiary importance: fisheries, forestry and the Saint-Maurice iron works. At first, agriculture was limited to subsistence, but, gradually and particularly during the second half of the eighteenth century, it had acquired a somewhat commercial character and, from that moment played an increasingly important role in exports, along with furs. At the beginning of the nineteenth century, with the decline of the fur trade and a crisis in Lower Canadian agriculture, overseas trade was transformed by the vibrantly expanding lumber industry, a situation destined to last until such time as greater quantities of grain began to arrive from Upper Canada and the United States.

Table 14   Value of Quebec exports by economic sector

	Agriculture %	Furs %	Fisheries %	Timber %	Various %	Total %
1770–1772	18.2	66.8	5.1	6.5	3.4	100
1773	38.6	37.6	4.2	19.2	0.4	100
1808	12.1	9.3	(?)	67.1	11.5	100

Source: PAC, MG 23, G. 1, 10.
Figures are approximations only.

One must add, that this break contributed to the radical alteration of the existing balance between the volume of exports and imports. As long as the fur trade remained the principal component of exports, ships sailing in ballast were to be found among those leaving port. In 1764, for example, the furs were carried out in 11 vessels when a total of 32 ships had arrived.[11] It is obvious, in view of the scant quantities of wood, fish and cereals exported during the same year, that the percentage of vessels which left port in ballast must have been considerable. But, with the growth in wheat exports and the moderate increase of wood and fish shipments, this situation was reversed: between 1801 and 1804, the proportion of ships which arrived unloaded was between 25 and 32 per cent. The spectacular rise in wood exports after 1805 decisively accentuated this disequilibrium: the proportion of ships arriving in ballast rose to 50 per cent, and, most often, stayed between 60 and 75 per cent. Massive immigration hardly modified this state of affairs save in 1831–32, as is shown by the percentage of vessels in ballast in 1847 (72 per cent) when 70,000 immigrants arrived in Quebec.

Thus, since the seventeenth century, the fur trade had been the principal base for exports from the St Lawrence Valley. From one period to another, the quantities exported had grown, and this increase had been due mostly to pelts other than those of beaver. This trade, strongly oriented towards France before 1760 and towards London thereafter, was the cause of the rapid white penetration of the continent's interior. In less than a century and a half, drawn by Indian tribes given to this activity, the traders had gone as far as New Orleans in the south and the Rockies in the west. After the British conquest, despite the constraints imposed by the government, this expansionist movement towards the south-west and west continued with even greater force. (see Appendix: table 34). The Mississippi route remained attractive for some time and was the source of an important clandestine trade for many years. These relations were sustained, up to a point, for four decades, even after the cession of Louisiana to Spain in 1763. The 1793 expedition from New Orleans to the upper Missouri of Jean-Baptiste Trudeau, a one-time student of the seminary of Quebec, like that of Jean-Baptiste Tabeau ten years later, illustrates quite well the surprising survival of this century-old contact.

The real expansion of the fur trade, however, took place towards the north-west, thanks to the impetus of the North-West Company. The Montreal firm, with offices in Quebec, New York and London, did not confine its sales to the London emporium. Rather, with its own ships and American ones, it established itself in the Chinese market and busied itself after 1790 by expanding its endeavors to the American one (see Appendix: table 34). The manpower used to gather these furs from the Indians and to transport them to Montreal was given its distinctive character by a rather small core of professional fur traders. Like most other local economic activities, however, the fur trade recruited the great majority of its work force from the peasants and their sons on a seasonal basis, from the rural parishes of Quebec. Around 1790 about 3,000 men were needed to transport the precious cargoes of fur, of which 80 per cent came from the countryside.

It is obvious that, until the onset of the decline of this risky but lucrative trade, the idea of a Quebec or Canada which spread from Atlantic to Pacific made sense, not only to the hundreds of merchants, *voyageurs* and *coureurs des bois*, who were used to the business, but also to an important proportion of the population which was drawn in, directly or indirectly, on an seasonal basis. The decline of this trade, heretofore always dominant, dates from the start of the nineteenth century. Internal rivalry and external competition, increased transport costs, inflation and high wages, account for the final bankruptcy of the North-West Company in 1821. Its demise redounded to the profit of the English-owned Hudson's Bay Company and to that of its American rivals. In any event, the evolving situation was of critical importance as it isolated the lowlands of the St Lawrence from the vast western spaces.

Side by side with this commercial activity which, albeit at different social levels and in substantial but limited numbers, drew in both urban and rural dwellers, was the agricultural sector, which involved the immense majority of the population as producers or consumers. Indeed, in the St Lawrence Valley, land was available in great abundance for over two centuries. Access to landed property was thereby facilitated for most people. At first, the development of agriculture took place in such a way as to exclusively satisfy the food needs of the local populations, which is why wheat growing became so fundamental an activity. To truly understand the role of wheat, one must add that it was then the most likely agricultural commodity to find eventually a ready market outside the colony. Indeed, the restricted needs of the fur trade and the small size of the cities prevented them from becoming effective internal propellants of commercial agriculture. During the 1730s a modest flow of flour exports to Ile Royale and the West Indies developed, but it was quickly interrupted. None the less, in 1740 some 50,000 *minots* of wheat were sent abroad.

This tendency towards commercialization began again after 1760, and became quite vigorous at the start of the second decade following the English conquest. Parenthetically, although exports receded after 1774 the commercial character of agriculture did not diminish on that account for, during the

American Revolution, the local market reached unheard of proportions because of the presence of British and foreign troops in the colony. After several critical years following 1779, a recovery in export levels began as the British market welcomed some colonial products. The overseas sale of Lower Canadian wheat products increased from 1785 to peak levels in 1802. Then, it diminished continuously until 1831, after which point Lower Canadian wheat production became largely insufficient even for colonial needs (see Appendix: table 35).[12]

The end to the overseas sale of wheat harvested in Lower Canada was due to a series of circumstances which contributed to the rise in local production costs and, consequently, encouraged bringing in for re-export wheat and flour from Upper Canada and the United States. In those areas, production costs were sufficiently low to compensate for high transport expenses from the interior, via the St Lawrence, towards Quebec. These regular shipments of alien wheat began in 1793: again, meat and dairy products arrived from the United States and Upper Canada at Côteau-du-Lac and, later, by the Lachine Canal. The few available statistics that refer to wheat and the other commodities for the years before 1817 indicate a progressive acceleration in these purchases from the start of the nineteenth century. These were not the only Canadian purchases of United States' agricultural products. As the New England countryside had already been transformed by cattle breeding, the massive importation of food-stuffs through the port of St Jean included very little wheat but large quantities of meat, dairy products and even cod. The same types of imports, although in reduced quantities, entered through Ste-Marie de Beauce and Stanstead (Lower Canada). Lastly, from 1832 onwards, substantial imports of wheat from Upper Canada arrived via the Rideau Canal (see Appendix: table 35). This relocation of grain-growing towards the west imposed such changes as the canalization of the river and the development of banking institutions, and favored the growth of Montreal.

Among the subsidiary economic sectors, one finds first of all the Saint-Maurice ironworks, an enterprise which, after the bankruptcy of F.-E. Cugnet, passed into the hands of the state. During the British regime the government farmed out this industrial establishment, which produced for the local market and had a modest exportable surplus.[13] Although brought into question by the defenders of pro-agricultural thought, because it encouraged use of land for charcoal production, the ironworks continued to operate with a certain degree of success down to 1850. By then, however, it was no more than a marginal operation (like the fur trade and fisheries) which used a seasonal rival work force for some of its operations.

The fisheries had, likewise, been a sector of subsidiary importance in an economy which was oriented towards overseas trade. In the French period, the international fisheries had been a domain struggled over by international rivals, one of which was New England. As far as the French were concerned, the fisheries had been controlled by metropolitan fishermen and by those of

Louisbourg.[14] The merchants and fishermen of Quebec had played a rather restricted role in this rivalry. Their share of the considerable French stake had been limited to supplying the local market and obtaining a rather mediocre opening into the West Indian zones. There is no doubt that after 1760 the exports of cod, salmon and fish oil increased substantially as the annual figures demonstrate. Moreover, certain ports like Gaspé and, later, New Carlisle became active during the second half of the eighteenth century. By 1820, exports from Quebec did not represent any more than one quarter of total cod shipments from these three ports. It has been reported that around 2,000 men found seasonal work in the fisheries at the start of the nineteenth century. None the less, after the independence of the United States, local fishermen increasingly objected to American trespass upon their fishing grounds, complaints which continued down to 1850. There is no doubt that export volume rose until 1820. One must note, however, that from the start of the nineteenth century Lower Canada also imported substantial quantities of cod every year from the United States via the port of St-Jean sur Richelieu.

In view of international rivalries, the forest industries did not stand much chance of occupying the first rank among Lower Canadian economic activities during the French period, or even in the last half of the eighteenth century. This is because neither England nor France would cease provisioning themselves with North European wood, which was cheaper than the colonial product. It is obvious that higher transport costs on the American side of the Atlantic weighed a great deal in the price disparities which dictated the metropolitan choice. Thus, in the eighteenth century the timber trade, despite a degree of expansion produced by colonial demographic growth and by the appearance of new foreign marketing possibilities, kept its status as a minor economic activity. The few tariff advantages conceded by Great Britain no doubt explain the modest progress of the industry. It is only with the continental blockade, when its traditional sources of supply were menaced that England took the decision to stimulate, through a tariff system adapted to the economic circumstances, the exploitation of forest resources in its North American colonies, and particularly in New Brunswick and Lower Canada. Within a few years after 1806, the wood trade became the principal cause of the growth in maritime activity and foreign trade (compare Appendix: tables 29 and 36). One should not believe, of course, that it had been enough for Great Britain to establish tariff protection, to suddenly launch an economic revolution in the St Lawrence valley. For many years, considerable quantities of potash and wood imports from the United States, via the port of St Jean, were required to sustain this overseas trade.[15] Similarly, a stream of imports from Upper Canada developed after 1806 which furthered the swift ongoing implantation of this industry in the St Lawrence Valley. It must be said that the decline of prices after 1815 contributed greatly to the protectionist effectiveness of the differential tariffs whose levels scarcely rose down to 1850. Lastly, it is important to point out that the forest resources could not be exploited on a large scale without a considerable reservoir of cheap seasonal manpower and an adequate core of professional woodsmen. The overpopulation of the Lower Canadian countryside, Quebec's agricultural problems and massive immigration from the British Isles facilitated a rapid transition. The abundance and great variety of local manpower, from the peasants and their sons to rural day laborers and immigrants in search of work and land, certainly aided the rapid diversification of forestry activities. As the growth in demand in Great Britain was generated by the needs of the English navy it was to be expected that the production of squared timber, which was principally concentrated in the Ottawa Valley and the Quebec region, would enjoy the greatest degree of priority. It played, of course, a role in the development of naval construction in the area around Quebec City. The construction lumber industry, for the domestic as for the overseas market, matured under the cover of the production of squared lumber. Further, as there was a strong demand for barrels in the West Indies and England, the production of staves, hoops and other barrel parts became an activity of considerable proportions, one which was more decentralized geographically than other types of forestry enterprises. Lastly, the production of potash in zones where the ground was being cleared for agriculture was a very profitable enterprise. Montreal had been the principal beneficiary of the fur trade. Under the new circumstances, however, Quebec City, even more than the Ottawa Valley, was to owe its growth to the forest industry; while Montreal was to depend upon the trade in agricultural products with the United States and Upper Canada and became, in this fashion, the true metropolis of the St Lawrence Valley.

Thus, the structure of the economy, while remaining oriented towards overseas trade, was substantially transformed at the start of the nineteenth century. From an economy dominated by the fur trade and valley agriculture, the area passed to one centered on lumbering and on agriculture carried out in the vaster spaces of Upper Canada and adjacent American States even further removed from external markets. All of this implied the establishment of banks, construction of roads and canals and, eventually, the railroads. The relationship between forestry and agriculture, however, was far more intimate than that which had existed between the fur trade and agriculture. Indeed, lumber companies could not carry on their activities without abundant supplies of agricultural products to feed the workers and horses. It should also be pointed out that, again compared to the fur trade, forest industries required more capital, more credit and some improvement in river routes.

After 1800, the industrial sector continued to develop very slowly. Leaving aside the Saint-Maurice ironworks and naval construction, only distilleries showed any growth, first in Upper Canada and (after 1830) in Lower Canada. Textile manufacturing began only around 1840.

This situation contributed to the growth of the import sector. During this entire period, the St Lawrence Valley brought in various products from outside the region: wines, spirits, tea, coffee, molasses, sugar, tobacco, salt, hardware, linens and other textiles (see Appendix: table 37). One should not forget, however, that as long as the fur trade survived a certain proportion of imported products were used as trade goods exchanged with the Indians for furs, and could therefore be considered as investments. Thus, in 1777, 26 per cent of the imported rum and 4 per cent of the wine were sent to the west. The canoes of the traders also carried that year: 2,580 guns, 122,010 pounds of powder and 186,631 bullets.[16]

What can one conclude from the above figures and analysis, if not to stress the importance of overseas trade for the local economy as a whole? To go further down this path, however, one must obtain a clearer idea of Lower Canada's trading partners.

2   The overseas trading partners of the St Lawrence Valley

As has already been indicated, the colony's import trade, which had reached considerable proportions by the end of the period, was comprised of a vast gamut of products from countries which were very different one from another, in terms of climate as well as of production. This situation, of itself, was a factor impelling a degree of diversification in trading partners. Likewise, the range of exported products was sufficiently broad to allow one to suppose that they were not all destined for a single market. Lastly, it is obvious that incoming and outgoing trade are never completely independent of one another. In consequence, the profitability of carrying cargo in both directions may have influenced the choice of a ship's destination. On such a basis, one can posit that there existed a rather complex and unexpected movement of goods, shaped additionally by the metropole's trade policies and by imperial and colonial market conditions. At that level of analysis, of course, one must begin by establishing the frequency of Lower Canada's contacts with its various overseas trading partners, and proceed subsequently to an evaluation of the weight of each trade. With such data in hand, one can then assess the importance of relations with the Spanish and Portuguese world.

In view of such statistics, one could conclude that, even as regards imports, the overseas trade of the St Lawrence Valley took place within an imperial context and that its commerce with foreign ports was strictly marginal. This conclusion seems all the more plausible as, over the course of the century covered, the metropole's share of the trade increased continuously even as that of the West Indies declined. Further, if one eliminates from the figures for the British Colonies the trade with the Thirteen Colonies before their independence, one can conclude that trade with the Maritime Provinces remained stagnant until just before 1850. This impression is even clearer, considering that the displacement of ships in the Atlantic varied greatly from one route to another (see table 32).

It is obvious that the technological change mentioned above did not touch all oceanic routes equally and that the trade with the West Indies was carried on

Table 15   Ship arrivals from the high seas at Quebec and Montreal by ports of origin

	Great Britain	British colonies[a]	West Indies	United States	Other foreign	Total percentage
1768−77	44.5	41.3	14.2			100
1778−83	66.3	14.4	19.3			100
1800−14			7.7			100
1828−32	77.2	12.4	7.5	1.1	1.8	100
1835−36	77.8	13.8	2.7			100
1841−42	74.0	13.7	1.4	4.1	6.8	100
1848−51	63.9	17.1		12.4	6.6	100

a In North America, only.

Sources: RAC, 1888, B.201; see the appendixes in JALBC and *JALC* for the years in question.

Table 16   Mean tonnage of ships arriving from overseas in Quebec and Montreal by ports of origin

	Great Britain	British colonies[a]	West Indies	United States	Other foreign	Total
1768−77	133.3	59.1	83.5			95.6
1778−83	164.3	86.4	108.7			142.4
1800−14			136.1			187.9
1828−32	304.0	116.4	118.8	243.9	232.4	264.9
1835−36	318.6	111.9	147.8	353.0	262.4	285.1
1841−42	366.8	164.9	201.3	497.0	273.8	335.7
1848−51	423.6	105.6		469.4	268.6	364.7

Sources: see table 15.

Table 17   Proportion by port of origin of tonnage of ships arriving from the overseas in Quebec and Montreal

	Great Britain	British colonies[a]	West Indies	United States	Other foreign	Total
1768−77	62.1	25.5	12.4			100
1778−83	76.6	8.7	14.7			100
1800−14			5.6			100
1828−32	88.6	5.5	3.3	1.0	1.6	100
1835−36	86.9	5.4	1.4	3.7	2.5	100
1841−42	80.8	6.7	0.9	6.0	5.6	100
1848−51	74.2	4.9		16.0	4.9	100

Source: see table 15.

by ships of relatively small size during the entire period. This means that Great Britain's domination of the import trade of the St Lawrence Valley was even more marked than indicated in table 15. Under such circumstances, one is entitled to ask where the international character of Lower Canada's commerce could truly be found, as it seems to have been more colonial and imperial.

This growing supremacy of Great Britain as channel and source of imports for the St Lawrence Valley is even more striking if one calculates it in terms of import values. These certainly passed the 70 per cent mark after 1760 while in 1833–50 the value of goods which arrived from Great Britain represented 93 per cent of the worth of sea-borne imports.[17] The growth of metropolitan participation in the trade, although continuous since 1760, seems to have become accentuated at the start of the nineteenth century, due to the expansion of the lumber industry which lowered the freight costs of imports. This development is somewhat surprising, of course, as the proportion of colonial and foreign goods in the sea-borne imports increased 19.7 per cent of value in 1799–1809, to 26.1 per cent in 1810–19.[18] This means that, in fact, Great Britain was becoming more and more a simple intermediary channeling non-English products towards the St Lawrence Valley.

There existed, therefore, two principal ways by which the Valley of the St Lawrence maintained economic contacts with the world overseas: a direct and official trade; and an indirect one, via the metropole as intermediary and under cover of the Navigation Acts, or via the mediation of some other parts of the empire, be it the West Indies, Gibraltar, Jersey or other British colonies. Parenthetically, of course, neither device excluded the possibility of contraband. In order to show the essential elements of the direct trade, and to get a glimpse of the role of the Spanish and Luso-Brazilian world in this commerce, I prepared table 18 which shows arrivals from overseas (save from the British Isles and West Indies).

These direct contacts with overseas ports had existed since 1760. In 1766, for example, out of 18 ships which left the port of Quebec, 5 had come from the Iberian Peninsula, 3 from Lisbon and 2 from Barcelona.[19] These first links with areas outside of the empire were never broken. Those with southern Europe took on greater importance after 1760, and they were perpetuated thereafter. From 1780 to 1783, 1,163,147 gallons of brandy were imported through Quebec and 16.4 per cent of the stock came directly from foreign ports.[20] At the start of the nineteenth century, this situation still prevailed. From October 1, 1800 to July 5, 1801, 100 ships put down anchor at the port of Quebec and 19 of them were of foreign origin.[21]

Seeing these figures concerning direct contacts with countries beyond the boundary of the empire, one could conclude that the United States was only the second most important commercial partner of the St Lawrence Valley, coming after Great Britain, the West Indies and the other British colonies. But, since 1790, trade by land between the United States and the Canadas had grown considerably. In this context, the river port of Saint-Jean sur Richelieu

Table 18 Arrival of ships from foreign ports in Quebec and Montreal

Port of origin	1828	1829	1830	1831	1832	1835	1836
United States	11 (3,045)	9 (1,971)	12 (3,224)	4 (822)	16 (5,323)	24 (6,507)	50 (19,619)
Europe	10 (1,402)						
China	1 (647)			1 (586)	2 (1,327)		1 (270)
Jersey[a]		1 (88)	2 (241)	1 (111)	1 (113)	1 (220)	2 (294)
Gibraltar[a]		1 (105)	8 (1,167)	3 (431)	6 (975)	5 (583)	1 (280)
France		1 (471)	6 (1,598)		2 (411)	9 (2,259)	24 (6,609)
Netherlands		4 (1,358)	4 (859)	3 (974)	3 (718)	3 (771)	4 (1,156)
Spain		2 (572)	2 (331)	2 (358)		1 (195)	2 (204)
Portugal		8 (1,290)	2 (202)	4 (879)	4 (694)	3 (498)	5 (1,331)
Sicily		2 (231)	2 (204)	1 (?)	1 (180)		
Sweden		1 (316)		1 (158)	1 (155)		
Tenerife		1 (104)	1 (?)		1 (106)		
Italy			1 (385)				
Canaries			1 (?)				
Mauritius[a]			1 (170)				
Azores				1 (?)	1 (356)		
Colombia				2 (266)	1 (145)		
Brazil				1 (457)	1 (289)	1 (437)	1 (86)
Madeira					1 (564)		
Hamburg						4 (1,075)	4 (1,179)
Russia							1 (226)
Algiers						1 (350)	1 (385)
Bremen						1 (270)	
Total	22 (5,094)	30 (6,506)	43 (8,360)	24 (5,042)	41 (11,356)	53 (13,165)	96 (31,639)

a British possessions.

Source: see table 15

played a decisive role in these commercial relations, particularly after 1800. During the nineteenth century this trade was characterized by an enormous disequilibrium between imports and exports, to the degree that the latter represented only 24 per cent of the former. In 1824–1840, these purchases made in the United States totalled on the average £255,055, about 10 per cent of all imports by sea via Montreal and Quebec. Although impressive, however, these figures are well below the real sums.[22] Indeed during these years, new internal ports were created at Ste-Marie de Beauce and at Stanstead. Around 1830, imports in these places amounted to about £15,000. This is without counting contraband carried out in all taxable items, particularly tea, coffee, sugar, molasses and salt.[23] At Stanstead, it was said, the value of clandestine trade equalled about two-thirds of official imports; at Ste-Marie, it was double the amount of legally imported goods; at St Jean it was equally substantial. It is obvious that this official and unofficial trade, by land and sea, was second only to that which the St Lawrence Valley maintained with Great Britain. The United States' role of first commercial partners after the British empire was all the more deserved as the transactions involved did not bear exclusively on consumer goods, produced locally or elsewhere, but also involved items which clarified relations with the Spanish and Portuguese world. Indeed, each year Lower Canadian banking institutions imported an average of about 150,000 pounds in coin, a much larger sum than was exported. This included, no doubt, large sums in English money. Mostly, however, Iberian coins were imported, particularly Spanish, often Portuguese, and sometimes Mexican.[24] This is not surprising as the Canadian monetary system was not unified and a great diversity of French, English, Spanish and other coins circulated throughout the province and were to be found in the amounts left in wills. The inventories after death attest to this situation and to the fact that the St Lawrence Valley was attached to an economic space and a monetary zone which overflowed the limited context of North America and the British empire.

Lower Canada's ties to the international market resulted, in large part, from the type of products sought in the colonial milieu. Thus, tea importers, who could choose between several sources of supply, had to either come to terms with the monopoly of the British East India Company or use clandestine means. Similarly, sugar, molasses and coffee theoretically came from the British West Indies, but the means of bringing in the products of the Spanish or French Antilles were numerous and efficacious. In fact, such goods did not necessarily arrive in Quebec from their zone of production. The rum trade responded to the same circumstances. Contemporaries, without making a point of it, were perhaps able to disentangle affairs. Today, however, how is one to distinguish between Jamaican, Leeward island and New England rum, when the documents merely indicate that it came from England, the West Indies or British colonies? The year 1835 provides a typical example of the plurality of routes these products took to get to the St Lawrence Valley.

Wine is another of these products which can be used to show the complexity of the networks by which the colony was forced to go outside of its economic frontiers and those of the empire. The St Lawrence Valley imported rum mostly for the lower classes, the *voyageurs*, their hired hands, and the Indians. Wine drinkers, however, were mainly recruited among the upper classes.

Table 19   Selected products imported in 1835 through Quebec and Montreal by port of origin

	Great Britain	British colonies	West Indies
Rum	78,183	383,191	514,684
Molasses	28,828	63,247	30,131
Sugar	2,000,032	1,923,817	
Tea	474,244	112,847	
Coffee	1,486		2,890

Source: *JALBC*, 1835–36, app. G.G.G.

The breadth of demand was rather considerable. Besides the wines of Spain, France, Italy and Portugal, consumers also had available those of Germany, Hungary, Greece, Malta, Algeria and even of the Cape of Good Hope. Four great producing countries shared the bulk of the local market: Spain, Portugal, France and Italy.

Table 20   Distribution of Canadian market share held by the principal wine supplying nations (*percentage of imports*)

	Spain	Portugal	France	Italy	Total
1823	51.3	30.6	14.4	3.7	100
1827	46.4	33.8	11.0	8.8	100
1828	55.6	36.6	6.4	1.4	100
1829	43.1	42.4	8.9	5.6	100
1830	54.2	27.8	10.1	7.9	100
1831	48.9	40.1	2.8	8.2	100

Source: see the appendixes to *JALBC* for years in question.

The fact that the market share of Madeira had not radically varied since 1793, allows one to posit that the equilibrium between the various producing countries had been stable since at least the end of the eighteenth century, after which period we have sound data concerning the ultimate origins of imported wines. As indicated above, Great Britain had a decisive role as the redistribution center for goods produced inside and outside the empire; and the St Lawrence Valley's direct trade with foreign countries, save in the case of the United States, accounted for a relatively small percentage of overseas exports. For wine imports table 21 clarifies the distinction between places of production and those of immediate provenance.

Great Britain functioned as an entrepôt for the distribution of metropolitan products and the redistribution of colonial and foreign goods throughout the empire and elsewhere. In the long term, this role no doubt facilitated the task of preparing well-balanced cargoes appropriate to each trade route. The end result, however, was to concentrate in British hands the opportunity to supply her colonies with needed imports, and ultimately, to allow the United Kingdom, in practice as in theory, to take charge of the exportation of colonial products. For this reason, as for others, British control of the trade of the St Lawrence Valley was even more marked for exports than for imports. The evolution of overseas trade demonstrates this fact, save for the period before 1783.

In the years immediately following 1760, Great Britain's domination of Lower Canadian trade was a good deal less evident for exports than for imports, to the point that one might conclude that the validity of the

Table 21   Wines imported into the St Lawrence Valley, 1829–1831
(*percentage of imports*)

| Provenance | Producing country | | | | Total |
	Spain	Portugal	France	Italy	
Great Britain	61.2	86.9	45.2	64.6	68.6
Ireland	5.4	1.4	2.2	2.3	3.8
British colonies	1.2	5.0	2.2	0.2	2.4
West Indies		0.3			0.1
Jersey	1.6	0.7	4.7		1.4
Gibraltar	13.4	0.3	42.7	3.1	10.4
France			3.0		0.2
Spain	3.3	0.5			2.0
Portugal		4.9			1.5
Sicily				29.8	1.9
Tenerife	13.9				7.7
Total	100	100	100	100	100

Source: see appendixes to the *JALBC* for the years in question.

Table 22   Departure of ships towards overseas from Quebec and Montreal according to their destinations (*percentage of ships*)

	Great Britain	British colonies[a]	West Indies	United States	Foreign	Total
1768–77	29.5	36.7	33.8			100
1778–83	43.4	38.2	18.4			100
1828–32	82.9	11.2	5.2	0.3	0.4	100
1835–36	81.8	15.6	2.0	0.2	0.4	100
1841–42	86.4	11.4	1.3		0.8	100
1848–51	75.7	18.1		5.3	0.9	100

Source: RAC, 1888, B.201; see also the appendixes to the *JALBC* and *JALC* for the years indicated.

documentary base is questionable. Up to a point, of course, it is questionable, as the figures available which establish the percentage of the export trade towards the West Indies, include not only the Antillan traffic but also that with southern Europe and even Africa. Obviously, the sudden development of commercial relations with the West Indies and the Iberian Peninsula was tied to exceptional, and more or less transitory, circumstances: the conflict between Great Britain and its old colonies on the Atlantic coast, and the unfortunate harvests of these years in southern Europe. The substantial exports of wheat and flour towards the West Indies, and most particularly towards Europe have to be accounted for in this fashion (see table 23). In this context, the shipment of agricultural products to the Maritime Provinces was a more durable phenomenon. Once these exceptional circumstances had passed, the trade between the St Lawrence Valley and the West Indies became once more what it had been previously, a very modest flow, while the direct trade with the Iberian Peninsula deflated to a size which was proper to it, becoming henceforth a marginal trade. Table 23 is quite clear in this regard.

Table 23   Proportion of wheat and flour exports towards the overseas from Quebec and Montreal (*percentage of minots of wheat exported*)

	Great Britain	British colonies	West Indies	Total
1768–77	15.9	14.2	69.9	100
1778–83	6.8	87.5	5.7	100
1829–36	71.0	24.3	4.4	100
1841–42	95.2	3.6	1.2	100

Source: *RAC*, 1888, B. 201; and see also the appendixes to the *JALBC* and *JALC* for the years in question.

For a time, therefore, there existed a demand in the West Indies for agricultural goods, forest products and fish which stimulated the overseas trade of the St Lawrence Valley with the Antilles. The growth of the forest-based economies of Nova Scotia and New Brunswick, however, provided significant competition. More importantly, the vigorous resumption of New England's activities in the marketing of wood, ships and agricultural products, in the fisheries and in the Antilles, seriously reduced the importance of the advantages enjoyed by the St Lawrence Valley in those markets. It is on this basis that one must explain the post 1783 decline in the sale of Lower Canadian beams and planks on the West Indies market.

Table 24   Proportion of deals and planks exported towards overseas from Quebec and Montreal (*percentage of exported pieces*)

	Great Britain	British colonies	West Indies	Total
1768–77	61.4	8.6	30.0	100
1778–83	29.9	8.8	61.3	100
1829–36	99.0	0.1	0.9	100
1841–42	99.7		0.3	100

Source: *RAC*, 1888, B. 201; and see also the appendixes to the *JALBC* and *JALC* for the years in question.

The survival of the West Indies sector of overseas trade was to depend, essentially, on a few products which were shipped in rather modest quantities: cod, fish oil, flour and, most particularly, wooden parts for barrels. The latter was an item which countries producing sugar, molasses, grains, tea, coffe, rum, wine and liqueurs needed in great quantities. As the St Lawrence Valley could produce them in great abundance and, it would seem, at competitive prices, staves, hoops and other barrel parts became, with fish and, to a certain degree, flour, the basic elements in the cargoes of ships sailing towards the West Indies to pick up sugar.

Table 25   Proportion of stave exports towards overseas from Quebec and Montreal (*as a percentage of exported pieces*)

	Great Britain	British colonies	West Indies	United States	Foreign	Total
1768−77	94.2	0.6	5.2			100
1778−83	89.6	0.2	10.2			100
1801−08	?		10.5			100
1829−36	77.4	3.9	17.6		11.1	100

Source: *RAC*, 1888, B. 201; and see the appendixes to the *JALBC* and *JALC* for the years indicated.

It must be understood, of course, that the number of ships involved in a trade link does not constitute an adequate measure of the real changes in trade volume along each of the routes taken by ships leaving the port of Quebec. The substantial modification in the size of the ships used in the different trade routes had a decisive impact on the amplitude of increases and decreases in the amount of traffic in one direction or another. After 1783, on the 'British colonies' route, the average size of ships decreased to the point where it begins to seem like more of a coastal trade than genuine oceanic navigation. On the West Indies run, on the other hand, the ships became larger. Their size increased by 48 per cent by 1850. This growth however, is minimal compared to that of ships going directly to Great Britain, whose dimension increased by a factor of 3.5 between 1768 and 1850. The contrast between the types of ships used for imports and those used for exports is most marked in the case of American ships, which illustrates rather well the fact that the St Lawrence Valley bought a great deal from the United States but sold them rather little. Table 26 provides eloquent evidence as to these disparities.

From all of the above, one must conclude that mercantilism was far from having been a vain doctrine, as its objectives were achieved in both directions of colonial-metropolitan trade: St Lawrence Valley — Great Britain and

Table 26 Average tonnage of ships departing towards overseas from Quebec and Montreal according to their destinations

	Great Britain	British colonies	West Indies	United States	Foreign	Total
1768–77	131.5	58.5	98.8			95.6
1778–83	158.7	112.2	137.1			136.9
1828–32	281.6	74.0	145.1	127.5	161.2	250.3
1835–36	335.7	69.5	141.4	96.0	176.3	289.1
1841–42	365.7	88.7	146.2	178.0	399.2	331.4
1848–51	456.2	78.6		114.9	186.6	367.3

Source: *RAC*, 1888, B. 201; and see also the appendixes to the *JALBC* and *JALC* for the years involved.

Table 27 Proportion of tonnage of ships departing towards overseas from Quebec and Montreal according to their destinations (*percentage of tonnage*)

	Great Britain	British colonies	West Indies	United States	Foreign	Total
1768–77	41.4	22.9	35.7			100
1778–83	50.3	31.3	18.4			100
1828–32	93.3	3.3	3.0	0.1	0.3	100
1835–36	95.0	3.7	0.9	0.1	0.3	100
1841–42	95.4	3.1	0.6		0.9	100
1848–51	94.0	3.9		1.7	0.4	100

Source: *RAC*, 1888, B. 201; and see the appendixes to the *JALBC* and *JALC* for the indicated years.

vice versa. The monopoly of Great Britain became so absolute, particularly as regards exports, that commercial relations with foreign countries were, at once, reduced to a minimum and masked by the massive intervention of the metropole in the trading process.

Under such conditions, what became of direct trade with foreign ports in Canadian products in general, and in staves and forest products in particular? The foreign export trade was even more marginal than the equivalent import trade.

The procedure chosen to bring out the international dimension of the Laurentian economy and the relationship which it maintained with Spain, Portugal and their possessions, has only allowed us to identify the nature and contours of a problem whose complexity is quite evident. The critical role played by overseas trade in the economic development of Canada in these

Table 28 Departure of foreign-bound ships from Quebec and Montreal (*Number of ships and* (*tonnage*))

Destination	1828	1829	1830	1831	1832	1835	1836
Europe	1 (105)						
United States	3 (609)		4 (432)	2 (158)	3 (331)	4 (397)	2 (179)
Portugal		1 (105)	1 (146)	1 (121)	2 (378)	6 (1,160)	
Fayal		1 (105)					
Cape of Good Hope[a]		1 (170)					
Jersey[a]			1 (113)	3 (352)			
Gibraltar[a]			2 (226)			1 (110)	
Spain			1 (105)	1 (53)			
France					2 (922)		
Madeira						1 (231)	
Brazil						1 (263)	

a British possessions.

Source: *JALBC*, appendixes of indicated years.

years is, without doubt, an indicator of its integration in the world market, even if through the mediation of the British empire. But this overseas trade, in the time of New France as later, remained so characterized by direct trade between the colony and the metropole that the development of direct contacts with countries outside of the empire, or even with colonies within it, did not really have a fair start. This was partially so as the mother country owned the immense majority of the ships transporting colonial exports and imports. The metropole remained an indispensable intermediary for the St Lawrence Valley. After 1840 foreign trade becomes an ever more important component of overseas commerce and the impact of this development is magnified by the booming inland trade with the United States. None the less, the new orientations were still so timid that one cannot see in them the true source of the fall of the old colonial trade system and the granting of a degree of political autonomy for the colonies. Rather, Great Britain itself repealed the Navigation Acts and preferential duties on St Lawrence Valley products. It seems that the principal reason for the change was that Great Britain was now ready to play the role of entrepôt on a vaster stage, that of the world as a whole, and that mercantilism could harm this new orientation.

Table 29   Port traffic with overseas (save for Gaspé and New Carlisle)

	Departures from Quebec and Montreal				Arrivals at Quebec and Montreal		
	Ships	Tonnage	Crew		Ships	Tonnage	Crew
1760							
1761					102		
1762							
1763	121[b]	7,534	955[b]		154	9,576	1,155[b]
1964	17[b]	1,560	137[b]		32	2,873[b]	252[b]
1765					52	4,814	456
1766	18	1,398	136[b]		66	6,999	601
1767					70	5,157	517
1768	31	3,149	261		39	3,614	322
1769	86	7,456	628		82	7,311	587
1770	51	4,200	382		48	4,170	364
1771	71	6,094	556		77	6,584	597
1772	63	5,455	492		62	5,313	504
1773	88	8,684	701		87	7,977	685
1774	151	14,998	1,161		156	14,172	1,133
1775	97	10,841	762		115	11,791	887
1776	50	4,646	409		49	6,358	544
1777	72	5,680	512		69	7,661	755
1778	72	8,882	1,047		76	9,545	1,077
1779	66	7,929	1,065		59	7,942	977
1780	46	6,290	705		42	6,350	676
1781	71	11,987	1,184		70	10,507	1,109
1782	70	10,690	1,420		72	12,247	1,760
1783	78	9,428	648		70	8,792	724
1784	36[b]	5,473	396[b]		32	5,164	356
1785	58[b]	9,364	638[b]		52	8,834	586
1786	93	15,335	687[b]		74	10,006	547
1787							
1788							
1789	91[b]	13,258	802[b]		86	12,508	733
1790					50	8,566	461
1791	84	14,631	714[b]		81	14,760	826
1792	66[b]	13,255	680[b]		63	12,505	653
1793	118	18,715	1,076		113	15,271	1,012
1794	116	16,126	764		114	16,827	982
1795	117	18,023	1,067		128	19,545	905

Table 29   *continued*

	Ships	Tonnage	Crew	Ships	Tonnage	Crew
1796	71	11,789	639	67	11,050	615
1797	105	15,668	901	88	13,349	780
1798	91	13,939	760	78	11,882	667
1799	138	19,537	1,089	125	17,941	1,017
1800	153	20,725	1,179	140	16,827	998
1801	188	27,986	1,522	175	25,736	1,548
1802	211	35,754	1,852	198	33,139	1,829
1803	175	30,483	1,573	167	28,837	1,553[b]
1804	173	26,883	1,390	162	25,021	1,506[b]
1805	170	26,506	1,342	138	21,333	1,283[b]
1806	193	33,996	1,603	186	33,104	1,729[b]
1807	239	42,293	2,039	212	37,962	2,014[b]
1808	334	70,275	3,330	295	60,783	2,802[b]
1809	435	88,056	3,915[b]	434	87,825	4,123[b]
1810	661	143,893	5,949[b]	635	138,057	6,032[b]
1811	532	116,687	5,553	495	107,075	5,593[b]
1812	439[a]	93,373	4,390[a]	415	86,227	3,895[a]
1813	205[a]	47,722	2,288[a]	179	37,485	1,753[a]
1814	194[a]	40,382	1,975[a]	186	33,433	1,569[a]
1815	234[a]	45,076	2,220[a]	219	41,044	1,960[a]
1816	336[a]	70,374	3,345[a]	344	70,797	3,473[a]
1817	369[a]	83,563	4,289[a]	378	86,330	4,076[a]
1818	449[a]	102,471	4,721[a]	440	100,677	4,545[a]
1819	691[a]	164,005	7,330[a]	699	160,862	7,486[a]
1820	643[a]	159,581	7,227[a]	647	160,806	7,400[a]
1821	476[a]	110,547	5,015[a]	487	117,810	5,133[a]
1822	684[a]	158,241	7,256[a]	668	157,647	7,017[a]
1823	644[a]	145,112	6,662[a]	615	141,703	6,570[a]
1824	722[a]	167,592	7,542[a]	674	160,433	7,340[a]
1825	941[a]	238,604	10,212[a]	873	207,936	9,668[a]
1826	839[a]	207,399	9,472[a]	764	191,200	8,809[a]
1827	727[a]	172,380	8,022[a]	684	166,245	7,742[a]
1828	828[a]	205,144	9,200[a]	805[a]	201,829	9,112[a]
1829	1,012[a]	259,420	11,642[a]	1,010[a]	260,221	11,774[a]
1830	1,054[a]	261,173	12,048[a]	992	238,991	11,380[a]
1831	1,148[a]	289,968	13,067[a]	1,163[a]	334,264	13,495[a]
1832	1,036	269,668	11,137	1,008	272,005	12,136
1833	1,103	279,495	12,421	1,074	276,353	12,308
1834	1,216	322,228	13,968	1,176	315,320	13,828

Table 29 *continued*

	Ships	Tonnage	Crew	Ships	Tonnage	Crew
1835	1,241	372,814	14,634	1,212	334,163	14,554
1836	1,214	372,814	15,859	1,229	360,662	15,122
1837	1,132	343,100	14,150[b]	1,068	329,858	13,971
1838	1,118	354,739	13,975[b]	1,091	347,574	14,250
1839	1,184	389,549	15,579	1,147	373,671	14,995
1840	1,433	478,906	18,639	1,348	450,345	17,739
1841	1,461	488,295	19,067	1,380	463,478	18,090
1842	1,040	340,651	13,381	988	326,284	12,704
1843	1,249	450,412	16,237[b]	1,228	443,087	15,964[b]
1844	1,483[b]	536,846[b]	19,427[b]	1,439	500,777	18,707[b]
1845	1,751[b]	633,862[b]	23,113[b]	1,699	628,389	22,087[b]
1846	1,751[b]	639,115[b]	23,288[b]	1,699	623,791	22,256[b]
1847	1,488[b]	543,120[b]	19,939[b]	1,444	542,505	18,916[b]
1848	1,392	521,604	18,643	1,350	494,247	18,214
1849	1,587	543,963	21,265[b]	1,328	502,513	18,118
1850	1,698	650,117	22,753[b]	1,196	465,804	16,092
1851	1,567	578,059	20,977[b]	1,305	533,821	17,765

a One of the numbers making up this total was estimated.
b Estimate based, as the case might be, on average number of ships, average size of crew, or average tonnage of the years preceding and following the year in question. This procedure was used in all estimates.

Source: 'Statistique sur le commerce de Québec (1768–1784)', RAC, 1888, B. 201, reproduced on the basis of documents in BM: 21,861 in the Haldimand Collection. See also J. Caron, *La colonisation de la province de Québec, 1760–1791* (Quebec, 1923), p. 169. For 1763 see APC, RG 4, A.3, vol. 1. For 1766–1819, see APC, RG 4, B.3, vol. 1 and B.58, vols. 6 and 7; and APC, MG 21, J.2, 3. For the 1786–1808 period, see the quarterly reports of the naval officer at Quebec, APC, MG 11, Q. For the 1793–1808 period see APC, MG 11, Q.89, Q.90, Q.109. See also J. Caron, *La colonisation de la province de Québec, 1791–1815* (Quebec, 1927), p. 245; and G. Paquet and J.-P. Wallot, 'Aperçu sur le commerce international et les prix domestiques (1793–1812)', *Revue d'histoire de l'Amérique française*, 21 (1967), 363–397. For the years 1807–22, see JALBC, 1823–24, appendix W. For the years 1817–28, JALBC, 1829–29, appendix U. For the years 1820–40, see *Le Canadien*, February 14, 1840. See also *JALBC*, 1808; *JALBD*, 1816; *JALBC*, 1825, appendix AA; *JALBC*, 1926, appendix U; *JALBC*, 1826–27; *JALBC*, 1828–29, appendix C; *JALBC*, 1830, appendix W; *JALBC*, 1831, appendix GG; *JALBC*, 1831–32, appendix SS; *JALBC*, 1832–33, appendices PP and Q; *JALBC*, 1835, appendix Z, *JALBC*, 1835–36, appendix GGG; *JALBC*, 1837, appendix E; *JALBC*, 1843, appendix SS; *JALBC*, 1849, appendices Z and XX; *JALBC*, 1850, appendix A; *JALBC*, 1851, appendix T; and *JALBC*, 1854–55.

Appendix table 30   Port traffic in Quebec and Montreal: ships and crew sizes

	Departures		Arrivals		
	Average tonnage	Average crew	Average tonnage	Average crew	Ballast (%)
1760					
1761					
1762					
1763	62.2[a]	7.9[b]	62.2	7.5[a]	
1764	91.8[a]	8.1[b]	89.8[a]	7.9[a]	
1765			92.6	8.8	
1766	77.6	7.6[a]	106.0	9.1	
1767			73.7	7.4	
1768	101.6	8.4	92.7	8.3	
1769	86.7	7.3	89.2	7.2	
1770	82.3	7.5	86.9	7.6	
average	83.7	7.8	86.6	7.9	
1771	85.8	7.8	85.5	7.8	
1772	86.6	7.8	85.7	8.1	
1773	98.7	7.9	91.7	7.9	
1774	99.3	7.7	90.8	7.3	
1775	111.8	7.9	102.5	7.7	
1776	92.9	8.2	129.7	11.1	
1777	78.8	7.1	111.0	10.9	
1778	123.4	14.5	125.6	14.2	
1779	120.1	16.1	134.6	16.6	
1780	136.7	15.3	151.2	16.1	
average	103.4	10.0	110.9	10.8	
1781	168.8	16.7	150.1	15.8	
1782	152.7	20.3	170.1	24.4	
1783	120.9	8.3	125.6	10.3	
1784	152.0[a]	11.0[b]	161.4	11.1	
1785	161.4[a]	11.0[b]	169.9	11.3	
1786	164.9	7.4[b]	135.2	7.4	
1787					
1788					
1789	145.6[b]	8.8[b]	145.4	8.5	
1790			171.3	9.2	
average	152.3	11.9	153.6	12.2	

Appendix table 30 *continued*

	Average tonnage	Average crew	Average tonnage	Average crew	Ballast (%)
1791	174.2	8.5[a]	182.2	10.2	
1792	200.8[a]	10.3[b]	190.5	10.4	
1793	158.6	9.1	135.1	9.6	
1794	139.0	6.6	147.6	8.6	
1795	154.0	9.1	132.6	7.1	
1796	166.0	9.0	164.9	9.2	
1797	149.2	8.6	151.6	8.9	
1798	153.2	8.3	152.3	8.6	
1799	141.6	7.9	143.5	8.1	
1800	135.5	7.7	120.2	7.1	
average	157.2	8.5	154.1	8.8	
1801	148.9	8.1	147.1	8.8	
1802	169.4	8.8	167.4	9.2	27.3
1803	174.2	8.9	172.7	9.3	
1804	155.4	8.0	154.5	9.3[a]	25.2
1805	155.9	7.9	154.5	9.3[a]	32.2
1806	176.1	8.3	177.9	9.3[a]	46.1
1807	176.9	8.5	179.1	9.5[a]	46.1
1808	210.4	9.9	206.0	9.5[a]	64.3
1809	202.4	9.0[a]	202.4	9.5[a]	60.7
1810	217.6	9.0[a]	217.4	9.5[a]	75.9
average	178.7	8.6	177.9	9.3	
1811	219.3	10.4	216.3	11.3[a]	
1812	212.6[a]	10.0[b]	207.8	9.4[a]	
1813	232.8[a]	11.2[b]	209.4	9.8[a]	
1814	218.5[a]	10.2[b]	179.7	8.4[a]	
1815	192.6[a]	9.5[b]	187.4	8.9[a]	
1816	209.4[a]	9.9[b]	205.8	10.1[a]	
1817	226.5[a]	11.6[b]	228.4	10.8[a]	
1818	228.2[a]	10.5[b]	228.8	10.3[a]	
1819	237.3[a]	10.6[b]	230.1	10.7[a]	
1820	248.2[a]	11.2[b]	248.5	11.4[a]	
average	222.5	10.5	214.2	10.1	
1821	232.2[a]	10.5[b]	241.9	10.5[a]	
1822	231.3[a]	10.6[b]	235.9	10.5[a]	
1823	225.3[a]	10.3[b]	230.4	10.7[a]	
1824	232.1[a]	10.5[b]	238.0	10.9[a]	
1825	253.6[a]	10.8[b]	238.2	11.1[a]	
1826	247.2[a]	11.8[b]	250.3	11.5[a]	

Appendix table 30   *continued*

	Average tonnage	Average crew	Average tonnage	Average crew	Ballast (%)
1827	237.1[a]	11.0[b]	243.0	11.3[a]	
1828	247.7[a]	11.1[b]	250.7	11.3[a]	
1829	256.3[a]	11.5[b]	257.6[a]	11.6[b]	57.9
1830	247.8[a]	11.4[b]	240.9[a]	11.5[b]	56.8
average	241.1	10.9	242.7	11.1	
1831	252.6[a]	11.4[b]	287.4[a]	11.6[b]	46.3
1832	260.3	10.7	269.8	12.0	53.5
1833	253.4	11.3	257.3	11.5	
1834	264.9	11.5	268.1	11.3	
1835	300.4	11.8	275.7	12.0	68.1
1836	307.1	13.1	293.4	12.3	68.1
1837	303.1	12.5[a]	308.8	13.1	
1838	317.3	12.5[a]	318.6	13.1	
1839	329.0	13.1	325.8	13.1	
1840	334.2	13.0	334.1	13.1	
average	292.2	12.1	293.9	12.3	
1841	334.2	13.1	335.8	13.1	
1842	327.5	13.3	330.2	12.8	
1843	360.6	13.0[a]	360.8	13.0[a]	
1844	362.0[b]	13.1[b]	348.0	13.0[a]	
1845	362.2[b]	13.2[b]	369.8	13.0[a]	
1846	365.0[b]	13.3[b]	367.1	13.1[a]	73.6
1847	365.0[b]	13.4[b]	375.7	13.1[a]	72.1
1848	374.7	13.4	366.1	13.5	72.5
1849	342.8	13.4[a]	370.4	13.6	61.8
1850	382.8	13.4[a]	389.5	13.4	62.4
average	357.7	13.3	361.3	13.2	
1851	368.8	13.4[a]	409.1	13.6	

a see same note, Appendix table 29
b see same note, Appendix table 29

Source: see Appendix table 29.

Appendix table 31   Port traffic: Montreal with the high seas

	Departures				Arrivals		
	Ships	Tonnage	Crew	Average tonnage	Ships	Tonnage	Crew
1812	40[b]	6,937	336[b]	172.2	53	9.127	443[b]
1813	7[b]	1,208	58[b]	176.5	9	1,589	76[b]
1814	10[b]	1,780	86[b]	180.0	13	2,341	113[b]
1815	40[b]	7,694	373[b]	194.6	52	10,123	490[b]
1816	48[b]	9,163	444[b]	191.4	63	12,056	584[b]
1817	35	7,004	339[b]	200.3	46	9,215	447[b]
1818	40	7,796	378[b]	197.2	52	10,259	497[b]
1819	41[b]	8,163	396[b]	198.8	54	10,740	521[b]
1820	47[b]	9,920	481[b]	210.5	62	13,052	633[b]
average	34.2	6,629	321	191.2	44.8	8,722	423
1821	40[b]	7,649	371[b]	189.8	53	10,064	488[b]
1822	43[b]	8,888	431[b]	208.8	56	11,694	567[b]
1823	35[b]	6,893	332[b]	197.1	46	9,069	440[b]
1824	42[b]	7,930	385[b]	189.6	55	10,433	506[b]
1825	58[b]	10,897	529[b]	186.2	77	14,338	695[b]
1826	38[b]	8,551	415[b]	225.0	50	11,251	546[b]
1827	49[b]	10,286	499[a]	208.2	65	13,533	656[b]
1828	65[b]	13,945	656[b]	215.0[b]	85[b]	18,348	890[b]
1829	84[b]	17,979	872[b]	215.0[b]	110[b]	23,656	1,147[b]
1830	73[b]	16,512	801[b]	225.0[b]	96[b]	21,726	1,053[b]
average	52.7	10,953	529	205.9	69.3	14,411	698
1831	103[b]	23,068	1,119[b]	225.0[b]	135[b]	30,352	1,472[b]
1832	89[b]	20,672	1,002[b]	232.4	117	27,200	1,319[b]
1833	101[b]	23,385	1,134[b]	231.3	133	30,769	1,492[b]
1834	68[b]	15,397	746[b]	227.6	89	20.259	982[b]
1835	82[b]	17,374	843[b]	211.8	108	22,873	1,109[b]
1836	64	17,437	846	227.4	98	22,289	1,082
1837	69	17,228	835[b]	249.1	91	22,668	1,099[b]
1838	49[b]	10,975	532[b]	222.1	65	14,441	700[b]
1839	103[b]	22,757	1,104[b]	221.0	110	24,311	1,179[b]
1840	129[b]	29,439	1,428[b]	228.2	137	31,266	1,516[b]
average	85.7	19,773	959	227.6	108.3	24,642	1,195
1841	130[b]	31,457	1,526[b]	241.7	208	50,277	2,438[b]
1842	131[b]	32,799	1,591[b]	250.9	172	43,156	2,093[b]
1843	115[b]	27,119	1,315[b]	236.3	151	35,682	1,730[b]
1844	157[b]	37,723	1,829[b]	239.7	207	49,635	2,407[b]
1845	160[b]	39,405	1,911[b]	246.8	210	51,848	2,516[b]
1846	167[b]	42,231	2,048[b]	253.3	219	55,566	2,695[b]
1847	178[b]	48,170	2,336[b]	270.8	234	63,381	3,074[b]
1848	123[b]	31,777	1,541[b]	258.1	162	41,811	2,028[b]
1849	155[b]	40,377	1,958[b]	259.8	144	37,425	1,815[b]
1850	270[b]	49,942	2,422[b]	185.2	304	56,312	2,731[b]
average	158.6	38,100	1,848	244.3	201.1	48,500	2,352
1851	313[b]	64,034	3,106[b]	204.3	332	67,848	3,291[b]

b See same note, Appendix table 29.

Source: see Appendix table 29 and also *JALBC*, 1832–33, appendix B, *JALBC*, 1835–36, appendix F; *JALBC*, 1837, appendix E; *JALBC*, 1846, appendix GG; *JALBC*, 1847, appendix KK; and *JALBC*, 1850, appendix A.

Appendix table 32   Port traffic in Gaspé (1811–1851)

	Departures			Arrivals		
	Ships	Tonnage	Crew	Ships	Tonnage	Crew
1811	10	831				
1812	1	78	49			
1814						
1815	16	1,904	103			
1816	29	2,231	154			
1817 (8 mo.)	8	863	57			
1818	13	1,280	102			
1819	20	1,630	130	30	4,376	141
1820	20	1,510		33	3,982	281
1821	22	2,420		33	3,608	259
1822	11	1,086		26	3,735	248
1823	25	2,029	148	27	2,073	151
1824	38	3,885	284	33	3,829	235
1825	26	2,757	180	24	2,405	152
1826 (8 mo.)	13	1,701	81	9	837	55
1827	25	3,310	208	28	3,073	174
1828						
1829	33	4,587	253	34	4,616	257
1830	43	6,711	351	35	4,661	280
1831	21	1,848	159	41	6,670	379
1832	23	2,892	160	34	4,700	274
1833	33	3,881	259	33	4,404	276
1834	31	3,583	254	34	4,187	263
1835	42	6,722	369	47	6,700	371
1836	47	6,341	362	50	5,583	364
1837	41	4,238	314	50	5,684	396
1838	40	4,858	309	36	3,802	287
1839	59	7,154	467	45	6,292	380
1840	41	5,200	318	44	5,593	342
1841				31	2,770	222
1842				42	3,283	248
1843						
1844						
1845						
1846						
1847						
1848						
1849						
1850	119	7,005	630	132	4,457	284
1851	103	7,799	576	85	6,939	431

Sources: for the years 1811–22, see *JALBC*, 1822–23, appendix W. See also, for the rest of the period, *JALBC*, 1825, appendix AA; *JALBC*, 1826, appendix U; *JALBC*, 1827; *JALBC*, 1828–29, appendix C; *JALBC*, 1830, appendix W; *JALBC*, 1831; appendix GG; *JALBC*, 1831–32, appendix SS; *JALBC*, 1832–33, appendix PP; *JALBC*, 1835, appendix Z; *JALBC*, 1835–36, appendix GGG; and *JALBC*, 1843, appendix SS.

Appendix table 33   Port traffic in New Carlisle (1811–1851)

	Departures			Arrivals		
	Ships	Tonnage	Crew	Ships	Tonnage	Crew
1811	15	1,381				
1812	15	2,205	112			
1813	20	1,675	85			
1814						
1815	13	1,459	77			
1816	25	2,737	163			
1817	12	1,406	88			
1818	16	2,010	109			
1819	27	4,492	264	30	4,376	241
1820	30	4,669	280			
1821	28	3,188	167			
1822	25	3,782	210			
1823	31	5,382	340	48	7,119	459
1824	34	5,900	868	36	6,389	366
1825	33	5,435	302	35	4,926	280
1826	30	4,787	261	29	5,307	295
1827	24	4,770	257	32	5,642	323
1828						
1829	31	5,925	302	33	3,701	252
1830	30	5,170	289	36	6,217	326
1831	36	6,926	362	43	7,651	395
1832	35	6,093	314	42	6,316	307
1833	25	4,715	247	28	4,477	233
1834	45	6,328	338	51	6,267	344
1835	22	3,946	203	38	5,561	289
1836	40	6,428	343	54	6,776	288
1837	28	4,728	251	27	3,711	192
1838	15	2,417	122	20	3,276	177
1839	76	10,865	583	56	7,676	431
1840	48	7,573	379	47	6,796	372
1841				47	6,649	358
1842				51	5,784	316
1843						
1844						
1845						
1846						
1847						
1848						
1849						
1850						
1851	56	6,759	366	65	7,216	386

Sources: same as in appendix table 32.

Table 34   Fur exports to Great Britain and the United States

	Furs exported from Quebec			Exported to the United States via St Jean			
	Beaver No. of Skins	Other No. of Skins	Total No. of Skins	Beaver No. of Skins	Other No. of Skins	Total No. of Skins	Total No. of Skins
1761							
1762							
1763							
1764	90,621	124,801	218,422				
1765	104,000	119,210	223,210				
1766	110,372	136,783	247,155				
1767	107,276	142,270	249,546				
1768	115,842	235,506	351,348				
1769	98,272	332,225	430,497				
1770	102,920	246,385	346,305				
1771	94,936	271,367	366,303				
1772	108,588	270,158	378,746				
1773	95,716	370,986	466,702				
1774	102,179	315,528	417,707				
1775	103,730	470,500	574,230				
1776	92,043	345,530	437,573				
1777	118,248	596,663	714,911				
1778	104,348	515,293	619,641				
1779	137,740	431,115	568,655				
1780	121,280	489,126	610,406				
1781	125,782	412,770	538,552				
1782	110,487	291,037	401,524				
1783	105,434	420,864	526,298				
1784	128,620	380,081	508,701				
1785	151,249	339,304	490,553				
1786	116,623	436,636	553,259				
1787							
1788	130,758	423,353	554,111				
1789							
1790							
1791				–	–	–	
1792				–	–	–	
1793	182,346	422,311	604,657	–	–	–	
1794	155,599	352,533	508,132	–	–	–	
1795	144,945	446,024	590,969	–	–	–	
1796	130,820	457,076	587,896	–	–	–	
1797	124,612	622,466	747,058	–	–	–	
1798	127,440	504,846	632,286	–	–	–	
1799	117,165	377,864	494,029	–	–	–	
1800	135,043	395,850	530,893	–	–	–	

Table 34 *continued*

	Beaver No. of Skins	Other No. of Skins	Total No. of Skins	Beaver No. of Skins	Other No. of Skins	Total No. of Skins	Total No. of Skins
1801	119,965	376,527	496,492	–	–	–	
1802	144,189	413,370	557,559	–	–	–	
1803	93,778	498,905	592,683	–	–	–	
1804	111,448	577,328	688,776	–	–	–	
1805	92,003	445,241	537,244	–	–	–	
1806	119,708	437,364	557,072	29,115	182,104	211,209	768,301
1807	114,363	311,695	425,058	51,876	219,639	271,515	696,573
1808	126,927	253,050	379,977	21,564	266,073	287,637	667,614
1809	105,032	164,400	269,432	12,676	260,907	273,583	543,015
1810	98,523	98,718	197,241	26,405	291,470	317,875	515,116
1811	80,123	112,780	192,803	1,072	11,201	12,273	215,076
1812	95,093	43,057	138,150				138,150
1813	71,928	98,960	170,888	5,702	621,503	627,205	798,092
1814	68,284	356,250	424,534				356,250
1815	56,562	95,158	151,720		349,440	349,440	501,160
1816	44,636	257,791	302,427				
1817	72,117	362,612	434,729				
1818	57,432	198,907	256,339				
1819	55,395	270,631	326,026				
1820	57,492	190,386	247,878				
1821	56,080	99,850	157,342				
1822	25,622	36,235	61,857				
1823	5,772	39,945	45,717		78,962	78,962	124,679
1824	20,799	22,630	43,429	13,990	142,681	156,671	200,100
1825	13,962	102,123	116,085	10,548	128,327	138,875	254,960
1826	7,510	75,376	82,886	10,769	36,947	47,716	130,602
1827	7,355	23,142	30,497		56,384	56,384	86,881
1828	10,660	73,005	83,665		47,654	47,654	131,319
1829	8,858	62,181	71,039		42,225	42,225	113,264
1830	10,650	53,231	64,081	2,711	42,215	44,925	109,006
1831	68,592	58,757	127,349		38,681	38,681	166,030
1832	13,376	77,065	90,941		1,584	1,584	92,525
1833	9,240	89,484	98,724	1,585	15,735	17,320	116,044
1834	7,319	96,358	103,677	790	18,777	19,567	123,244
1835	9,150	75,074	84,224	519	9,225	9,744	93,968

Sources: APC, MG 23, G.I., 10; RAC, 1888, B. 201, p. 12s; APC, MG 11, Q. 29, Q. 90, and Q. 109; *JALBC*, 1822–23, appendix W. See also *JALBC*, 1808; *JALBC*, 1824, appendix AA; *JALBC*, 1826, appendix U; *JALBC*, 1827; *JALBC*, 1828–29, appendix C; *JALBC*, 1830, appendix W; *JALBC*, 1831, appendix GG; *JALBC*, 1831–32, appendix SS; *JALBC*, 1832–33, appendix PP; *JALBC*, 1834, appendix NN; *JALBC*· 1835, *appendix Z; JALBC*, 1835–36, appendix GGG; *JALBC*, 1837, appendix E.

Appendix table 35   Exports and imports of wheat and flour: Lower Canada[a]

	Exports	Imports from the United States, Upper Canada and others			
	Quebec and Montreal	St Jean	C. du Lac and Lachine Canal	Rideau Canal	Others
1761					
1762					
1763	57,195				
1764	29,205				
1765					
1766					
1767	16,505				
1768	24,052				
1769					78,115
1770	59,247				
1771	197,929				
1772	240,486				
1773	276,830				
1774	467,370				
1775	187,490				
1776	61,280				
1777	56,600				
1778	83,145				
1779					
1790					
1781					
1782	300				
1783	22,905				
1784	19,680				
1785	5,200				
1786	156,200				
1787	285,475				
1788	249,900				
1789					67,365[b]
1790	150,000				
1791	224,740				
1792	350,000				
1793	541,500				
1794	482,500		18,910		
1795	485,000		—		
1796	24,605		—		
1797	101,000		—		
1798	139,500		—		
1799	151,000		—		
1800	317,000		—		

Appendix table 35   *continued*

	Quebec and Montreal	St Jean	C. du Lac and Lachine Canal	Rideau Canal	Others
1801	663,000			70, 165	
1802	1,151,000		57,110		
1803	447,450		–		
1804	273,135		–		
1805	114,965		–		
1806	151,895	470	12,255		
1807	333,750	7,180	107,607		
1808	399,010	195	–		
1809	301,845	300	–		
1810	233,495	625	–		
1811	97,555	6,470	–		
1812	451,435		–		
1813	2,585	35	–		
1814	6,085		–		
1815	9,600	12,090	–		
1816	5,685	31,540	–		
1817	335,895		220,606		
1818	554,475	3,610	230,371		
1819	98,325	250	83,491		
1820	545,890	25	415,626		
1821	431,655		419,901		
1822	380,655	10	326,161		
1823	237,400	15,348	201,308		
1824	214,900	c	139,004		
1825	918,850	50	291,541		
1826	396,965	650	371,072		
1827	661,420	172	626,875		
1828	290,910	598	516,472		
1829	168,905	46,889	336,871		
1830	940,845		929,230		
1831	1,734,575	440	1,069,343		
1832	912,530	5,820	753,275		
1833	404,105	510	1,146,350	18,263	
1834	467,380	109	1,083,878	67,566	
1835	349,115	271	622,255	86,088	
1836	421,560	15	900,250	51,430	
1837	146,965	1,345	231,500	59,696	
1838	221,730	111,430	642,535	c	
1839	133,380		1,042,594	c	
1840	1,043,775		2,940,957		

Appendix table 35   *continued*

	Quebec and Montreal	St Jean	C. du Lac and Lachine Canal	Rideau Canal	Others
1841	2,342,910	79,045	3,435,691		
1842	1,678,000	6,845	3,193,900		
1843	1,194,015		2,030,100		
1844	2,309,515	3,740	2,852,255		
1845	2,607,390		3,341,610		
1846	3,312,755		4,686,430		
1847	3,883,150		4,979,715		
1848	2,156,015		3,787,485		
1849	3,891,335		4,144,120		
1850	1,829,460		2,570,890		
1851	2,158,690		−		

a Flour converted to wheat at the ratio of 5 *minots* per barrel
b Partial amount
c In 1824, exports to the United States via St Jean surpassed imports by 48 *minots*; in 1838, wheat exports to Upper Canada via the Rideau Canal surpassed imports by 17,119 *minots*; in 1839, this surplus was 6,140 *minots*.

Sources: *RAC*, 1888, B.201, p. 1419; APC, MG 23; G.I., 10; APC, MG 11, Q, vol. 89, 90, 109; *JALBC*, 1823–24, appendix W; APC, RG 1, 'Report on Inland Navigation, 1839.'; *JALBC*, 1808; *JALBC*, 1825, appendix AA; *JALBC*, 1826, appendix U; *JALBC*, 1827; *JALBC*, 1828–29, appendix C; *JALBC*, 1830, appendixes D and W; *JALBC*, 1831, appendix GG; *JALBC*, 1831–32, appendixes Q and SS; *JALBC*, 1832–33, appendix PP; *JALBC*, 1834, appendixes E and NN; *JALBC*, 1835, appendixes F and Z; *JALBC*, 1835–36, appendixes Q and GGG; *JALBC*, 1836, appendix E; *JALBC*, 1837, appendix E; *JALBC*, 1842, appendix F; *JALBC*, 1843, appendix SS; *JALBC*, 1844–45, appendix AA; *JALBC*, 1946, appendix GG; *JALBC*, 1849, appendix Z.

Appendix table 36   Exports of forest products: Quebec

	Potash (quintals)	Squared logs (pine and oak) (pieces)	Planks and deals (pieces)	Staves, Hoops and ends (pieces)
1761				
1762				
1763				
1764	100	1	970	
1765				
1766				
1767	96	868	23,423	128,164
1768	456	957	2,670	184,093
1769	546	395	83,471	198,340
1770	625	6,297	88,405	55,740
1771	733		9,884	213,998
1772	1,491		8,155	185,795
1773	1,951	425	2,823	118,470
1774	1,856	1,070	26,428	250,359
1775	1,417	1,834	58,545	68,624
1776	992	81	40,071	6,899
1777	930		67,297	72,920
1778	805	503	48,082	48,645
1779	776	5,570	115,065	140,304
1790	630	218	101,105	213,783
1781	1,537	418	64,683	336,118
1782	1,548	1,528	59,002	150,463
1783	1,828	830	73,210	68,774
1784	1,533		41,567	25,960
1785	1,215	2,302	85,792	251,739
1786	1,724	706	76,791	138,647
1787	5,680	610	30,979	144,015
1788	7,700	7,230	69,000	462,000
1789				
1790				
1791		3,635	34,913	244,263
1792				
1793	9,702	1,240	22,059	294,608
1794	7,824	729	15,863	151,354
1795	7,746	936	30,000	593,652
1796	12,358	1,405	18,286	818,799
1797	14,933	3,063	47,691	734,198
1798	22,051	2,224	11,769	446,469
1799	24,355	2,403	52,140	705,178
1800	29,142	1,645	34,863	542,656

Appendix table 36   *continued*

	Potash (quintals)	Squared logs (pine and oak) (pieces)	Planks and deals (pieces)	Staves, Hoops and ends (pieces)
1801	25,620	2,617	60,033	535,547
1802	16,920	4,241	104,735	764,312
1803	17,896	6,972	125,322	776,898
1804	21,946	8,783	78,391	1,085,267
1805	27,291	5,431	42,820	1,061,836
1806	36,450	10,308	66,116	1,821,922
1807	107,652	14,528	107,642	1,831,700
1808	30,838	26,882	194,676	1,887,314
1809	30,942	33,842	262,280	3,079,979
1810	29,407	103,069	312,423	3,934,421
1811	22,734	93,316	396,674	2,396,127
1812	9,613	48,507	297,631	1,870,737
1813	5,541	23,312		1,886,381
1814	2,722	17,647	188,000	2,033,844
1815	4,326	19,394	190,567	1,074,730
1816	19,267	29,630	389,975	1,306,586
1817	23,886	31,177	470,728	1,908,837
1818	24,251	40,733	642,160	1,895,915
1819	31,928	94,205	1,236,296	3,585,523
1820	28,678	103,275	890,129	4,333,747
1821	35,765	40,659	996,154	3,861,562
1822	36,269	104,532	930,759	5,486,189
1823	55,170	95,223	880,826	3,543,313
1824	55,108	98,020	1,052,147	3,687,604
1825	62,502	161,230	1,579,142	3,953,685
1826	39,589	152,973	873,973	4,164,688
1827	27,303	107,826	1,621,648	5,445,160
1828	32,817	135,489	1,500,830	4,112,795
1829	33,041	193,566	1,717,239	6,821,311
1830	46,354	168,740	1,645,522	6,156,587
1831	49,916	205,269	1,715,546	5,569,111
1832	30,278	214,818	1,665,584	4,917,740
1833	37,098	210,554	2,260,959	5,027,184
1834	22,279	259,742	2,635,742	2,767,856
1835	29,140	323,147	2,133,125	6,558,674
1836	33,689	338,754	2,750,536	6,640,085
1837	33,756	300,383	2,792,011	6,155,410
1838	29,454	326,864	2,886,635	5,459,261
1839	25,480	395,254	3,046,248	6,037,747
1840	17,478	399,545	2,422,407	7,847,765

Appendix table 36 *continued*

	Potash (quintals)	Squared logs (pine and oak) (pieces)	Planks and deals (pieces)	Staves, Hoops and ends (pieces)
1841	22,012	409,283	2,829,069	7,601,550
1842	27,621	248,866	2,478,870	3,492,990
1843	34,916			
1844	35,743	298,166	2,928,377	3,323,174
1845	30,916	383,286	3,539,274	5,711,000
1846	26,011	373,824	2,468,067	3,455,000
1847	19,243	277,871	3,399,529	2,830,000
1848	18,282	277,338	2,846,891	3,043,000
1849	23,717	421,147	2,940,008	5,020,393
1850	2,435	443,204	2,998,608	4,804,000
1851	3,082	527,290	3,526,647	5,705,200

Sources: *RAC*, 1888, B.201, pp. 14–19; APC, MG 23, G.I., 10; APC, MG 11, Q. 89, 90, 109, *JALBC*, 1823–24, appendix W; *JALBC*, 1808, *JALBC*, 1828–29, appendix C; *JALBC*, 1830, appendix W; *JALBC*, 1831–32, appendix SS; *JALBC*, 1831, appendix GG; *JALBC*, 1832–33, appendix PP; *JALBC*, 1835, appendix Z; *JALBC*, 1837, appendix E; JCS, 1841, appendix EE; *JALC*, 1842, appendix T; *JALC*, 1843, appendix SS; *JALC*, 1844–45, appendixes K and P; *JALC*, 1847, appendix AA; *JALC*, 1852–53, appendix MMM.

Appendix table 37   Imports to Quebec and Montreal

	Rum and spirits (gallons)	Wines (gallons)	Sugar (pounds)	Molasses (gallons)	Tea and coffee (pounds)	Salt (minots)
1761	467,539					
1762	63,460	8,064				
1763	37,769	116,096				
1764	74,528	112,374				
1765						
1766						
1767	110,310	49,273		69,621	33,824	13,168
1768	258,754	153,875	23,744	18,692	20,719	17,000
1769	268,328	153,875	21,924	54,487	29,601	9,100
1770	233,368	132,100	57,932	81,224	22,289	5,929
1771	220,587	83,444	72,266	70,152	49,784	52,089
1772	285,395	49,268	56,392	62,073	41,068	76,323
1773	378,633	212,436	108,024	100,280	34,387	5,500
1774	752,442	112,381	121,744	193,559	33,268	72,046
1775	74,000	306,936	66,976	64,701	16,432	14,376
1776	116,144	81,848	76,648	78,504	66,959	
1777	263,911	213,241	146,720	60,250	87,545	4,500
1778	378,582	205,932	7,984	160,774	111,012	29,669
1779	450,842	198,811	162,764	83,199	81,520	12,350
1780	265,607	309,204	183,456	104,658	97,502	13,920
1781	734,263	297,108	285,264	80,331	147,644	51,849
1782	728,915	179,928	110,880	58,072	59,001	
1783	289,186	202,860		139,481	30,213	20,800
1784	41,817	130,347	29,924[a]	15,540	8,436[a]	15,290
1785	208,691	123,039	93,555[a]	165,900	1,436[a]	102,869
1786	333,528	287,658	240,030[a]	179,760	6,804[a]	38,835
1787				81,504		
1788						
1789						
1790						
1791						
1792	256,725					
1793	321,280	194,000	126,170	25,740	16,540	150,732
1794	395,100	88,350	143,305	50,220	11,450	58,004
1795	116,450	121,590	183,643	17,767	18,404	35,450
1796	249,867	153,503	246,788	62,898	75,746	31,606
1797	178,727	91,146	138,538	63,525	21,814	38,513
1798	251,986	225,505	300,404	19,422	34,080	69,444
1799	525,926	153,382	269,783	69,165	48,847	83,536
1800	233,128	159,937	324,983	37,073	35,079	102,975

Appendix table 37 *continued*

	Rum and spirits (gallons)	Wines (gallons)	Sugar (pounds)	Molasses (gallons)	Tea and coffee (pounds)	Salt (minots)
1801	310,044	161,253	221,780	65,693	50,816	136,010
1802	398,743	192,454	119,440	49,094	29,359	101,064
1803						
1804	514,931	248,202	74	1,278		104,168
1805	538,887	188,310	506,935	61,814	59,971	100,787
1806						
1807	389,532	51,870	563,681	36,068	24,846	212,850
1808	454,055	59,608	1,614,645		140,015	154,722
1809		201,129		46,874		218,349
1810	756,678	316,437	1,747,339	59,346	36,976	81,121
1811	814,970	136,408	3,852,528	71,075	393,421	100,755
1812	861,684	107,498	1,247,752	15,997	86,763	117,361
1813	868,299	138,274	1,724,796	115,822	414,201	74,980
1814	1,777,411	448,300	2,831,682		168,962	85,904
1815	1,286,638	538,438	1,772,165	21,434	544,798	114,525
1816	1,261,955	300,470	2,248,095	135,241	554,410	219,826
1817	1,183,154	231,935	2,920,137	60,547	290,243	186,247
1818	1,102,618	185,977	967,481	33,977	398,786	139,242
1819	1,219,639	119,584	2,220,983	105,334	323,588	162,911
1820	1,734,663	250,501	2,963,140	88,215	222,445	106,423
1821	1,207,823	305,685	1,750,621	60,187	240,028	198,855
1822	1,326,630	110,712	2,237,502	115,413	229,308	243,486
1823	1,054,379	193,638	2,252,050	37,822	111,625	198,108
1824	1,104,379	242,704	2,928,278	79,689	424,126	150,801
1825	1,809,379	263,443	3,146,897	39,906	1,212,626	231,570
1826	1,208,031	287,082	2,600,850	100,875	1,150,658	209,783
1827	1,084,155	230,273	3,347,403	48,779	1,213,570	198,824
1828	1,058,509	261,061	2,818,976	73,279	874,741	181,160
1829	1,218,506	139,346	5,484,690	74,455	87,223	352,917
1830	1,590,524	352,985	4,962,936	82,108	940,616	239,856
1831	1,559,649	348,934	7,008,398	97,813	703,764	267,173
1832	1,334,390	412,247	6,727,044	123,024	1,156,907	260,227
1833	1,880,512	1,067,630	11,216,825	104,150	2,191,918	238,500
1834	1,409,494	629,786	7,952,965	92,962	1,042,173	329,644
1835	1,858,831	421,469	10,214,617	175,772	1,046,706	228,137
1836	977,576	384,243	8,147,721	56,417	1,351,653	290,808
1837	616,691	275,944	6,596,998	78,922	1,251,125	
1838	1,062,054	267,425	6,542,210	70,335	1,085,054	308,203
1839	777,246	392,984	6,969,853	82,820	996,520	484,662
1840	602,716	310,479	9,170,143	174,387	903,910	360,135

Appendix table 37   *continued*

	Rum and spirits (gallons)	Wines (gallons)	Sugar (pounds)	Molasses (gallons)	Tea and coffee (pounds)	Salt (minots)
1841	377,023	215,002	12,485,249	69,494	1,271,179	322,692
1842	277,749	399,984	8,724,389	109,326	1,528,962	417,060
1843	227,168	246,764	6,325,199	132,250	620,971	641,100
1844	474,407	392,279	10,912,340	212,240	1,145,367	835,560
1845	367,207	221,015	8,101,371	352,970	826,493	373,830
1846	375,295	523,265	11,959,651	151,675	1,028,345	353,976
1847	679,027	372,298	12,725,133	365,450	1,787,274	104,494
1848	249,636	124,563	6,525,560	321,643	722,452	415,145
1849						
1850	206,890	188,567		556,620	1,712,388	413,309

a Incomplete data

These figures do not include imports at Gaspé and New Carlisle, nor the occasionally substantial imports to the port of St Jean from the United States.

Sources: *RAC*, 1888, B. 201, pp. 5–7; APC, RG 23, G.I., 10; APC, RG 11, Q. 89, 90, and 109; *JALBC*, 1823–24; appendix W; APC, RG 4, 32, *JALBC*, 1808; *JALBC*, 1825, appendix AA; *JALBC*, 1825, appendix U; *JALBC*, 1827; *JALBC*, 1828–29, appendix C; *JALBC*, 1830, appendix W; *JALBC*, 1831, appendix GG and AAA; *JALBC*, 1831–32, appendix SS; *JALBC*, 1832–33, appendix PP; *JALBC*, 1835, appendix Z; *JALBC*, 1835–36, appendix GGG; *JALBC*, 1837, appendix E; *JALC*, 1843, appendix SS; *JALBC*, 1846, appendix Z; *JALBC*, 1849, appendix SS.

PART THREE
Cuba: origins and modalities

Anglo-American entrepreneurs in Havana: the background and significance of the expulsion of 1784–1785

The war between England and the Thirteen Colonies from 1775 to 1783 brought numerous changes to the New World, but few were more lasting than the economic links that developed between Cuba and the struggling English colonies. Although economic exchanges between Cuba and the English mainland possessions antedate the American Revolution, this earlier trade was sporadic, often indirect, and seldom of any duration. Indeed, merchants in the thirteen colonies had far more experience trading with Spanish possessions like Puerto Rico, Santo Domingo and Florida, all of which were isolated and off the heavily-travelled trade routes, than with Cuba.[1] Moreover, existing trade with Cuba was often carried out through merchant houses in Jamaica which served as middlemen in the exchange of goods. The American Revolution, however, shattered this traditional pattern. During the war Cuba grew to be a significant market for North American exports and an even more important source for hard currency. At the same time, the United States represented an ideal temporary market for Cuban products which could not be sold in Europe because of the vicissitudes of war. So mutually profitable was this trade during the war years that the Spanish government took the most extreme measures to stop it in 1784–1785 but with only limited success.

The foundation of the wartime commerce between Cuba and the United States was flour. Havana was a garrison city, the principal military outpost of the Spanish empire in the New World. The Crown deliberately stationed the bulk of its army and navy in Spanish America there. At the same time, Havana was also the premier commercial port in the empire. The number of merchant vessels with a Havana port-of-call surpassed that of any other Spanish coastal city in the New World.[2] Havana, thus, was a thriving military and commercial center in the latter half of the eighteenth century, yet it could not feed its population. Although the island had a dynamic agricultural sector, Cuba's major crops were sugar, tobacco and coffee — lucrative exports but not the foodstuffs needed to feed a large urban population. Like Spaniards in the mother country, residents of Havana considered bread to be a basic staple of their diet.[3] The flour to make this stapel had to be imported.

The flour trade in Havana during the 1770s and 1780s was a complicated business. In addition to the problems associated with importing the product, there were two separate flour markets in the city — one for the private sector and another for the purchases made by the government. Although in theory serving different groups of people, the two markets overlapped and often competed for the same flour. Flour itself had to be baked into bread, hardtack, or some edible form before it could be consumed. The baking of bread was a very lucrative part of the business. Some entrepreneurs participated in all aspects of the flour trade, from importing to baking, but most confined their work to one phase or another. It was, in other words, a highly specialized industry touching the lives of many people.

In the 1770s and 1780s the flour business had a certain pattern that made it very vulnerable to the fortunes of war. In theory, the government purchased all its flour from New Spain and used it to feed the garrison, fleet, prison laborers, and the king's slaves. New Spain produced an abundant crop of wheat in the region around Puebla and Atlixco, and the viceroyalty was ideally situated to supply Havana with this valuable export. Until 1776, the viceregal government farmed out to a single *asentista* (royal contractor) the task of supplying the government in Havana. Because of dissatisfaction with the *asentistas*, the Crown took over direct administration of this function as part of the royal exchequer.[4] Whether run as a private or public monopoly, however, there were so many problems in transporting flour from Mexico to Havana that New Spain never adequately supplied the royal needs in Cuba.[5] As a result, the government often bought its flour from the same sources which served the private market in Havana.

In some ways, the private market was hardly less monopolistic than that of the government. A baker's guild (*gremio de panaderos*) controlled all private purchases of flour in Havana. The *gremio* came into existence in the early 1770s when the king granted the bankers of the city the right to monopolize the production of breadstuffs in return for an annual contribution to finance the clothing and arming of militia units in the island's capital. Since the cost of maintaining these militia units would obviously rise during wartime, the guild received an exemption from this duty should Spain actually engage in a war — something, of course, that happened all too soon and which made the contract rather one-sided in its benefits. The *gremio* could control the number of bakers doing business in Havana and the prices charged for bread. Not surprisingly, the *gremio* kept its membership as low as it possibly could.[6]

A representative of the bakers did all the buying for the guild. He obtained his flour from several sources. On occasion, some privately owned flour came from Veracruz aboard the infrequent military and commercial ships sailing from that port.[7] The *gremio*'s most important source for flour, however, was the ships arriving from Spain. Flour made up a significant part of many cargoes crossing the Atlantic. It was safe to carry, lasted a long time (even in the tropics) and had almost a guaranteed market in Havana. Some of the trans-Atlantic flour came directly from Spain, grown and milled in Galacia, Andalucia, and Santander. At least half, if not more, however, originated in foreign countries, particularly France and to a lesser extent in the British colonies (from whence it had been shipped east to Spain and then eventually back west to reach Cuba).[8] There existed one other important source of flour for the *gremio* in the 1770s — the *asiento de negros* (the royal slave trade monopoly). The rapidly expanding domestic economy in Cuba desperately needed laborers in the eighteenth century and this meant slaves. Although often profitable, the slave trade often proved to be a risky business which frequently resulted in substantial losses for its practitioners. In order to encourage the slave trade in Cuba and other parts of the Spanish Caribbean, the king permitted the *asiento* to import flour at a set rate for each slave delivered. The ratio varied in the 1760s and 1770s from one to three barrels of flour for each imported slave. Although it was clear that slave traders frequently found flour the more profitable half of their two-sided business, the *asiento*'s flour supposedly came from Spanish ports and did not equal in volume individual shipments coming from that direction.[9]

During the 1770s the king's advisors recognized many of the potential problems inherent in the way Havana received its food supplies. It certainly was not desirable to have the most important Spanish military post in the New World dependent upon a life-line stretching across the Atlantic. Spain's traditional foe since the sixteenth century had been England, the world's greatest sea power. No prescience was required to foresee what might happen to the Cuban capital if it could not be re-supplied by sea. Officials in Spain periodically inquired as to why the population of Havana could not live off the agricultural products of the island, particularly *pan de casaba*.[10] At the very least, the Crown hoped that Havana could depend upon the shorter sea run from Veracruz for its supplies. Yet the government ultimately tolerated the existing system. It was unlikely that even England could mount a long-term naval blockade of Havana, and there was always enough flour and other supplies on hand for shorter emergencies.[11] The Crown did try to increase exports from Mexico, but the exchequer earned considerable revenue in Spain from foreign grain that was taxed passing through Peninsular ports on its way to the New World.[12] Rarely could royal officials muster the political courage necessary to stop an activity which produced tax revenues in the mother country. Most significant, however, was the fact that Havana got the flour it needed through the existing system. With shortages only a potentiality, there were far more pressing problems for the Spanish bureaucracy to address.

The war between England and the Thirteen Colonies ended this familiar system. Since Spain delayed her entrance into this conflict until 1779, the war did not immediately affect flour supplies in Havana. The shipping lanes between Havana, Veracruz and Spain remained open. Only the flour normally shipped through the *asiento de negros* seemed affected by the conflict, but the other sources easily compensated for this shortage.[13] Spanish ambivalence about the war itself, torn between a desire to see England humbled and a natural repugnance for the ideas and objectives of the rebellious English colonies, resulted in a policy that permitted Anglo-American ships in distress to visit Spanish ports but refused these vessels the privilege of staying any longer than was necessary or permission to conduct business. Once Spain declared war against Great Britain, however, old practices changed rapidly.

During the first year of the war, food supplies for Havana grew increasingly scarce. Spanish merchants felt that the sea lanes between Havana and Europe were vulnerable, particularly to privateers patrolling the coast of Spain or cruising in the Caribbean. Moreover, no one knew the intentions of the English fleet in the Caribbean. As a result, the number of ships reaching Havana declined. In addition, the Spanish government mobilized the island's militia, reinforced the garrison and fleet in Havana, and assigned the Spanish commanders there a number of ambitious tasks, most notably the recapture of Pensacola and Jamaica.[14] Food supplies not only had to be sufficient for an increased population in the colony, but officials had to stockpile provisions for the numerous expeditions planned for the Spanish military. By the end of 1780, military and exchequer officials in Havana had no choice but to turn to the rebellious English colonies for flour and other food-stuffs. For the next four years, the Anglo-Americans poured into Havana in unprecedented numbers.

The first significant arrival of Anglo-American ships carrying needed supplies occurred during the last four months of 1780.[15] Although Havana welcomed other foreigners at the same time, the Anglo-Americans were the only outsiders who could supply the island and its bloated wartime population with flour. The table below gives graphic evidence of how abruptly the flour trade changed in 1780.

The first merchant vessels sailed under the direction of Robert Morris, Secretary of the Treasury for the Continental Congress, and various merchants from Philadelphia.[16] Thereafter, other merchants and other cities became involved in the trade. Since the major export for the Anglo-Americans always remained flour, merchants in Philadelphia and Baltimore, the major ports for the export of flour, dominated the trade (see table 39). At the same time that Anglo-American ships were welcomed in Havana, the Continental Congress appointed an official representative in Havana. He was Robert Smith, son of a prominent Baltimore merchant and a friend of Robert Morris. Although Smith spoke little Spanish when he went to Cuba, he performed innumerable services for his fellow countrymen doing business in Havana. Smith received no salary in his position, but his government expected him to use his position and talents to meet expenses and provide an income.[17] He continued in this post in Havana until late 1782 when he died unexpectedly.

Table 38   Flour imports in Havana, 1779–1783

Year	Tercios[a]	Barrels	Total
1779	10,152	10,128	20,280
1780	26,998	6,484	33,482
1781	3,241	43,301	46,542
1782	8,847	57,545	66,392
1783	9,955	64,334	74,289
	59,193	181,792	240,985

a The *tercio* was the dry measure used for flour from New Spain. The barrel was the dry unit for all other flour (although the actual weight could vary greatly). From 1780 to 1783, flour in barrels was overwhelmingly from the Thirteen Colonies. If anything, this chart underestimates the amount of flour purchased in Havana. It is doubtful whether the navy's purchases are here since that branch of the service kept its own records. Moreover, flour for the Spanish expeditionary army stationed in Cap Français in 1782 is not included here even though it was purchased through the Havana treasury.

Source: AGI, Santo Domingo 1240, exp. 451, fs. 30–4, 'Certificación de José Alvarez,' Havana 3 Sept., 1784. AGI, Santo Domingo, 1864–1865. 'Cajas cuentas de la marina, Havana.' AGI, Mexico, 2483. 'Estado en que manifesta la compra de viveres y pertrechos en ... [Guarico para la esquadra del dn. José Solano], [Guarico].'

His replacement, Oliver Pollock, found Smith's post far more than he could handle.

Although the evidence is not conclusive, American merchants often worked in partnership with Cuban entrepreneurs in Havana. Since American ships gained little by remaining long in port, the supercargoes or factors that came with most Anglo-American vessels and who were in charge of selling the ship's cargo tried to do business rapidly. Cuban merchants bought the cargo and held it until the best price from the government or *gremio* could be obtained. There were times, nevertheless, when the Americans bypassed the middle-man.[18] There were also occasions when Cuban merchants sent their own boats to the Thirteen Colonies to buy flour.[19] Flour offered such a chance to make money during the war that neither the foreign nor the native entrepreneur experienced much difficulty in working or competing with each other.

Like all commercial exchanges, flour had to be paid for, and this was done in a number of ways. Since Cuba was a prime producer of sugar, the Anglo-Americans often bartered flour for this crop. The English colonies traditionally obtained their sugar from the British West Indies, but the war had interrupted this commerce. Cuban sugar was a valuable substitute.[20] At times, the Spanish government covered its purchases by granting foreign merchants the right to carry trade from Cuba to other parts of the empire, particularly peninsular ports. Yet the most common form of compensation, and the most

				Ports of origin and destination[b]				
Year	Arrivals	Departures	Total	Carolinas and Georgia	Chesapeake Bay	New York	New England	Other
1775[c]	2	2	4	0%	0%	0%	50%	50%
1776[c]	2	2	4	0%	25%	0%	0%	75%
1777	9	9	18	17%	28% (Phil. 22%)	0%	0%	55% (Corsair 17%) (Fr. islands 11%)
1778	22	14 (1Br)	36 (1)	28%	6% (Phil. 6%)	0%	6%	61% (Corsair 42%) (Fr. islands 8%) (Dut. islands 6%)
1779	22 (1Sp)	25	47 (1)	17%	34% (Phil. 23%)	2%	13% (Boston 13%)	34% (Corsair 17%) (Cayo de San Luis 13%)
1780[d]	32 (1Sp) (1Br)	26 (1Br)	58 (3)	24% (Charl. 12%) (Edenton 7%)	45% (Phil. 35%) (Balt. 7%)	0%	3% (Boston 3%)	28% (N. Orleans 9%) (Dut. islands 7%) (Fr. islands 5%)
1781[d]	126 (12Sp) (2Br)	101 (3Sp)	227 (17)	7% (N. Car. 5%)	65% (Phil. 60%)	6% (All Sp. ships)	10%	12%
1782	211 (9Sp) (3Br) (1Fr)	157 (5Sp) (1Br) (1Fr)	368 (20)	12% (N.Car. 7%)	41% (Phil. 22%) (Balt. 15%)	3%	15% (Boston 5%)	31% (Providence 11%) (Sp. ports 6%)
1783	173 (5Sp) (2Dut) (1Br)	128 (8Br) (2Dut) (1Sp)	302 (19)	11%	44% (Phil. 25%) (Balt. 12%) (Va. 6%)	3%	10%	32% (St. Thomas 9%)
1784	19 (1Sp) (1Fr)	23 (3Br)	42 (5)	17% (Charl. 17%)	50% (Phil. 43%) (Balt. 5%)	0%	5%	29% (Jamaica 7%) (N. Amer. 7%) (Curacao 5%) (Fr. Islands 5%) (N. Orleans 5%)
1785	4 (4Sp)	6 (5Sp) (1Br)	10 (10)	20% (Charl. 20%)	60% (Phil. 60%)	20%	0%	0%

a English, Spanish, Dutch, and French ships are indicated in parentheses if they arrived from or departed for a port in the Thirteen Colonies. By subtracting the number of foreign ships in each column, the reader can determine the exact figure for American ships. If a sea captain listed several ports of origin or destination (which was rare), each port is counted. The totals, thus, are slightly higher than the true number of ships.

b Ship captains and Spanish officials conspired to make it very difficult to determine in many cases a vessel's port of origin or destination. The *entradas* and *salidas* might list a ship as coming, for example, from Carolina, South Carolina or Charleston. These may well have been all coming from Charleston or from different cities along the coast. For the purposes of this chart, the English colonies are divided into four geographical areas — the one exception being New York since it was under British control for most of the war. If any single port had 5 per cent or more of the total trade for any year after 1776, it is listed in parentheses. Percentages are rounded to the nearest whole number, making the total in some cases more than 100 per cent.

c Spanish port records in Havana do not distinguish between American and English ships until 1777. In 1775 and 1776, hence, only ships in direct transit to and from the Thirteen Colonies are listed. There were, of course, many more English ships (some of which were probably American) which entered Havana during those years. Even after 1777, the records do not always indicate the nationality of ships from the mainland ports. The figures in this chart include all vessels from the Thirteen Colonies, plus whatever other ports of origin or destination that are indicated for American ships.

d Shipping records are missing for February 1780, and August 1781.

Sources: AGI, Indif., 2421; Cuba, 1331, 1332, 1365, 1416; Santo Domingo, 1217, 1227, 1230, 1232–1243, 2083A, 'Entradas y Salidas', 1775–1785.

welcomed, was specie. Historians cannot precisely determine the amount of cash generated by the flour trade, but in a ten month period from 1780 to 1781 one Spanish treasury official estimated that the Anglo-Americans had already received 3,000,000 pesos.[21] This figure is suspect for a number of reasons, but the flour trade undoubtedly generated large sums of money. Robert Smith alone, for example, earned 300,000 pesos in 1782 through supplying only part of the Spanish army.[22]

It should be noted that much of this specie did not actually find its way back to the Thirteen Colonies. Hard currency in large amounts was difficult and awkward to transport. Moreover, it was extremely dangerous to move money by sea during wartime. Ships carrying flour were not as tempting a target for corsairs and privateers as ships carrying specie. As a result, private and public purchases of flour in Havana were often made in *letras de cambio* and *libramientos* (bills of exchange redeemable in specie). This paper was safe, light-weight, easily negotiable, usually corsair-proof and often non-taxable. When payment was made in hard currency, many Anglo-Americans chose to keep it in Havana by lending the specie to Cuban merchants and the exchequer rather than risking its transportation back to the mainland.[23] In the same fashion, Cuban traders operating ships in the Thirteen Colonies rarely sent money by sea but lent their profits out in the American ports.[24] Regardless of whether payment was made in currency or bills of exchange, the credit of Cuban merchants and the Havana exchequer was excellent, and the amount of money that Cuba spent on flour demonstrates why some parts of the rebellious English colonies felt little economic pain during their separation from England — at least for the moment.

The door, however, that had swung open so wide in 1780 to the Americans and other foreigners began to close in 1782, the last year of the war. The Spanish government, of course, had never intended to make permanent the commercial changes brought on by the necessities of war. By 1782 the need for foreign flour and other food-stuffs decreased. It was apparent that the British were losing the war and could not maintain control of the Caribbean long enough to blockade Havana effectively. The stockpile of food necessary for this emergency, hence, was no longer necessary.[25] At the same time, the Spanish military began to anticipate the end of the war and scaled down serious preparations for additional expeditions against loyal British colonies, further lessening the need for large quantities of flour. With only nature rather than British sea power to fear, hundreds of ships (mostly Anglo-American, but some from as far away as the Baltic) entered the harbor of Havana lured by the high prices paid for flour.[26] For a time in 1782, Havana was glutted with flour, a product that had been so valuable and scarce in previous years.[27]

It was not just the grain surplus that changed the climate for foreigners in Havana. Spanish bureaucrats in New Spain anguished over the plentiful harvests of wheat in their viceroyalty and their inability to satisfy the needs of the Havana market. The flour was available in New Spain, and it had only to be transported to Havana. Ramón de Posada, *fiscal* of the royal exchequer in New Spain and probably the most powerful figure in the viceroyalty during the early 1780s, led a personal crusade to remedy this problem. In a series of reports written during the war, Posada predicted that free trade in grains (*comercio libre*) would supply Havana with the flour that the viceregal monopolies, both private and public, had failed to do. Whether or not Posada was right, he was advocating an economic theory popular at the Spanish court, particularly with José de Gálvez, the minister of the indies. In 1782 Gálvez accepted the Posada proposals and ordered the viceroy of New Spain to take the steps necessary to implement them. Since the changes proposed by Posada promised an end to the need for foreign flour in Havana, Gálvez supported the reforms by starting to restrict foreigners from doing business in Havana. The government intended free trade only for citizens of the empire.[28]

Even peninsular merchants contributed their part to closing Havana to foreign entrepreneurs. The profitable flour market on the island had not escaped their attention during the war and they had continued reduced shipments from Spain throughout the conflict. With the trip to Havana relatively safe by 1782, these businessmen only awaited the removal of foreign competition to resume large shipments of flour across the Atlantic. Spanish merchants and lobbyists started to apply pressure in Madrid and in Havana to have the Anglo-Americans barred from colonial ports.[29]

With hindsight, only an unexpected extension of the war and a revival of British sea power could have kept Havana open to foreigners much after 1782, but the actions of the Anglo-Americans and other outsiders on the island during the last years of the conflict contributed to the events that were shortly to follow. To begin with, the Americans hardly acted as if their presence in Cuba was temporary, raising to some extent the ugly specter of the previous war with England in 1763 when it proved so hard to remove English merchants from Havana.[30] Not content to be transporters of raw materials, many Anglo-Americans opened commercial houses in Havana where they represented themselves and other foreigners. The extent of their businesses is not clear, but some ventured into commercial enterprises that had little to do with imports or exports. David Beveridge, a Scotch-American from Philadelphia, for example, owned two stores selling salted meat.[31] Those who did confine their commerce to imports, moreover, refused to restrict their trade to flour, other food-stuffs and naval wares (all legal imports). It was common for Anglo-American sea captains to sell their boats after unloading their cargoes in Havana, a business that might have involved up to one-fourth of their ships at its peak.[32] The ships' officers and crew then found other ways home. Although illegal, the government tolerated this type of activity because Havana always needed more vessels. Some American merchants started to compete with the *asiento de negros* by importing slaves, evidently straight from the former English colonies.[33]

The most disturbing business of the Anglo-Americans, however, was their propensity to traffic in contraband, a habit that played no small role in their country's break with England. Few issues in Cuban colonial history are more controversial than contraband and there is no other issue which historians must handle with greater care. Scholars often give the impression that contraband trade was the predominant economic activity and that legal trade was the exception. This was certainly not true in the 1770s and 1780s. Although important, the amount of contraband trade had much to do with the willingness of governmental officials to permit it. During the 1770s and 1780s, Havana had public servants, particularly Juan Ignacio de Urriza, intendant of the exchequer, willing to stop illegal trade. Urriza was an acerbic, honest and ambitious official who instinctively knew which laws to enforce in order to gain favor at the Spanish court. He zealously enforced the laws against contraband and used the issue to destroy other public servants less dedicated to controlling this problem.[34] As long as Urriza was intendant, other officials in Havana found it politically expedient to match his zeal in this area.

The Anglo-Americans came under Urriza's scrutiny during the war. He soon found them guilty of smuggling illegal goods into the country and of under-reporting what they took out in order to avoid export duties. In both instances, there was a similar pattern. To bring illegal goods into Havana, traders usually filled the bottom half of a flour barrel with contraband and the top half with flour.[35] As long as the people handling the merchandise did not make note of any weight discrepancies, the system was usually successful. Flour barrels customarily weighed two hundred pounds and few exchequer employees chose to lift them as part of an inspection. Moreover, any inspection could be a lengthy ordeal since a single ship might unload a thousand or more barrels of flour at one time. The same procedure was followed with sugar barrels when goods were smuggled out of Cuba. Exporters stuffed the bottom of the barrels with pesos, the usual contraband in this case, and the top with sugar.[36] Again, employees of the exchequer rarely checked the weight of the barrels.

Although all nationalities dabbled in contraband in Havana, it was the Anglo-Americans who were the most numerous and who at the end of the war participated in the most notorious case to come before Urriza. Like most crimes of this nature, chance (rather than diligent police work) exposed the smugglers. After the death in 1782 of Robert Smith, the first American diplomatic representative in Havana, the Continental Congress appointed Oliver Pollock to replace him. Pollock seemed to be a better choice than Smith had been. He had extensive experience dealing with Spanish officials in Louisiana during the war. He spoke Spanish and was born in Ireland (a land with many historic ties to Spain). Not the least of his qualifications was his personal friendship with Bernardo de Gálvez, whose uncle was José de Gálvez, the minister of the Indies.[37] As was the case with Smith, Congress granted Pollock no salary for his work but expected him to earn his livelihood through the many business opportunities presented by his diplomatic post.[38]

It was these apparent opportunities that brought about the downfall of Pollock. Chartering two boats to take his family and employees to Havana in August 1783, Pollock loaded his ships with flour and household goods, enough household goods to furnish numerous homes in Havana. He also packed many of the flour barrels with contraband. Pollock obviously meant to do a great deal of business immediately. Once in Havana, however, he suffered all types of misfortune. Some of the contraband barrels burst during unloading, exposing the contents to all who happened to be near. For once, the extreme differences in weight of some flour barrels caught the attention of a diligent treasury official.[39] Pollock's employees panicked and tried to bribe a custom agent to ignore their crime. Rejecting the proffered money, the Spanish official reported the offer instead to Intendant Urriza. In a desperate effort to get rid of the damaging evidence before being caught, sailors dumped some of the contraband on shore. Fate could not have been worse for Pollock since most of the valuable barrels, those containing the contraband, had his initials stenciled on them. Although Pollock lost most of his legal and contraband property in the judicial proceedings that followed, he never endured imprisonment for his crime, primarily because of his diplomatic position. His employees, however, felt the wrath of Spanish justice and confessed their guilt in order to receive lighter punishments.[40] With the highest ranking member of the Anglo-American community guilty of a flagrant violation of the law, Spanish patience towards the presence of other Anglo-Americans in the port, suspected of doing the same thing, was remarkable.

In August 1782, the minister of the Indies reminded officials in Havana that the city could not accept foreigners after the war ended.[41] Yet he delegated enforcement of this policy to the governor and intendant on the island. When the official declaration of peace reached Havana, Urriza and other officials began cautiously to implement the new policy. They realized that time would be required to liquidate inventories and collect debts. Ships clearing foreign ports for Havana or already at sea obviously had no way of knowing that they were no longer welcome in Cuba. Moreover, an abrupt termination of trade with the newly independent English colonies without a corresponding rise in ships coming from Spain and New Spain with flour would leave the island exposed to starvation. At the end of the war Havana once again bulged with people, merchants who had waited until the end of the war to ship their most valuable cargo back to Spain and the expeditionary army and fleet preparing to leave the island. Nevertheless, in May 1783, the government notified all foreign ship captains in Havana that they could not return to the city once they departed.[42] At the same time, Francisco Rendón, the Spanish representative in Philadelphia, had instructions to issue no more permits to ship captains wanting to sail to Havana and to announce in the American gazettes that Havana no longer accepted foreign ships.[43] The only exception to this rule would be foreign men-of-war on official duty and private vessels in distress. These exceptions, particularly the latter, shortly became the rule.

These initial steps failed to have the desired effect for a number of reasons. Havana still needed a steady supply of flour and Spanish merchants waited for word that the Anglo-Americans were gone before venturing large shipments of flour from Europe. The *comercio libre* reform in New Spain had just been instituted and its practical results could not yet be determined. Until Spanish merchants began shipping grain at whatever price, Cuban officials could hardly enforce the expulsion of foreigners. Moreover, there were many Cuban entrepreneurs who did not wish foreigners to be excluded. Time after time, the *gremio* and others petitioned to buy foreign flour since there was no other available. The Anglo-Americans themselves were not going to give up such an important market without a struggle, especially since independence from England ushered in a period of great economic uncertainty in the former colonies. Many ship captains soon discovered that naval officials made little effort to monitor the level of distress that might require a foreign vessel to stop at Havana. Foreign ships, hence, found all types of reasons to stop in Cuba, the most common being the need to careen. Once there, it was very easy to discover a way to sell the ship's cargo.[44]

By the end of 1783, officials in Spain and Cuba felt compelled to end this untenable situation in Havana. The population in the city had decreased with the departure of the expeditionary army and navy. Ships from Spain came on a regular basis and many began to carry some food-stuffs. The intendant Urriza complained bitterly to José de Gálvez in Spain and to his fellow officials on the island about the presence of the Anglo-Americans and the constant violations of the spirit of the law. In January and February of 1784, the minister of the Indies sent two Royal Orders to the governor and intendant in Havana ordering them to refuse admission to all foreign ships no matter what the circumstances.[45] At the same time, the minister of the Indies expected the Anglo-Americans already in the city to leave immediately. Although it had been the intendant who had inspired these orders, it was the Governor of Havana, Luis de Unzaga, who carried them out.[46] Unzaga notified each foreign ship captain in the port to leave immediately. Those supposedly needing repairs had to have them done at once and depart. Naval officials refused permission to foreign ships to enter the harbor, while those already in the harbor had to have Spanish guards aboard until they left in order to prevent any last minute attempt to sell their cargo. Under threat of imprisonment, the king specifically prohibited any Cuban merchant, especially the purchaser for the *gremio*, from petitioning the governor to buy foreign flour. Indeed, the king would shortly disband the *gremio*.[47] The governor summoned the Anglo-Americans living in the city and ordered them to leave the island within a month. The combination of these various Spanish efforts influenced most Americans to depart.

Yet some stayed on finding it very difficult to terminate their businesses overnight and tempting fate that there would be a change in attitude. Unzaga, however, aware of the royal position on this question and interested in his own future, was not willing to allow a few laggards to be exceptions. At the end of March 1784, he sent soldiers to patrol the streets and arrest any Americans found in public. Those who had ships were escorted under armed guard to their vessels and ordered to leave. In at least one case, Spanish sailors forcibly lifted a ship's anchor and pushed it out to sea. Other soldiers hunted down Americans who had stayed in their homes and avoided earlier patrols. The governor forced these individuals to book passage out of Havana on the first available ship and to appoint Spanish attorneys to handle their businesses once they were gone. He threatened, if the Americans refused, to place them on any ship leaving Havana (no matter what the destination) or to keep them in jail until they complied. Some were jailed anyway. Anglo-American ships, even those on official business, that appeared outside the port could not gain admission, and the forts guarding the harbor entrance threatened to fire upon several which did not depart as rapidly as port officials wanted.[48] By the end of 1784, the only Anglo-Americans in Havana were Oliver Pollock, the disgraced envoy under house arrest partly for his trafficking in contraband and partly because of his indebtedness, and the Anglo-Americans serving prison terms because of their contraband activities. All of these left Havana in the spring of 1785 when Bernardo de Gálvez arrived in Cuba as the new governor of the island. Gálvez, a personal friend of Pollock, decided to send all the Anglo-Americans, diplomats and criminals alike, to the United States as a good will gesture towards the Confederation. This action was timed to coincide with the arrival of Diego de Gardoqui, the new Spanish envoy to the United States.[49] For a brief moment, Havana was free of its neighbors to the north.

The importance of the wartime trade with Cuba, however, was not underestimated by either side. For the Anglo-Americans, it had come at a crucial time in their history and dramatically showed the possibility of new markets to the south. Indeed, it could be argued that the war commerce with Cuba prepared American merchants for the 1790s when trade with all parts of Latin America began to open up. Yet even in the 1780s the Anglo-Americans had not completely lost the flour trade to Havana. They would have to share it, but many merchants started shipping flour to Spain where it was once again transported back across the Atlantic to Havana.[50] Moreover, the expulsion of 1785 did not include everyone, and some Anglo-Americans remained clandestinely in the city.[51] Within a year, at least one prominent Philadelphia merchant was back in Havana doing business and feeling secure enough to complain about his mistreatment in the *residencia* of Governor Unzaga, the official who had expelled him in 1784.[52] Others drifted back later, although the Anglo-American community did not regain its wartime size until the 1790s.

Spanish officials likewise appreciated the significance of the trade. It had been a necessary evil during the war, but one that had to be stopped if there was any hope of keeping the island within the economic sphere of the empire.

Spanish bureaucrats realized how important this trade was to the Thirteen Colonies, and at least one speculated whether independence would have resulted without the massive injection of Spanish currency into the empty coffers of the rebels.[53] Cuban merchants, furthermore, had tasted a highly profitable market in the north. Although the Crown prohibited Anglo-American merchants from trading and residing in Havana, it did not directly address itself to Cuban merchants doing business with the United States. In the years after the war, the governor and intendant in Havana received numerous petitions from entrepreneurs in Havana seeking permission to conduct business with their former trade partners.[54] In the 1790s, when the French Revolution made sea traffic between the New and Old World dangerous once again, American and Cuban entrepreneurs were well prepared to resume the lucrative trading system established during the American Revolution.

Appendix table 40   Ship arrivals and departures in Havana: 1780–1786

Year	Total	Foreign ships
1780	347	40 (12%)
1781	782	261 (33%)
1782	1208	387 (32%)
1783	1284	463 (36%)
1784	700	74 (11%)
1785	680	38 (6%)
1786	617	31 (5%)

Sources: 'Nota de la entrada y salida de embracaciones ... de la Havana en ... 1780', Juan Ignacio de Urriza, Havana, 1781, AGI, Santo Domingo, leg. 1658, num. 793; 'Nota de la entrada y salida de embarcaciones en ... la Habana en ... 1781', Urriza, Havana, January 3, 1782, AGI, Santo Domingo, leg. 1659, num. 888; 'Estado de las embarcaciones que han entrado y salido ... de la Havana en ... 1783', Urriza, Havana, December 31, 1783, AGI, Santo Domingo, leg. 1664, num. 1267; 'Nota de las embarcaciones que han estrado y salido de ... la Havana, 1784', Urriza, Havana, January 1, 1785, AGI, Santo Domingo, leg. 1665, num. 1533; 'Noticia de las embarcaciones que han entrado y salido ... de la Havana, 1786', Francisco Antonio Astigarreta, Havana, January 1, 1787, AGI, Santo Domingo, leg. 1668A. The figures for 1782 and 1785 come from AGI, Indif., leg. 2421; AGI, Cuba, legs. 1331–2, 1416; and AGI, Santo Domingo, legs. 1234–6, 1242–3, 'Entradas y salidas'.

Appendix table 41   Private shipments of flour from Veracruz to Havana (*Measurements in tercios*)

Year	Amount carried in men-of-war	Total
1779	892 (28%)	3,174
1780	3,459 (20%)	17,386
1781	551 (24%)	2,259
1782	2,321 (28%)	8,367

Source: 'Noticia individual ... de arina que han extraido ...', Carrion *et al.*, Veracruz, September 11, 1782, AGI, Santo Domingo, leg. 1393, num. 1902.

Appendix table 42   Flour shipped to Havana in 1778–1779 from Spanish ports (*Measurements in quintales*)

Origin of flour	1778	1779
France	4,693 (38%)	6,244 (85%)
Thirteen Colonies	1,260 (10%)	0 (0%)
England	700 (6%)	0 (0%)
Domestic	638 (5%)	645 (9%)
Foreign (origin undetermined)	5,075 (41%)	350 (5%)
Unknown origin	0 (0%)	31 (1%)
Total	12,366	7,270

Sources: 'Relaciones de generos y frutos para La Habana', AGS, DGR, leg. 568; 'Relaciones de la carga de embarcaciones del comercio libre, 1778–9', AGI Indif., legs. 2415–8.

Appendix table 43   Flour exports from Veracruz to Havana, 1774–1778 (*Measurements in tercios*)

Year	Flour shipped by the government	Flour shipped by individuals	Total
1774	5,022	1,097	6,099
1775	3,939	1,723	5,662
1776	8,145	4,304	12,449
1777	15,225	7,394	22,619
1778	7,567	12,084	19,651

Source: 'Martín de Mayorga to Gálvez', México, November 20, 1782, AGI, Mexico, leg. 1393, num. 1902.

Appendix table 44   Flour shipped to Havana from Spanish ports, 1785–1788
(*Measurements in quintales*)

Origin of flour	1785	1786	1787	1788
Domestic	19,130 (44%)	21,253 (36%)		27,866 (34%)
Thirteen Colonies	9,021 (21%)	19,578 (33%)	Not available	20,714 (25%)
France	14,841 (34%)	14,429 (24%)		24,591 (30%)
Foreign flour (origin unknown)	462 (1%)	3,072 (5%)		8,006 (10%)
England	0	1,103 (2%)		1,662 (2%)
Total	43,454	59,435		89,839

Sources: 'Relaciones de generos y frutos para la Habana', 1785–1788, AGS, DGR, legs. 572–5. One of the effects of the war, as can be seen by the chart, was to stimulate Spain's domestic exports of flour of Havana. See Fernando Berreda, *Comercio marítimo entre los Estados Unidos y Santander (1778–1829)* (Santander, 1950), p. 12.

CHAPTER SIX

Anglo-American merchants and stratagems for success in Spanish imperial markets, 1783 – 1807*

But the Spanish Colonies, being wholly cloathed and in a great degree *fed* by our nation, should they like the tyger be suffered to cripple the hand whose bounty *feed* them? Has not the *second* nation on the Globe in commercial tonnage, and the *first* in exports for the necessaries of life, a right to demand with firmness, the respect due to her Flag and Citizens ...?

When Josiah Blakeley, consul of the United States at Santiago de Cuba, wrote these lines to Secretary of State James Madison on November 1, 1801 he had recently been jailed by administrators on that island.[1] This remarkable situation notwithstanding, his sentiments still neatly express the paradox of trade between the United States and Spanish Caribbean ports. The expanding hinterlands of New York, Philadelphia and Baltimore furnished North American merchants with ever increasing, exportable food supplies and led to fierce competition for new markets at the end of the eighteenth century.[2] At the same time, Spain's American colonies remained chronically, often desperately, short of food-stuffs. Imperial bureaucrats at many levels consistently recognized this problem, yet they imposed numerous trade restrictions.[3] Even more than the dizzying pace of war and peace itself after 1793, these restrictions made North American commerce with the Spanish Caribbean volatile, risky and undesirable for many.[4] This essay focuses not upon those who were deterred from the trade, but rather upon a small network of North Americans who, despite the uncertainties, chose to operate within these markets. First, the salient characteristics of their businesses are outlined. Then, it is argued that their behavior departed from the models postulated for American merchants that have been developed by students of the period. As opposed to luck or 'imaginative innovation' or aggressive individualism, the key factor emphasized here is cultural flexibility.[5] Moreover, the research is drawn from archives, both foreign and domestic, that are not often consulted by Anglo-Americanists. At the very least, this strategy allows a more correct identification of the individuals involved in trade with the Spanish Empire.

The example of John Leamy provides a case in point. Countless *expedientes* in several Spanish archives attest to his commanding presence in U.S. trade with Spanish America after 1792. At times when no other North American received the necessary licenses, Spanish imperial officials made sure that Leamy was able to land his cargoes. Moreover, his ships were the first foreign ones admitted to the Rio de la Plata in 1798.[6] Yet, the most commonly consulted North American sources yield only the barest indications of his existence. If Leamy's personal or business papers have been preserved, they have yet to be found. But, since he was a founder and director of the Insurance Company of North America, it is possible to reconstruct some of his activities through less direct sources, such as minutes of directors' meetings and maritime insurance policies. While certain types of questions regarding the rate of return on a particular venture, for example, still cannot be answered with precision, these alternate sources do add new insights into entrepreneurial behavior in this commercial sphere. In addition to John Leamy of Philadelphia, John and Thomas Stoughton, based in New York, are also treated here in some detail. Again, Spanish archival sources attest to their importance; in this instance, fortunately, two sets of their letterbooks have also been preserved in New York. Finally, Stuart Bruchey's thorough treatment of the Olivers of Baltimore provides the opportunity to assess the business practices of a spectacularly successful firm from that port.[7]

In brief, the operations of these merchants shared the following characteristics: 1) they were built upon personal contacts cultivated over many years with high-ranking peninsular officials as opposed to Spanish merchants; 2) they preferred to rely upon relatives on the scene rather than native correspondents or United States' consuls; 3) they often worked in concert with, instead of competing against, other North Americans from nearby ports; 4) they exhibited extreme flexibility in business dealings, including the willingness to ship provisions by indirect routes, to pay off corrupt bureaucrats, and even to transport slaves to gain admittance to ports that were officially closed. If such behavior failed to qualify as modern entrepreneurship in the fullest sense, it is clear nevertheless that, given the context of the Spanish commercial system, the Leamys, Stoughtons and Olivers acted quite rationally to maximize their trading opportunities. Those who acted differently simply did not succeed.

In the forefront of Spanish imperial trade in the 1790s, these men had steadily nurtured Spanish contacts throughout the preceding decade. With Spain's overt participation in the Revolutionary War after 1779 came the legalization of direct trade to key Spanish Caribbean ports. This was due primarily to the influx of troops that needed to be fed.[8] The Spanish initiated deals with prominent rebel merchants, offering Robert Morris one of the first trading licenses to Cuba. Morris jumped at this opportunity, but his principal contact, Juan de Miralles, soon died. Morris served as executor of the estate, but then turned his attention to governmental affairs and other, less fortunate business schemes.[9] At the same time, John Leamy took his cue from the Spaniards, assiduously cultivating the deceased agent's secretary, Francisco de Rendón. Of Irish origin, Leamy had been educated in Spain, where he lived for several years prior to establishing himself in business in Philadelphia around 1781. Leamy had won the trust of some Spanish officials by that time, since he carried letters, luxury items and funds to Rendón, who was eventually named the new agent. Seven years later, the highest-ranking Spanish diplomat in the United States, Diego de Gardoqui, admitted that Leamy performed favors for him, such as recruiting Pennsylvania artisans to settle in Spanish Louisiana.[10] Likewise, the up-and-coming merchant ingratiated himself with Gardoqui's two subordinates, Josef de Jáudenes and José Ignacio Viar. Charged with obtaining food supplies for Santo Domingo late in 1791, these young Spaniards were duly impressed when Leamy diverted one of his ships, already loaded and destined for a French Caribbean port, to the Spanish colony instead. Jáudenes and Viar noted Leamy's zeal and partiality for Spain, as well as the fact that he declined to take excessive profits from the switch. A few years later, Jáudenes moved into a house in Philadelphia owned by Leamy. And, as late as 1820, Leamy served as a clandestine conduit for privileged information from peninsular authorities to Spanish representatives in North America. Unlike the Stoughtons, then, Leamy never held the title of Spanish consul, but it is clear none the less that he often functioned in a similar capacity over the course of four decades.[11]

Like John Leamy, the Stoughtons also did favors over the years for Spaniards stationed in North America. For example, the son of Felipe Fatío, a long-time Spanish commercial agent, owed the North Americans money as early as 1792.[12] But if Leamy provided a residence for Jáudenes, John Stoughton went one step further by giving his daughter in marriage to the only man with authority to sell trading permits to Cuba in the early 1790s. The bride of Jáudenes' successor, the Marqués de Casa Irujo, came from a distinguished Pennsylvania family, the McKeans. That tie kept him living in Philadelphia even after the capital had moved to Washington, D.C., no doubt a convenient arrangement for his business partner, James Barry. And surely it was no coincidence that, following the marriage of his sister to Francisco Sarmiento, John Craig of Philadelphia received promising trade concessions to Venezuela.[13] Most of the persons discussed above were Roman Catholics, a fact that obviously facilitated these alliances. Undoubtedly, it would be difficult to overstate the influence of religion in cementing official trust. For example, it was none other than Bishop John Carroll himself who introduced James Barry to Jáudenes and Viar. And the hapless Spaniard Rendón was recalled to Madrid when he sought to marry the daughter of a New York merchant who was Protestant. Still, it must be emphasized that these North Americans went out of their way to pattern their behavior along Spanish, as opposed to strictly Catholic, lines. When Jáudenes went to drink at City Tavern, it was for the expressed purpose of ingratiating himself with Thomas Jefferson and other members of the government. Obviously, this lesson was not lost on another frequent patron of that establishment, John Leamy.[14]

Cultivating the right Spanish officials was more efficient than seeking to establish close relations with Spanish mercantile firms. In the decade following the revolution, the Stoughtons sent out several feelers to houses in the peninsula and in the colonies. However, they do not appear to have maintained successful, long-term arrangements with specific individuals or businesses. The difficulties involved are illustrated by the case of Pedro Juan de Erice of Havana. Late in 1793, the Stoughtons consigned some goods to him. A series of increasingly stiff letters followed, demanding more prompt unloading of cargoes, quicker return shipments and payment of expired accounts. Finally, an exasperated John Stoughton went himself on a trading voyage to the Spanish Caribbean. He intended to settle with Erice in person: whether or not he succeeded is unknown.[15] John Leamy solved the problems of unreliable correspondents by working through his brother James, a long-term resident of that Cuban port. And, on at least one occasion, local Spanish functionaries smoothed the arrival of consignments to him.[16] This last point is a telling one. Historians often assume that the 'latin personality' helped to keep Hispanic businessmen from serving as competent correspondents. In truth, however, it was the Spanish commercial system, defined by policymakers in Madrid, that really circumscribed their role. Spanish imperial merchants simply did not have the freedom to make decisions, the ability to guarantee performance, or even the access to reliable shipping information that were enjoyed by their North American counterparts. Leamy and the Stoughtons recognized this fact and consequently directed their attention towards other, more productive channels.

While this circle of North American traders depended upon Bourbon functionaries in conducting their various commercial affairs, and even assumed Spanish offices themselves, they did not as a rule rely upon the services of American consuls stationed in Spanish colonial ports. This was an understandable and wise course of action. For many of the United States' consuls were themselves aspiring merchants who regarded official duties as secondary to their own business interests. Under such circumstances, it made little sense for them to aid competitors who already enjoyed strong influence in high places. More to the point, however, was the fact that the consuls were in the extremely unenviable position of not being legally recognized by the Spanish government. Thus, at the same time that the United States required them to protect the interests of its traders and seamen, Spain gave them little room to maneuver. Moreover, the consuls were often required to record formal protests against Spanish commercial policy, which subsequently limited their ability to work behind the scenes to alleviate specific problems. So, while stranded American sailors complained that their maintenance allowances, paid out of the consul's own pocket, were inadequate, local administrators harassed these representatives. On occasion, they had their papers confiscated, were asked to leave the colonies, and even were thrown into jail. Not surprisingly, the turn-over rate in this office was high. As a rule, then, its occupants never established the powerful connections that Leamy, Craig and the Stoughtons had built up over the years.[17]

Regarding their relationships with each other, the degree to which Leamy and the Stoughtons worked in concert to further their respective commercial ends is striking. They were never formal partners, but they did send business each others' way and each party performed vital services for the other. For example, Leamy functioned as an insurance broker, often purchasing maritime policies for his counterparts in New York and elsewhere. The Stoughtons, in turn, chartered and provisioned ships for Leamy around the time of the outbreak of yellow fever in Philadelphia in 1793.[18] They cooperated in much the same way as did John Craig and the Olivers, who at least were related by marriage.[19] In short, when Spaniards like Jáudenes presented the opportunities, Leamy and the Stoughtons responded by trusting each other to advance their individual interests. This occurred, it should be pointed out, at a time when their respective home ports, Philadelphia and New York, rivalled each other for national supremacy in foreign trade.

From the examples presented above, it is obvious that success did not come easily to North Americans trading with the Spanish Empire. On occasion, even the operations of men as well-connected as Leamy and the Stoughtons did not proceed smoothly. When John Stoughton travelled as supercargo to Santo Domingo and Cuba during the summer of 1794, he carried numerous passports and letters of introduction to the proper authorities, each duly noting his relationship to Jáudenes. Furthermore, the New Yorker's grasp of Spanish was strong enough to write appropriately flattering petitions to local dignitaries. Nevertheless, Stoughton was given the runaround, or at least caught in the middle of a dispute between the military commander, who wanted to buy flour to feed his troops, and the local economic authority, who opposed this. To complicate matters, the latter official had gone off on vacation on a remote part of Hispaniola. It took Stoughton over two weeks of difficult and dangerous travel through the backcountry to track him down. With a smile, the official finally suggested that the cargoes be sent to Cuba. Stoughton had sent one of his ship captains ahead already, with instructions to deliver gratis one dozen bottles of mustard to the highest-ranking functionary on the island. Then, perceiving the market at Havana to be temporarily weak due to speculation and multiple arrivals from the United States, Stoughton himself proceeded with another ship to the smaller port of Santiago. He intended to sell most of the cargo there, using the proceeds to purchase sugar, hides and brandy of higher quality and lower price than were available in Havana. However, he was not allowed to sell much flour there and ultimately sailed for the capital anyway. This particular letterbook ended with notices to his partners that Stoughton would winter in Havana, and that the venture would probably not live up to expectations after all.[20]

If John Stoughton had to endure such costly delays, they were undoubtedly even more common for other North American traders. For example, some twenty-two U.S. ships were suddenly embargoed in Havana harbor in June 1797, for reasons connected with military security. By the third week in port, the captains estimated that they had collectively lost over sixteen thousand dollars. Major expenses included: seamen's wages, provisions, and medical fees; damages to vessels caused by worms and unrepaired leaks; and spoiled cargoes. Moreover, they complained that ships already loaded with sugar for the return voyage would not arrive home in time to avoid an increased rate of duties on that item.[21] This case is but one example of how costly disruptions of commerce could not always be blamed on cruisers and pirates. Again, it was Spanish imperial policy that caused uncertainty, risk and loss for North American merchants. And, for most of the years under consideration here, direct trade with the colonies had been strictly prohibited. Under those circumstances, Leamy, the Stoughtons and the Olivers had to endure the inconveniences of indirect shipping — via New Orleans or to a nearby French island where trade with both the United States and Spanish colonies was permitted. Alternately, traders could misrepresent their true destinations on official documents or entrust their cargoes to smugglers.[22] Leamy and the Stoughtons accepted these conditions, but in an era when other markets existed, those who found the conditions distasteful simply turned elsewhere.

In fact, there was one aspect of trade with the Spanish Empire that for some North Americans was clearly unacceptable, even though it facilitated entrance to Spanish colonial ports. For years, foreign merchants transporting slaves were allowed to sell a proportionate number of barrels of flour at substantial rates of profit. This policy was extended to Cuba, desperately short of labor, in 1789. Throughout the next fifteen years, blacks were delivered to that island regularly; by far the majority of ships involved were identified as Anglo-American.[23] While many of the slaves had probably been picked up on adjacent Caribbean islands, at least some were transported directly from the African coast. Furthermore, although such evidence is sketchy, there was at least one recorded instance of a black from Maryland being sold into slavery in Havana.[24] More research needs to be done, but at this stage it is clear that most of the aforementioned merchants engaged in this activity. The Stoughtons, clearly, did. Moreover, they worried about obtaining insurance for ships carrying human cargoes.[25] How the majority of their peers reacted to their involvement in the slave trade is unknown. However, it is interesting to compare the operations of men like Leamy with those of others less successful or less visible in the Spanish Caribbean trade. Thanks to Jules Boymel's unpublished analysis of the rich Boone Papers at the Historical Society of Pennsylvania, it is possible to use the career of Jeremiah Boone as an example.[26] Coincidentally, Boone arrived in Philadelphia the same year that John Leamy did; from 1781 on, both worked to build up their respective businesses. Yet, while Leamy cultivated contacts in the manner described above, Boone seems merely to have dispatched his ships to various Spanish and non-Spanish ports in the Caribbean. His son, William, occasionally travelled as supercargo to Havana. While there, the younger Boone complained strongly about official corruption. Contrast this attitude with John Stoughton's, as he methodically sought to smooth his own way. And, given the fact that Jeremiah Boone was a Quaker who once wrote an anti-slavery tract, it is unlikely that he used slaves to gain entrance to colonial ports. In short, Boone was unwilling to behave in the manner best calculated to insure high returns from Spanish imperial trade. Not surprisingly, his businesses failed three times. While these losses corresponded with the terminations of three wars, the evidence indicates that, even in the good years, he never enjoyed Leamy's and the Stoughtons' strong links to Spanish markets.

To conclude, we cannot fully understand trade between the United States and the Spanish Empire in the 1790s simply by focusing upon traditional market mechanisms. For, in general, demand in the Spanish Caribbean for North American products was high, at the same time that east coast merchants needed Mexican specie to trade with other parts of the world.[27] Given the geographical proximity, these areas should have been prime trading partners. However, constraints imposed upon foreign merchants by Spanish imperial policy obscured this relationship and molded entrepreneurial behavior along distinctive, sometimes contradictory lines. Leamy and his counterparts were often forced to act in ways reminiscent of seventeenth-century traders. Their methods were highly personalized; they relied upon relatives and patrons at the start of a century that saw the rise of the independent, less kin-oriented entrepreneur.[28] At the same time, they were modern men, whose behavior was eminently rational and, in some instances, pioneering. Both Leamy and John Craig were original subscribers to and directors of the Insurance Company of North America, founded in 1792. Leamy also had the distinction of being that agency's best customer during its first years; in so doing, he showed himself to be a risk-taker who took some of the risk out of his own operations.[29] Perhaps his greatest talent was his ability and willingness to act like a 'Spaniard' when circumstances so warranted, and like an 'Anglo-American' when the opportunity was there. Of such was successful entrepreneurship made in the Napoleonic era.

CHAPTER SEVEN

Anglo-American investors and payments on Spanish imperial treasuries, 1795–1808

1

Among our enduring images of Spanish colonial history are those of a treasure ship sinking in heavy seas or being captured after a spirited action with Dutch, English or French enemies. At the root of such stereotypic views is the well-known fact that Madrid ordered its colonial treasures to be moved to their appointed destinations on ships and in coin. So familiar, indeed, are we with this phenomenon that it rarely strikes us as being at all remarkable. Yet, it should be a cause for wonder. After all, Hapsburgs and Bourbons both transferred their funds around Europe through paper transactions when the need arose. Further, other colonial powers, the British for instance, made extensive use of this device to transfer needed funds to their American possessions. Why were such precedents and examples not heeded and the technique applied to the Indies? The advantages of doing so were surely compelling: greater security, as even warships were vulnerable; increased economic activity, as the circulating medium would have been kept circulating; potential for remissions even in wartime, when the Spanish navy was usually kept in harbor by superior naval forces.

In fact, of course, the systematic transfer of royal funds from the Indies to Spain by means of bills of exchange (*libranzas* or *letras de cambio*) was not entirely unknown, although it did develop at a comparatively late date. The reason for this delay in adopting a practice long known in the world of private business is a matter for speculation. Bullionist prejudices may have played a role, but it may well be that the predominant reason was that commercial life was restricted in such a way as to provide merchants with little incentive to obtain funds in the colonies by paying out cash in the peninsula. In most instances the sale of outward-bound cargo more than paid for the in-bound shipment, the difference being made up by sending American coins to Spain. Indeed, in general, the Spanish colonies suffered from a balance of trade deficit which, as they received almost no European capital, implied a permanent outflow of specie. The necessary studies have yet to be undertaken and specific evidence is therefore lacking. None the less, it would seem that bills of exchange had to be relatively minor players in the Indies trade, at least compared to the role that they played elsewhere in the Atlantic economy. What is certain is that they did not figure in the calculations of government officials.

This situation corresponds to a phase lasting over nearly all of the colonial period, one characterized by Spanish America's relative isolation from the mainstream of western economic life. Compared to the trade of the Portuguese East that of the Spanish West was surely substantial. Yet, when the commerce of Castile's Indies is weighed against that of the British or French Antilles or of Anglo-America (save for its bullion component) it pales in significance. It is this relative isolation which allowed the region to develop and preserve its own manufacturing industries, but which also maintained certain Indian sectors in an inefficient and oppressive subsistence/labor extractive type of economy and which prevented the 'normal' growth of Spain's tropical colonies into slave societies producing specialized agricultural products for Europe.

The use of bills of exchange by the Bourbon colonial state is one of the indicators of the absorption of Spanish America into the mainstream of the Atlantic economy. In view of the role that Anglo-American merchants and ship-owners played in that economy at the turn of the eighteenth and nine-teenth centuries, it is hardly surprising that they figured prominently among the factors which induced the Spanish Crown to pay more attention to paper and less to silver. The details of their involvement, none the less, do not lack interest.

2

The Crown's tardy adoption of bills of exchange does not mean that Anglo-Americans were denied access to Spanish silver. Indeed, payments were ordered in their favor but in the traditional form of a *Real Cédula de Libranza*. Typical is that expedited for William Walton of New York on August 31, 1752, by which the Mexico City treasury was ordered to pay 63,001 pesos, 2-½ reales for supplies he had provided St Augustine (Florida) in 1731–1738. This document, however, was specific to Walton and his agent. It could not be discounted or sold to a third party.[1] Research in this domain being as underdeveloped as it is, of course, these findings must be considered tentative. What is beyond question is that by the middle of the eighteenth century the peninsular administration already enjoyed the services of a government-owned office of *Real Giro* charged with making payments in all of the great financial centers of Europe.[2]

Although reluctant to issue bills of exchange against American treasuries or to take them in return for colonial funds, officials seem to have accepted them under certain circumstances. Thus, in the 1730s the Caracas Company, which held a monopoly of trade with Venezuela, paid off some of its obligations in this form.[3] This was hardly the first firm to make this type of payment, of course, for we find fines paid in bills from the earliest days of Bourbon rule. The practice may be safely considered to have dated from the earliest Hapsburg period. Negotiable bills do not seem to have been issued on government treasuries, however, nor were private ones systematically used to patriate colonial funds. The breakthrough may have come with the *real negociación extraordinaria* launched by François Cabarrus, founder of the Bank of San Carlos, to help finance the Spanish war effort during the War of American Revolution. This complex operation involved floating the first issue of *vales reales* (interest-bearing but money-like instruments) and patriating silver from Havana, with payment to the Crown in both cases largely made by means of bills of exchange.[4] In any event, during the war Intendant José Avalos bought *letras* expedited from the Netherland West Indies and by 1785 his replacement, Francisco de Saavedra, was doing the same from Venezuela itself.[5] It was in the latter year also that the governor of the Philippines was ordered to turn over to the Manila factor of the *Cinco Gremios Mayores* of Madrid all sums bound for Spain, accepting bills in return, an order which was never executed.[6] The essential point is that the Crown seems to have learned to accept the use of the device in the colonial sphere from its dealings with its own privileged companies. One might well wonder, however, why a negotiable instrument came to be used in preference to a simple receipt. In fact, of course, both types of documents were used side by side for a considerable time.[7] The *letra*, however, had the advantage, from the Crown's point of view, of being negotiable which meant that refusal to pay (protesting the bill of exchange) could have an impact on a firm's entire credit position. It was less likely than a receipt to become the subject of endless litigation. Similarly, there were advantages for the firms involved, as they could include provisions for delayed payment of the sometimes considerable sums involved.

Bills of exchange became a standard device in colonial fiscal administration. They were used to transfer funds from one part of a colony to another, as by the tobacco monopoly of Guatemala;[8] to pass funds between colonies, as in the case of Havana and New Orleans;[9] and in semi-colonial situations, as with the Canaries.[10] The latter case involved the proposition of the firm of John Paisley and Archibald Little to accept the surplus of the insular treasury, giving in return *letras de cambio* on Madrid houses. The device was also employed to collect for services rendered to foreign ships in colonial harbors. Thus, in the closing years of the French Old Regime the La Perouse expedition was aided in this fashion in Manila, a practice repeated subsequently with republican vessels.[11] Similarly, after the settlement of the Nootka Sound controversy, Spanish officials on the Pacific coast of South America found themselves giving aid to foreign vessels and accepting bills of exchange in payment. In 1792 alone, the Viceroy of Peru sent a total of ten such *letras* to Madrid, for a total value of 2,718 pesos (clearly, no great sum), many of which were payable on the British consul in Cadiz, who protested them.[12] One has the impression that the administration was experimenting with a new toy.

The most fruitful use of the new device, of course, was likely to be in the realm of transatlantic payments. This was recognized even before the Crown accepted the idea of using *libranzas* in the colonial world. Thus in 1780 one Melchor de Guardia proposed to the Count of Floridablanca that a *Real banco de giro de letras de España a Indias* be established.[13] It was in Venezuela and in the Philippines, however, that the practice became established. Having dealt with the question elsewhere, I will limit myself here to a brief resumé.[14] The situation in both regions was the same, the Crown wanted to send money from the colonies while the Philippines Company needed to send coins to them. The latter situation arose because sale of company exports to each of these areas would not buy enough for the return cargo. Having inherited the assets of the Caracas Company and the interests of the *Gremios* in the Philippines trade, the new company was able to obtain the right to take funds in the colonies in return for *libranzas*. In the Philippines the matter was straightforward and lasted to the end of the century. In Venezuela, however, complex changes took place which tended to generalize usage of the bills. From 1788 through 1790 only the company was allowed to pay for cash by means of *letras*. As more funds were available than the Philippines Company could absorb, however, from 1791 into 1793 the privilege was shared with a number of Madrid and Cadiz firms designated by the ministry of finance. Lastly, in October of 1793 Venezuelan producers (*cosecheros*) were allowed to share in the scheme to the temporary end of the trade in 1797.[15] In this fashion, the government became accustomed to dealing with many individuals and small firms, as opposed to a few large ones.[16]

The Crown was also involved in transatlantic bills of exchange in this period in another locale. Wishing to prepare its Caribbean posessions for the upcoming war with Great Britain, Spain authorized its agent in the United States, José de Jaudenes, to emit bills against Treasurer General Francisco Montes in Madrid. These were to be used to pay for the goods and transport charges to Puerto Rico and Puerto Cabello.[17] It may be, however, that there were problems placing the *libranzas* for in the following years Madrid's envoy, Marqués de Casa Yrujo, used the medium of bills on D. Manuel Torres in London. Torres was the British agent of *Cinco Gremios Mayores* and received the needed funds by means of the *giro* operations of the Bank of San Carlos.[18] Spanish government bills of exchange ceased to be an unknown commodity in North America.

3

The coalescence of the various elements thus far treated took place in the port of Havana. Given the presence in harbor of a substantial Spanish squadron, and Great Britain's far-flung naval obligations, the port remained largely open and welcomed neutral vessels which brought in supplies and took away the fruits of the island's rich tropical agriculture. The sea lanes to Europe, however, were dangerous even for Bourbon men-of-war. In consequence, silver shipments, which safely made it through the still-Spanish Gulf of Mexico, tended to be stopped in Havana to await a safer day. These funds, and those produced in Cuba itself, exercised a magnetic attraction upon a Crown rendered ever more penurious by each passing day of war.

As early as 1795, the Spanish government authorized Antonio Lasqueti to take up to 60,000 *pesos fuertes* in Havana, giving *letras* in return. This license was used only in 1797 and 1798, however.[19] In the latter years, and in conjunction with the legalization of the neutral flags trade, Minister of Finance Francisco de Saavedra authorized the payment to George Adler of Altoona (Germany) 200,000 *pesos fuertes* in *libranzas* on Havana.[20] The business never took effect and the *libranzas*, which are clearly bills of exchange, remain to this day in their virginal state and multiple copies exist in the General Archives of the Indies in Seville.[21] The single largest transactions in Havana in these years were connected to the tortured affairs of Spain's *Caja de Amortización de Vales Reales*. To maintain the value of these debt instruments the Crown had laid hold of the funds and properties of the peninsula's chantries and charitable foundations. The needs of the General Treasury being more pressing, however, these monies were diverted to operational expenditures, the *Caja de Amortización* being indemnified with *libranzas* on American treasuries. Of these, Havana was made responsible for 500,000 *pesos fuertes*.[22] The collection was routed through the Bank of San Carlos, and its Havana agent the House of Sta María y Cuesta. The beneficiaries had the right to take the coins out duty free, on a neutral ship, to any port in the world. Ultimate payment was guaranteed by making the viceroy of Mexico responsible for putting the necessary specie in Havana.

Another major source of bills on Havana in this period of war with Great Britain, was the Treaty of San Lorenzo. As provided by the treaty, United States' claims against Spain were examined by commissioners who were authorized to render judgements against Madrid's Treasurer General. In fact, however, the Spanish minister in North America turned these judgements into *libranzas* against Havana, the first of which was paid in September of 1798. The agent for the United States' firm, again the House of Sta María y Cuesta, offered to export the value in sugar rather than coin and aboard an Anglo-American vessel then in port, which was accepted by Intendant Valiente.[23] From October 30, 1798 to February 9, 1801, a total of 122,271 *pesos fuertes* were paid out in this fashion in Havana, and payments continued to be registered thereafter.[24]

The most striking development, however, was the start of peninsular sales of *letras* against Havana predominantly to Anglo-American houses. The first such was to the House of 'D. Enrique Dowell y Co.' of Cadiz, which offered to give *pesos fuertes* in Spain in return for the capital, plus a ten per cent bonus, in Havana. The bill of exchange, which had cost 32,202 *pesos fuertes* in Cadiz, brought Kirk and Luckens of Charleston, to whom it was endorsed, about 35,422 *pesos fuertes* in Havana.[25]

These original terms of sale did not prove capable of withstanding market pressures. By the time the trade became well-established, *libranzas* on Havana were sold at a rate of fifteen *reales de vellón* to fifteen *reales*, two *maravedis de vellón* per *peso fuerte* (of twenty *reales de vellón*). A commission of one-half of one per cent, and brokerage fees of two-tenths of one per cent were also normal. In moments of need, an additional agent's fee of two per cent of net value was also allowed. On one typical contract the discount and fees were such that they amounted to 26.7 per cent of the Havana payout. On such terms bills worth some 437,516 *pesos fuertes* were negotiated on Havana in 1799–1800. To put that in perspective, that is about as much as a naval frigate would carry to Spain on a run from Veracruz. If one adds to this, however, the larger *libranzas* issued in the name of the *Caja de Amortización*, the smaller ones of the Philadelphia commissioners and those issued to Lasqueti, something over 1,200,000 *pesos fuertes* were delivered in Havana down to the end of 1800.

It is fairly difficult to form an idea of the real buyers of these bills because in many instances the money was supplied by someone other than the purchaser of record. Thus, the first firm to become involved, that of 'Enrique Dowell', refused one set of bills because 'not being so arranged ... as to satisfy the true owners of the money, I am duty-bound to return them, and solicit others in their place'.[26] In many instances, North American firms were overtly involved. Among others, were the firms of Lloyd Buchanan and Courtenay of Baltimore and Kirk and Luckens of Charleston. The origins of other firms cannot be established from the Spanish documentation, even if the names are suggestive. Typical are those of John Mayne, Jones and Clark, Christopher Fitzsimon and John Teasdale. Most telling of all is the fact that United States' consuls in Spain were direct buyers, as were William Wills of Barcelona and Robert Montgomery of Alicante. In addition, Anglo-American merchants often bought bills from Spaniards who acquired large lots of them in the hope of making profits by endorsing them to others in smaller quantities. The most important of these jobbers was Antonio Montenegro, *ministro de real hacienda* in Alicante.[27]

Given the role of North American firms, it was not surprising that United States' government agencies should become involved in seeing to it that Havana authorities be solvent enough to pay the *libranzas* against them. Thus it was that Intendant Viguri was able to convince the captain of the American warship *Warren* to sail to Veracruz to pick up silver. To Viguri's indignation, however, the Viceroy refused to put royal pesos aboard a foreign naval vessel.[28] Even more ambitious was the proposition of the United States' consul in Alicante, Robert Montgomery. In May of 1801 the latter proposed to go to Charleston and from there to send ships to Havana and other Spanish American ports to pick up as much as 10,000,000 *pesos fuertes*, and to pay out the same number of *pesos sencillos* in Spanish ports. The proposition was countersigned by the United States' Consul General in Madrid, Moses Young, and led to a complicated series of negotiations which culminated in Minister of Finance Soler accepting the offer of seventeen and one-half *reales de vellón* per *peso fuerte*. The onset of peace negated the transaction.[29] In any event, by that time the North American role was well established. When the Crown sought to give some overlying structure to its sale of bills on America early in 1801, by placing everything in the hands of the *Real Giro*, three of the five overseas agents named were in United States' ports (Charleston, Baltimore and New York).[30]

4

With the Peace of Amiens, Havana's delivery of silver to Anglo-Americans came to an abrupt end. Outstanding bills were paid, but no more were issued. Their loss, however, was the French's gain. Cuban authorities were distrustful of the latter's willingness to repay sums advanced. None the less, at Madrid's behest, they agreed to supply Leclerc's expedition in Haiti with cash and goods. In payment, the French authorities provided *libranzas* on Paris. By mid year of 1804 some 728,000 *pesos fuertes* worth of these bills had been sent to Spain.[31] Along with these French bills the Havana administration also sent back *letras* on private Spanish houses. This form of patriation of insular surpluses was chosen in reaction to the increased tendency of Veracruz treasure ships to avoid putting into Cuban harbors.[32] In any event, bills of exchange continued to play a central role in treasury affairs.

Anglo–Spanish hostilities were renewed in late 1804. As formal allies of the French, the Spaniards were obligated to provide help to the troops fleeing Haiti,[33] to aid passing Napoleonic vessels[34] and to pay a renewed flow of *libranzas* — this time issued by the *Caja de Consolidación de Vales Reales* in favor of the French imperial treasury. At first, these were made payable to the Napoleonic forces in Santo Domingo.[35] With the winding down of Haitian operations, however, the French Emperor tried to get the money to Europe by using Anglo-American intermediaries. Thus, in 1807 Thomas Stoughton, son of the Spanish consul in New York, arrived in Havana with 700,000 *pesos fuertes* worth of *letras* on *consolidación* funds. Stoughton died before endorsing them, so Havana officials did not have to pay.[36] Overall, this was fortunate for the Crown as funds were lacking in Cuba, and as the viceroy of Mexico was so hard pressed paying *libranzas* on his own treasury that he refused to help.[37] By that stage, of course, Anglo-American attention had largely been redirected towards New Spain, the ultimate source of silver. Thus, houses from United States' ports were used in one of the largest *libranzas* operations of the 1804–1808 period — David Parish's activities on behalf of Hope and Co., head of an Anglo–Dutch consortium serving the interests of Napoleon.[38]

What may we conclude from the Spanish Crown's acceptance of bills of exchange in treasury transactions? Clearly, over the two decades preceding the fall of Charles IV in 1808 paper transactions did replace treasure shipments as the main device for patriating royal silver from the Americas. The shift was symbolic of the transformation taking place in the Spanish imperial economy, which was at last being drawn into the type of relationships typical of the interchanges between other ports of the Atlantic world. In that transformation Anglo-American entrepreneurs played an important role, as was normal given the importance of the United States' merchant marine in these years. In Havana, and more tardily in other Spanish American harbors, theirs was to act as intermediaries between industrializing Britain and her future economic dependencies and to cement long-lasting relationships binding the Anglo-American world with the Hispanic one. In any event, the era of treasure ships came to an end because more sophisticated means of patriating surpluses were at last adopted. The irony, of course, is that this should have taken place on the eve of the emancipatory wars which were to consume all surpluses.

Los Llorones Cubanos: the socio-military basis of commercial privilege in the American trade under Charles IV*

No Spanish vassals have been more indulged, enriched, and favored than those of Havana, but they still clamor and complain ....
Intendant Roubaud 1809[1]

Of all the Spanish colonies in America, Cuba probably enjoyed the broadest commercial privileges under Charles IV. During the French Revolutionary and Napoleonic Wars, Cubans repeatedly extracted the right to engage in neutral trade, a commerce directed largely to the United States which absorbed Cuban sugar while providing grain food supplies and lumber for sugar crates. While the Spanish government, under the stress of war, frequently granted similar concessions to its other colonies, the Cubans, wailing and moaning about their unique situation, specialized in anticipating these arrangements and extending them into periods of general prohibition, even peacetime, and, in the process, they often won special tax exemptions to support their burgeoning sugar industry. At times, Cubans simply prevailed upon the local colonial authorities to contravene disadvantageous royal instructions. More frequently, the Crown itself acceded to colonial pressure to legalize neutral commerce. With few exceptions, Cubans traded freely with the United States from 1793 to 1808 and beyond. Cuba might well be viewed as a spoiled colony.

Part of the explanation for this phenomenon lies with the strong connections that the planter elite was able to sustain at Court and with its ability to exploit those relationships through effective lobbying tactics. But such connections, although important, were more symptom than cause, for much deeper forces were at work. Since Charles III first began to rearm the colony following the Seven Years' War, the Cuban planter aristocracy and the Spanish Crown had operated under a special compact through which Cubans assumed major military responsibilities but in return received compensatory commercial privileges. Events during the reign of Charles IV would reaffirm this historic understanding.

The present essay will not treat specifically the privileged commercial arrangements that Cubans enjoyed during the reign of Charles IV, a task already completed elsewhere.[2] It will instead examine the larger political and military realities that help explain why Cubans so frequently had their way in commercial affairs. The analysis necessarily will focus upon Havana and Matanzas, the economic and demographic core of the island, because events in those districts bore most directly upon the shaping of royal policy.

When Charles III entered the Seven Years' War in a vain attempt to turn the tide in favor of his French cousin, his empire was poorly prepared for the challenge that awaited it. Dependant upon small veteran garrisons supported by an untrained militia and operating behind poorly maintained fortifications, his forces were no match for the British who possessed the capacity to send thousands of men against any objective. In the summer of 1762, the loss of Havana, the strategic outer bastion of the empire, brought this point home with merciless reality. When Charles recovered Havana at the price of Florida in the Treaty of Paris, he took sweeping measures to insure that the catastrophe of 1762 would not recur.

The central military problem for land operations was to produce enough trained manpower at a manageable cost to counter a possible invasion or, if the opportunity should develop, to exact revenge upon the British. To this end, Charles sent to Cuba the Conde de Ricla as captain general and Field Marshal Alejandro O'Reilly as inspector general with instructions to establish a disciplined militia based upon a system developed in Spain during the War of the Polish Succession. This system provided volunteer units with a standard table of organization, with firearms, uniforms and other equipment, and with veteran cadres that were directly integrated into the command structure to impart systematic training through weekly drills. Finally, the disciplined militia enjoyed military corporate privileges. The Crown also expanded the veteran garrison of Cuba from an authorized strength of 2,112 to 3,208 men, including a fixed infantry regiment (1,358), a Spanish rotating regiment (1,358), a regiment of dragoons (320) and two artillery companies (172). But the bulk of the trained manpower came from the reorganized militia. Spain's success in restructuring Cuba's defenses depended, therefore, upon its ability to make the militia system work.[3]

During late 1763 and early 1764, O'Reilly in his capacity as inspector general raised eight 800-man battalions of white and colored infantry. The whites included two battalions organized as a regiment in Havana and its sister city, Guanabacoa, and single battalions in Cuatro Villas in the south-central region of the island, in Puerto Principe, and in Santiago. The colored units consisted of single battalions of *pardos* (mulattoes) in Havana and Santiago and of *morenos* (blacks) in Havana. O'Reilly also raised a 650-man cavalry regiment for Havana and a 450-man regiment of dragoons in strategic Matanzas a short distance east of Havana. The volunteer forces numbered 7,500 soldiers.[4]

A judicious selection of the leadership for the white units, especially those of the economic and administrative center, Havana, was absolutely essential.

Under the disciplined militia system, the command positions, i.e. the colonelcies and the captaincies, were volunteer offices as were the sublieutenancies. Veterans completed the remainder of the command and staff group as well as the lieutenancies. In a like manner, veterans also shared authority with volunteer non-commissioned officers.[5] As commanders of their units, the colonels in particular held politically sensitive positions that required close cooperation with the local municipal governments. The *ayuntamiento* mustered 'volunteers' to fill the ranks, financed uniforms and firearms, and represented ordinary justice which, in the event of antagonism, could obstruct the military judicial privileges with jurisdictional challenges. O'Reilly, therefore, recruited his officers from the principal families of the island.

By 1763, Cuba had a well-defined elite. Five men held titles of Castile: Juan Francisco Núñez del Castillo, the Marqués de San Felipe y Santiago; Manuel José Aparicio del Manzano y Jústiz, the Marqués de Jústiz de Santa Ana; Gonzalo Francisco Recio de Oquendo, the Marqués de la Real Proclamación; Gonzalo Luis de Herrera, the Marqués de Villalta; and Francisco Chacón y Torres, the Conde de Casa Bayona. Four more gained titles during the later 1760s: Pedro José Calvo de la Puerta y Arango, the Conde de Buena Vista; Augustín de Cárdenas, the Marqués de Cárdenas de Montehermoso; Gerónimo Espinosa de Contreras y Jústiz, the Conde de Gibacoa; and Gabriel Antonio Beltrán de Santa Cruz, the Conde de San Juan de Jaruco. Moreover, two Spaniards, who had become *radicados* (nativized) into creole society through marriage acquired titles: Lorenzo Montalvo, the Conde de Macuriges, who was marine intendant; and Domingo de Lizundia y Odria de Echevarría, the Marqués del Real Agrado, who was treasurer of the tobacco monopoly. Others distinguished their social reputations by acquiring habits in Spanish crusading orders or by establishing entailed estates.[6]

Although the sugar revolution is usually associated with the postwar period, cane was well on its way to becoming Cuba's dominant crop by the eve of the Seven Years' War. Most if not all of the titled nobles had begun to convert to sugar production and, among them, the Calvo de la Puerta, Cárdenas, Chacón, Herrera, Núñez del Castillo, and Santa Cruz families were leading producers. Other leading planters were the Arango, O'Farrill, Peñalver and Zayas families. Juan O'Farrill, whose father had arrived early in the century as a factor of the South Sea Company was one of the wealthiest and most powerful men in Havana.[7] Although he never acquired a title of Castile, he married Luisa Herrera y Chacón, the daughter of the Marqués de Villalta; he was the brother-in-law through his sister of the first Conde de Buena Vista; and four of his sons-in-law would obtain titles: Antonio José de Beitia y Castro, the second Marqués del Real Socorro; Ignacio Montalvo y Ambulodi, the first Conde de Casa Montalvo; Jose María Chacón y Herrera, the third Conde de Casa Bayona; and Sebastián Peñalver y Barreto, the second Marqués de Casa Peñalver. This clan would be a dominant political, economic and military influence well past the turn of the century. Ignacio Peñalver, who was also immensely wealthy, unlike O'Farrill eventually acquired his own title as the Marqués de Arcos in 1792.[8]

Many of these families had made their commitment to sugar under the auspices of the *Real Compañía de Comercio de La Habana*, a creole-dominated enterprise organized in 1740 to promote Cuban commerce. Original shareholders included the O'Farrill, Peñalver, Jústiz, Beitia, Calvo de la Puerta and Oquendo families as well as the Marqueses de Villalta and San Felipe and the Conde de Casa Bayona.[9] Hence, it was commonplace for the planter aristocracy to be involved in marketing or to have close relatives committed to mercantile careers. Not surprisingly, these same families also dominated the *ayuntamiento* of Havana.[10]

O'Reilly brought this planter aristocracy into the disciplined militia. Either personally or through close relatives, all of those who held titles of Castile during the 1760s were represented in the officer corps except the Marqués de la Real Proclamación, who was childless, and the Marqués del Real Agrado, whose primary commitment was to the tobacco monopoly. The Conde de Gibacoa became colonel of the Matanzas dragoons and the Conde de Casa Bayona became lieutenant colonel of the Cavalry Regiment, while others served in company grade offices or had close relatives who did so. From the leading planter families without titles, Juan O'Farrill served as lieutenant colonel of the infantry regiment, while Ignacio Peñalver, an Arango and three Zayas served in company grade offices.[11]

To the planter aristocracy, military titles represented a highly coveted status in Havana society. Military commands evoked images of a feudal past, which seemed especially appropriate to landed magnates who powered their industries with slave labor. The sugarocracy's quest for military office would be a continuous theme throughout the late eighteenth and early nineteenth centuries. Although some exceptions developed, maritime merchants ordinarily did not serve in the militia. Their occupational demands, including travel, and probably also their unique relationship to society made the military option less attractive. By order of June 18, 1779, the Crown officially exempted maritime merchants from the obligation to serve in the militia.[12]

Commercial and revenue reform completed the emerging compact between the sugarocracy and the Crown. When Ricla left Spain for Cuba, the Marqués de Esquilache, who as minister of war and finance took a direct hand in the Cuban reforms, instructed him to seek the economic and financial means to support the expanded military establishment and to do so in consultation with the colonial patriciate. Mexican monies would finance fortification construction but Cuban revenues should fund the army. The results were a delicate series of meetings with the Havana elite concerning possible reforms, a fact-finding *visita* of the island by O'Reilly, and, finally, a Royal Order of April 25, 1764, and two of October 16, 1765, which addressed boldly the problems of finance and commerce. The *alcabala* (sales tax) was increased from two to six per cent and special levies were placed on the sale of *aguardiente* and a local liquor called *sambumbia*. Although these measures represented a stiff tax increase, compensation came elsewhere, especially for planters. The October orders opened nine ports of Spain to the Cuban trade, thus breaking the Cádiz monopoly, and consolidated Spanish export duties to six per cent ad valorem for national products, seven per cent for foreign. Equally significant, cumbersome export duties on sugar were also consolidated at six per cent, while import duties on slaves were abolished.[13] Sugar producers thus enjoyed access to broader legal markets, reduced levies on the export of their product and lower purchase costs for slaves. Cubans had assumed a major responsibility for the defense of their island and for financing that defense, but they were rewarded with broad commercial provileges. Defense realities and commercial policy were thus closely intertwined.

The image of Cuba that emerges from these innovations is that of a colony where special arrangements prevailed. Another boost for Cuban privileges was the Royal Declaration of April 15, 1771, which defined the *fuero* or judicial privilege of the disciplined militia as active as well as passive. In the Spanish militia regulation, the *fuero* applied only when the holder was a defendant, i.e. passively, and that was the interpretation of militia law in New Spain as well. Using a rather weak precedent, Cuban volunteers had petitioned for the active *fuero* and, as indicated, won for officers and sergeants the right to use their privilege even when plaintiffs, a privilege heretofore exercised only by the Royal Guard at Court. The planters who served as officers in the militia could thus bring legal cases against civilians and have them tried before military authorities, a comfortable arrangement indeed![14]

The ensuing decades brought very little change in the composition of the militia. As Cuba entered the 1790s, the reign of Charles IV, the same regiments and battalions of horse and foot that O'Reilly had established remained in place and basically the same families led by the O'Farrills, controlled the officer corps. In 1791, José Ricardo O'Farrill, son of Juan, became lieutenant colonel of the cavalry regiment, the position that his father had long occupied. His uncle, the Conde de Buena Vista, was colonel; his brother-in-law, the Marqués del Real Socorro, had become colonel of the infantry regiment in 1783, while in that same year the Conde de Casa Bayona, another brother-in-law was promoted to lieutenant colonel; and a third brother-in-law, the Conde de Casa Montalvo, was colonel of the Matanzas dragoons. Upon the death of the Conde de Casa Montalvo in 1795, a younger O'Farrill brother, Juan Manuel, became lieutenant colonel of dragoons. The second Conde de Gibacoa, son of the first colonel of dragoons, an acting lieutenant colonel, became colonel. Company grade offices continued to include members of the Arango, Beitia, Cárdenas, Chacón, Herrera, Montalvo, Santa Cruz and Zayas families.[15]

The high degree of continuity within the disciplined militia was expressive of special conditions in Cuba. José de Gálvez, minister of the Indies from 1776 to 1787, was noted in colonial politics for his anti-Americanism, an orientation that became especially evident in the colonial armies following the violent resistance to his administrative and revenue reforms in Peru and New Granada during the War of the American Revolution. In both viceroyalties, he advanced blatant policies designed to limit creole officerships as he reshaped the colonial armies during the later 1780s.[16] Cubans, however, had cooperated at various levels with the war effort. When mobilized to replace veterans units that were sent onto the offensive in Florida, the Cuban militia had, despite hardship, answered the call effectively, manning the local defenses while Spanish victory unfolded in the north.[17] Cuban planters, who benefited from the commercial concessions of 1765 and whose lands lay on the exposed rim of the empire, had much to gain by imperial success and had behaved accordingly. Moreover, Havana residents extended critical emergency loans to the royal treasury which helped fund the French action at the final victory at Yorktown.[18] Consequently, during the 1780s, when the Crown sought to restructure the American armies to a politically suitable composition and when creoles were being factored out of the defense systems in Peru and New Granada, the traditional elite families continued their domination in Havana.

Cuban continuity was also noteworthy at another level. Following the death of Gálvez in 1787, the emphasis in colonial policy shifted toward cutting costs in the colonies and maximizing remissions to Spain. The War of the American Revolution had placed a considerable strain on the royal treasury and, in any event, following its colonial victories in 1783 Spain began to shift its military emphasis to European priorities.[19] At this time, Charles III divided the Ministry of the Indies between two men, Minister of the Navy Antonio Valdés, who acquired War, Finance and Commerce, and Antonio Porlier, who assumed control of Grace and Justice. Both met regularly with the other ministers in what amounted to a Spanish cabinet, the *Junta de Estado*. By 1790, Charles IV had integrated the Indies' portfolios directly into the appropriate Spanish ministries, a further step toward coordinating the affairs of America and Spain.[20] As part of its program, the *Junta* sought to curtail inflated American military establishments, both to minimize costs and to reduce local conflicts generated by the exercise of military privilege and by ill-will arising in the militia ranks from the drudgery of weekly drills and other obligations. Charles IV continued this orientation when he became king in 1788. A Circular Order of January 12, 1790 instructed colonial officials to review carefully all units to determine where reductions could be made, and in due course substantial cuts were effected in Peru, New Granada and New Spain.[21]

Captain General Luis de Las Casas made no such changes in Cuba.[22] Costs for the royal treasury were not a serious problem because the several municipalities levied local taxes to fund the uniforming of their units. The Havana *ayuntamiento* was also able to finance the weapons for its volunteers and beyond that produced surpluses that the captains general used to build barracks and to advance various kinds of public works.[23] With an interlocking directory operating both the civil and military jurisdictions, judicial conflicts at this point did not pose a significant problem and men regularly appeared to fill the volunteer ranks.[24] Moreover, every unit of the Cuban militia had proved its worth during the last war. The Cuban regiments and battalions thus survived without change.

Cuba also continued to receive commercial privileges beneficial to the planter aristocracy. Following the regulation of 'free trade' of 1778 which, excluding New Spain and Caracas, extended to the rest of the empire substantially the same rights that Cuba had gained in 1765, Cuba for a time no longer enjoyed a special position. That situation changed in 1789 when Cuban lobbyists won yet another major concession for the sugar industry. By Order of February 28, 1789 Charles IV and the *Junta de Estado* opened the Cuban slave trade to all Spanish subjects, thus dispossessing official monopolists, and even opened the island to foreign dealers for a two-year period.[25] An inflow of slaves at unprecedented levels resulted and in 1792 Cuban planters won a six-year extension of the order.[26] The new commercial privilege when combined with the retention of the traditional militia establishment amounted to a reaffirmation by Charles IV of the compact that his father had established with the Cuban sugarocracy twenty-five years earlier.

Despite the continued cooperation between Crown and patriciate, indeed partly because of it, new difficulties emerged. As the sugar industry grew, so too did the number of successful planters who under the existing arrangement deserved consideration for promotions or appointments to new military positions. By 1796, there were twenty-three titles of Castile in the island, all but one in Havana. Although some represented new families, most of the newcomers were close relatives of previously titled nobles. Further, Pedro O'Reilly, the son of Alejandro O'Reilly and nephew of Captain General Las Casas (1790–96), emigrated to Cuba where in 1792 he married María-Francisca Calvo de la Puerta y Aparicio del Manzano O'Farrill y Jústiz, the daughter of the Conde de Buena Vista, himself becoming the second Conde de O'Reilly in 1794.[27] The O'Farrill clan had done very well, as was to be expected, but other men of condition who had achieved the same kind of prominence demanded recognition through proper military offices. In 1792, the colonel of the Havana cavalry regiment, the Conde de Buena Vista, proposed to remedy this problem by creating a line of supernumerary captains for the cavalry, an obvious ruse to manufacture additional military titles for deserving planters. During this same period, unsuccessful offers abounded to raise or to expand at personal expense volunteer and veteran units in return for military commissions. Although the Crown rejected Buena Vista's proposal '*por estraño*', the authorities addressed the problem of recognition and advancement through very similar action, albeit on a piecemeal basis.[28]

To achieve promotion through normal channels was most difficult. Only six militia colonelcies existed in the Havana–Matanzas district. Even the number of captaincies was quite limited because the second infantry battalion of the Havana regiment was based across the bay in Guanabacoa where few of the distinguished resided and the dragoons were farther east in Matanzas. While colonels might dwell in Havana, captains were expected to live in the district of their companies. Moreover, colonels and captains usually served until an advanced age, until death or infirmities intervened. To accommodate service merit or to find places for new aspirants, the Crown might simply have expanded the militia, but at a time when it was reducing the number of disciplined units elsewhere, such a step was inappropriate, even for Cuba.

During the early 1790s, the Ministry of War alleviated the problem of advancement by promoting officers to grades above their actual positions of command. Under such arrangements, a man elevated to the rank of lieutenant colonel might still act as company captain or a captain might still function as a sublieutenant. By 1795, the Havana infantry regiment had six lieutenant colonels commanding companies and several men of higher grades acting as sublieutenants. The cavalry had a colonel and lieutenant colonel serving as captains.[29] While this practice did not originate under Charles IV, it became far more prevalent.

As the decade advanced, the Ministry of War created additional space for aspirants by simply attaching colonels and captains to the regiments as supernumeraries. Under this system, a creole could hold a title of rank and enjoy the prestige of his uniform but he would not actually occupy a position of command. By 1805, the volunteer infantry regiment had as supernumeraries two colonels, one lieutenant colonel and six captains. In addition, two lieutenant colonels commanded companies. The acting colonel of the regiment held the grade of brigadier, while the lieutenant colonel was a colonel. The cavalry regiment had two lieutenant colonel and two captain supernumeraries. A colonel and a lieutenant colonel acted as company commanders.[30] While this phenomenon may appear a bit absurd to the modern observer its political significance should not be underestimated.

The Crown also had other means of rewarding deserving planter-officers. A common practice was to promote an officer upon his retirement or, occasionally, to grant him a habit in a crusading order.[31] Habits or titles of Castile might, of course, also come during the course of an individual's active years.[32] Although based upon broad considerations, including a substantial fee, distinguished military service by an applicant and usually also his father was an important part of the process. On another level, the sons of noble officers might receive special consideration in Spain. Two sons of the Conde de Casa Montalvo, for example, and one son of the Marqués del Real Socorro (thus grandchildren of Juan O'Farrill) gained admission to the College of Royal Nobles in Madrid.[33] Still other Cubans received commissions in the Spanish army. The most famous of these was Gonzalo O'Farrill, son of Juan and, therefore, the brother, brother-in-law or nephew of most of the colonels in Havana during the 1790s, who rose to the rank of lieutenant general.[34] These connections, obviously, had the important effect of tying the Cuban elite more closely to Court where lobbying opportunities abounded.

The means by which creoles acquired higher office might simply be faithful service reinforced or accelerated by a distinguished social reputation, but as the 1790s progressed the practice of lubricating the promotion process through *beneficio* or purchase became increasingly common. The Cuban militia regulation, which had been drafted by O'Reilly, expressly forbade the sale of offices: 'Under no ... pretext will a fee be exacted ... for the awarding of commissions ...; they will be given and registered free.'[35] However, faced by mounting financial pressure arising from Spain's disastrous involvement in the French Revolutionary Wars and by an incessant creole clamor for military offices, the Ministry of War soon forgot O'Reilly's admonition.

As the process developed in Cuba, sales occurred less by grand design than by a kind of piecemeal, opportunistic accommodation to the pressures of the 1790s. The modern practice of selling offices began in the regular army. In 1786, Gálvez had ordered the formation of a second fixed regiment of three battalions for Cuba, known as the Infantry Regiment of Cuba. To reduce transportation costs and other difficulties, the first two battalions replaced the Spanish regiments that since 1763 had been rotated in and out of Havana to supplement the fixed garrison. The third battalion served in St Augustine. In accord with practice in Spain, where the offices in the third battalion of regiments raised since the last British war had been sold, four fusilier captaincies of the Florida battalion were offered at 5,000 pesos to individuals in Cuba with at least six years military experience. Qualified buyers soon purchased all four offices.[36] A short time later, when the Fixed Infantry Regiment of Havana was expanded to include a third battalion, three of the captains transferred to that unit and at least one lieutenancy and four sublieutenancies were sold.[37] This action set a precedent. Thereafter, purchase became one more route to military office both in the regular army and in the militia.

Fearing with good reason that the sale of offices might undermine the Cuban army, Charles IV's government was never fully comfortable with the practice. Yet, the temptation was great, especially when Spain found itself in a costly war with revolutionary France, 1793–95, and then in the First British War, 1796–1802. In accepting offers, the Ministry of War attempted to ascertain that the bidder was otherwise generally qualified and should therefore be permitted the 'honor' of advancement at a fee. Past service, social status, age and price were all considerations, and the Ministry rejected more offers than it accepted.[38]

Official qualms should not lead to the conclusion, however, that all purchasers were fully qualified. The general rule was that the higher the jump the higher the cost and as the extent of the demand became evident prices went up.[39] While the original fee for a captaincy in the regular army, which carried a salary, had been 5,000 pesos, it required at least 8,000 pesos by 1800 to buy that same office in the militia.[40] The prestige office was, of course, a colonelcy. As an unnamed official in the Ministry of War observed, 'the grade of colonel is much esteemed in that district [Cuba], perhaps more than in any other place.'[41] In 1799, Francisco Chacón, son and heir of the Conde de Casa Bayona and currently a supernumerary captain in the volunteer infantry, and Joaquín de Santa Cruz y Chacón, the grandson of the same Conde and a sublieutenant in the infantry, both acquired supernumerary colonelcies for 10,000 pesos. Yet later that year, the Ministry of War rejected an offer of 12,000 pesos from Joaquín de Ortiz y Ozeguera, who came from a prestigious family but one not quite as well-connected as the Chacón and Santa Cruz families. The Ministry observed that given the current level of demand, he should have made a better offer.[42]

Offices in the regular army, which carried salaries, cost more. In 1797, the father of Anastasio de Armenteros y Zaldívar paid 30,000 pesos to give his son a supernumerary colonelcy in the Squadron of Dragoons of America as did the Marqués of San Felipe y Santiago for his heir, Juan Francisco del Castillo, in the Regiment of Havana.[43] Yet in 1799, the Conde de Casa Barreto paid 55,000 pesos for a supernumerary colonelcy in the veteran dragoons, an earlier offer of 40,000 having failed to move the Ministry of War.[44] Seen from a purely financial angle, this type of sale amounted to a cheap way for the Crown to acquire funds. The sale for 30,000 pesos of a colonelcy, which carried a salary of 2,400, cost the Royal Tresury eight per cent annually with no obligation to repay the principal. Given current interest rates, the Crown in 1795 had been willing to go as high as thirteen per cent for the salary of a lieutenancy, and militia offices carried no salary unless the unit was mobilized.[45]

The total number of sales does not appear to have been great, yet it was large enough. For those who craved for themselves or their children title of rank and the accompanying honors and who were willing to pay a high enough price, flexibility existed in the system. The top-heavy officer corps of the Cuban army was eloquent of the Crown's willingness to accommodate the planter aristocracy, even if at a price, an historical pattern that remained very much alive at the turn of the nineteenth century.

As suggested by the above analysis, the regular army had also become an outlet for planter military aspirations. The Crown had traditionally attempted to limit creole offices in veteran units to twenty per cent or less, but reality was something else.[46] Creoles enlisted in large numbers of cadets and, as Spain failed to provide enough officers for Cuba owing to transportation difficulties and various pressures in Europe, they acquired commissions. Some advanced by merit, others, as has been seen, by special arrangement.

By 1799, creoles held 102 of 179 offices in the two infantry regiments, the three companies of light infantry, and the squadron of dragoons which at that time garrisoned the island.[47] The greatest creole penetration occurred in the lower ranks, but natives had also made significant gains above. A majority of the captains in the Infantry Regiment of Havana were creoles and natives showed real strength in the colonelcies, both in positions of command and, of course, as supernumeraries. The commanding officers of both infantry units came from Havana: Brigadier Francisco Montalvo, the third son of the Conde de Macuriges, for the Regiment of Havana, and Juan Lleonart, an *hidalgo*, for the Regiment of Cuba. Montalvo, eventually became field marshal and in 1813 viceroy of New Granada. Of the four subordinate battalion commands, Spaniards held three, but the Marqués de Casa Calvo (Sebastián Calvo de la Puerta y O'Farrill) was colonel of the second battalion of the Regiment of Cuba, meaning that Havana patricians held half of the six battalion commands. These men had served in various veteran and volunteer units as they advanced in rank without the benefit of purchase.

In the supernumerary category, the two regiments possessed one creole colonel, the son of the Marqués de San Felipe y Santiago, and two lieutenant colonels, including Juan de Montalvo y O'Farrill, the brother of the second Conde de Casa Montalvo. The other creole lieutenant colonels held company commands. And the Conde de O'Reilly, who had married the daughter of the Conde de Buena Vista but who was technically a Spaniard, was a supernumerary lieutenant colonel. Not including the Conde de Casa Barreto, whose purchase of a colonelcy was not yet completed, the cavalry had one supernumerary colonel, the previously discussed Anastasio Armenteros y Zaldívar.[48] The regular army thus joined the disciplined militia as a creole vehicle for prestigious titles of rank and, significantly, had begun to show substantial creole power in the central command structure. With a multitude of creole cadets awaiting commissions while Spain's capacity to provide officers declined, creoles would continue to advance steadily after the turn of the century.

The most intriguing example of the creole penetration of the military establishment was the meteoric rise of Joaquín Beltrán de Santa Cruz y Cárdenas. The heir to vast sugar holdings, Beltrán de Santa Cruz in 1785 entered the Volunteer Infantry Regiment of Havana as a sublieutenant, although only sixteen. In 1786, he married María Teresa Montalvo y O'Farrill, who was the daughter of the first Conde de Casa Montalvo, Colonel of Dragoons Ignacio Montalvo, and the granddaughter of Juan O'Farrill. In the following year he succeeded to a captaincy in his regiment. Soon thereafter, young Joaquín, who was heir to the Condado de San Juan de Jaruco, a title which he would claim in 1804, journeyed to Court with his wife to pursue his opportunities. In Spain, an attempt to acquire a lieutenant colonelcy in the Havana cavalry failed both because he lacked proper military merit and because he possessed insufficient time in rank as captain. Nevertheless, he used his wealth and position to become a *gentilhombre de cámara* (gentleman of the Royal Bedchamber) with entrance in 1792. The turning point in his career came when he somehow won the friendship and patronage of the fast rising Manuel Godoy, perhaps through his brief service with the *Real Compañía de Guardias de Corps* against the French in 1793. Through Godoy's intervention, the Ministry of War promoted him to brigadier general of the army and, more significantly, named him inspector general of the army of Cuba, a position that no creole had ever held! At this same time, Beltrán de Santa Cruz became the first Conde de Santa Cruz de Mopox and won royal authorization to undertake an incredibly ambitious development plan for Cuba which included the founding of towns, the construction of roads and new port facilities, and even a project to dig a trans-insular canal.

Eventually rising to the rank of field marshal and making at least one more trip to Spain, the conde continued to advance his projects, albeit mainly for nothing, and to function as inspector general until his premature death in 1807. In the meantime, his wife, Teresa, remained at Court where she quite successfully lobbied for private concessions to help her husband finance his work. Among the many favors she secured for the conde were the right to introduce 100,000 barrels of flour from the United States into Cuba in exchange for sugar and even the privilege of shipping cane to the peninsula on returning Spanish warships! While the gains of the Conde de Santa Cruz de Mopox y San Juan de Jaruco did not always please rival planters, his successes illustrate the intimate connection between Court politics, the military and commerce.[49]

The military realities that evolved during the French Revolutionary and Napoleonic Wars related closely to commercial policy. In terms of manpower, the most significant development was the decline of the regular army. As discussed earlier, when the Ministry of the Indies reorganized the Cuban garrison during 1786–89, it expanded the fixed forces while discontinuing the practice of deploying a Spanish regiment of two battalions on the island. This reorganization converted the Infantry Regiment of Havana from two battalions of 679 men each, not counting officers, into three battalions of 615. The first two battalions of the newly-created Infantry Regiment of Cuba stood at the same strength while the third, that for Florida, possessed 396. These measures brought the authorized strength of the infantry to 3,075, without the Florida battalion, compared to 2,716 beforehand, including the Spanish regiment. In addition, the Cavalry Squadron of America and the Three Companies of Catalonian Light Infantry claimed 164 and 306 men respectively, bringing the authorized strength of Cuba's infantry and cavalry to 3,545 soldiers.

By drawing from European units and sending fresh recruits to Cuba, Spain was able to bring the island's units to nearly full strength by 1791, but troop levels declined steadily thereafter. Tropical diseases inflicted a steady toll, some men died in combat and others deserted or completed their terms of enlistment. Moreover, the Ministry of War repeatedly transferred men from Cuban units to the Fixed Infantry Regiment of Louisiana to alleviate its manpower difficulties. The Cuban regiments maintained recruiting parties in the Canary Islands but returns were small. And once Spain became entangled in war its capacity to supply fresh recruits diminished sharply. The Havana regiment, which accounted for over half of Cuba's authorized garrison, declined to 1,142 effectives by November 1794, 863 by October 1797, 510 (not including the second battalion which was deployed in Santiago) by August 1805, and 572 by May 1810. By 1805, the first two battalions of the Infantry Regiment of Cuba had only 484 men out of an authorized strength of 1,230 and by 1810 only 332. The other units followed a similar pattern.[50]

In times of crisis, Spain had traditionally deployed two or three extra Spanish regiments in Cuba to bring the garrison to a full wartime footing.[51] When war broke out with France, however, the Ministry of War, which could ill-afford to spare European troops, ordered two regiments from New Spain, those of Mexico and Puebla, to Cuba. No fact testifies more eloquently to the condition of the fixed garrison than the refusal of the Cuban authorities to return these Mexican units to New Spain after the war, nor, for that matter, after the First or Second British Wars, despite repeated entreaties from the viceroys. The captains general, citing the wretched state of the fixed Havana garrison and their higher duty to defend the island, were able during the brief periods of peace to postpone the return of the troops through bureaucratic delay until the next conflict began and the issue again died.[52] Nevertheless, the Mexican regiments themselves withered quickly, standing at less than half their authorized strength by 1803 and at merely some twenty per cent by 1810.[53] Thus, as the stress of war mounted, the veteran forces counted for less and less.

As the regular army declined, the disciplined militia gained in relative importance and with it those commitments that since 1763 had welded the Cuban sugarocracy to Spain. The French War much resembled the American Revolutionary War in that the captain general mobilized the militia to send the veteran infantry regiments on the offensive, in this instance in an unsuccessful campaign in Saint Domingue where both the Regiments of Havana and Cuba saw action.[54] Moreover, one battalion of the Regiment of Mexico was redeployed in Louisiana and over 200 Mexicans helped garrison the fleet, steps which occasioned further militia service at home.[55] Characteristically, the Havana officers of the militia infantry regiment volunteered to serve without pay.[56] As a result of the British Wars, which featured a number of attacks on Spanish possessions including Puerto Rico, the veteran garrison was so weak that the militia, in the face of very real danger, served regularly to fill the gaps left by deficiencies in the regular army, duty that frequently also continued well into peacetime. Local authorities alleviated this hardship by alternating units to limit the duration of mobilization.[57] Nevertheless, during the nearly endless international turmoil that persisted from 1793 on, the cooperation of the planter aristocracy to sustain the militia system through leadership, recruitment and finance was absolutely essential.[58] This fact explains much about imperial-colonial politics.

A singularly revealing incident developed during this same period which graphically demonstrates the political power at Court of the disciplined militia and its planter officer corps. In 1791, José Ylincheta, who as deputy governor held appellate jurisdiction for ordinary justice in Havana, raised a challenge to the militia officers' active *fuero*, that is, the right to bring legal action against others in military courts.[59] Ylincheta, an ambitious young Spaniard, complained that 'almost all the nobility is included in the militia units', a situation that deprived him of the income through court fees to live decently.[60] Ylincheta also hosted *tertulias* (intellectual social gatherings) where he marshalled support for his stand against the militia privilege, a development that suggests somewhat broader discontent over military justice, perhaps on the part of Cadiz-oriented merchants.[61] Captain General Las Casas forwarded the complaint to Spain where in 1793 the king appointed a special commission to review the Cuban *fuero*. Two officers from the Ministry of War and two officials from the Council of the Indies comprised the committee.[62] At this time, the Ministry of War was in the process of promulgating a new regulation for the disciplined militia of New Granada, which presumably contained the latest royal thinking on military law. This code deleted the active *fuero* from the privilege in that colony, a right that the officers had enjoyed since 1773 when the militia was reorganized under the policies prescribed by the regulation for Cuba.[63]

Led by the Conde de Buena Vista and the Marqués del Real Socorro, the Havana officers protested Ylincheta's action vigorously.[64] Real Socorro personally journeyed to Court in 1796, ostensibly to attend to pressing private matters but in all likelihood also to lobby for the preservation of militia rights.[65] What specific action the marqués, Teresa Montalvo y O'Farrill de Beltrán de Santa Cruz, or others might have taken is unknown, but events strongly suggest that substantial political pressure was brought to bear on the Crown. When, in conformity to practice in New Granada, the special commission in 1798 recommended the retraction of the active *fuero* from Cuba, the King, acting through Minister of War Juan Manuel Alvarez, suspended the proposal, 'not finding it presently [during wartime] propitious to remove privileges'.[66]

The search for a final resolution to the case lingered into the nineteenth century, as deaths, transfers and vacillation delayed a final committee recommendation. Incredibly, as one replacement, the King appointed Gonzalo O'Farrill to the commission, a Cuban who, as discussed earlier, had pursued a highly successful military career in Spain and was the brother or brother-in-law of most of the colonels of the Havana militia, including the Marqués del Real Socorro.[67] The final decision, which came by Order of December 17, 1804, predictably sustained the traditional privileges of the Cuban militia, thus reaffirming the pattern of special arrangements for that island.[68] As for Ylincheta, the decision was hardly a serious personal reverse, for in the meantime he had found a surer path to power and fortune, having become engaged in 1803 to Gabriela O'Farrill, daughter of Lieutenant Colonel José Ricardo O'Farrill, with whom he eventually contracted marriage.[69]

It is understandable, therefore, that the planter-military elite was also able under conditions of war to continue its special relationship in the area of commerce. Created in 1794, the major vehicle for advancing planter interests was the Havana consulado (maritime merchant guild) which was internally constituted to insure agrarian dominance over merchant representation.[70] Not surprisingly, the first three priors of the consulado were the Conde de Casa Montalvo, the Marqués del Real Socorro and José Ricardo O'Farrill, all three colonels of the Havana militia, and in later years prominent military representation continued.[71] The consulado thus completed an interlocking directory that dominated the ever more important disciplined militia and the *ayuntamiento*, and commanded a strong presence in the regular army as well. The consulado thus spoke for the same planter elite that commanded the armed forces. In the face of this reality, the Crown faced tremendous pressure to pay large dividends to those who historically had cooperated in sustaining the defense of the island and, as observed earlier, it did so through repeated concessions in the area of neutral trade.

Cuba was, then, a unique colony where special arrangements prevailed. Located on the strategic rim of the empire, extensive concessions to local interests on behalf of defense became the rule after the loss of Havana to the British in 1762. These concessions led to a creole assumption of major military responsibilities, a commitment made quite willingly as an expression of a broadly desired social image. But in return for its contribution the sugarocracy expected and received liberal commercial privileges. *Los llorones cubanos* wailed for more and more, but in a very real sense they paid more and more for their privileges by assuming through repeated mobilization heavy responsibilities to sustain the sovereignty of the Spanish Crown in their colony. To appreciate the connection between military realities and commercial policy is to grasp the essence of the political chemistry that governed relations between Spain and its most favored colony.

PART FOUR
Louisiana and Venezuela: case studies

CHAPTER NINE

The commerce of La Guaira with the United States during the Venezuelan revolutionary juncture: 1807–1812

Before addressing the theme of the present work, some introductory comments about its scope and title are in order. In the first place, commerce is the essential component for an historical understanding of Venezuela during the seventeenth and eighteenth centuries for the simple reason that this colony enjoyed an open economy whose existence depended upon its imports and exports.[1] The area produced an excellent variety of tropical crops (principally cacao, indigo, coffee, cotton, sugar and tobacco) as well as ample livestock (mainly cattle and mules). These products were sold on the international market to obtain manufactured goods, certain food-stuffs (mainly flour) and the specie that lubricated its economy.[2] Because it lacked gold and silver mines, the money that circulated in the colony necessarily came from the outside through commerce. In this respect, Venezuela was a very different type compared with other Hispanic American territories, except Cuba which was very analogous in nature.[3] In any case, trade volume is a good means, albeit not perfect, to measure the country's economic vitality, with its profound implications for the social, political and even military aspects of Venezuelan life.

Secondly, the province of Caracas was the core of Venezuelan dynamics: it possessed half of its population (nearly 400,000 inhabitants),[4] the creole obligarchy (the great *cacaos*), great capital (commerce and ranching), the principal institutions (university, consulado or maritime merchant guild, audiencia, tribunal of accounts), and the seat of the Spanish administration and, later, of the republic. The province also sported the best port in Venezuela, La Guaira, the capital port par excellence. Suffice it to say that by the end of the eighteenth century, La Guaira controlled 94.3 per cent of all the cargo that entered or left the captaincy general and that maritime traffic amounted to 87 per cent of the total.[5] During the period encompassed in the present study, this activity diminished, but in terms of value, it still handled 51.9 per cent of the merchandise and crops that entered and left Venezuela. The other port in the province of Caracas was Puerto Cabello, which accounted for 14.1 per cent of the value of foreign trade.[6] These considerations justify the view that La Guaira was representative of that which, on a larger scale, took place in Venezuela. Another reason for choosing La Guaira as the focus of this study is that it has the most complete and serialized documentation for the period, precisely because it was, indeed, the most important port.

Finally, the period under consideration corresponds to the revolutionary era. Usual chronology places the revolutionary period between the years 1810 (the April *cabildo* and the *Junta de Gobierno*) and 1821 (the Battle of Carabobo) or 1823 (the final expulsion of the Spaniards from Puerto Cabello), but never between the years 1807 and 1812, the limits of this study. The difficulty is that the revolutionary period is usually associated with the time when a series of political, principally military, events unfolded to secure independence for the country. But from the economic or more specifically, commercial, perspective of the present study, revolutionary ideology is manifested by the reform of the colonial commercial system which occurred between June 1806 and April 1812. In fact, on June 25, 1806, the captain general of Venezuela, Guevara de Vasconcelos, decreed the opening of Venezuelan ports to trade with vessels of neutral or friendly nations.[7] Thus ended the Spanish monopoly, the true bondage of the colonial period, and thereafter any merchant from a non-belligerent power could freely enter the ports of the captaincy general and trade in competition with Spain's own ships. Another important step was taken in 1808 in the form of a new customs regulation which substantially lowered existing duties, although the Crown rescinded this act a few months later. The same year saw an unusual concession, the lowering of the duties on English vessels by 20 per cent.[8] The culmination of revolutionary measures for commercial affairs came in 1810 and 1811 when the patriots, now free from metropolitan pressures, ratified the free trade conceded in 1806, reestablished the customs regulation of 1808, lowered the duties on British ships by 25 per cent (all of which had been initiated before the political movement of 1810), abolished the *alcabala* on a number of popular foodstuffs, abolished the levies on agricultural tools and implements, rationalized customs procedures, banned the outflow of specie, etc.[9]

The reformist enthusiasm began to wane by the end of 1811, and in 1812 events went so badly that Generalísimo Miranda decided to militarize the economy. His emergence as dictator on April 26, 1812, marks this article's limit *ad quem* because it signals the transition from a revolutionary to a wartime economy. Miranda described the change clearly when he wrote: 'It is necessary that the very government, in its economy and in its form, assume the military character that circumstances dictate ... Foreign affairs, internal relations among the provinces, the administration of public revenue, and all the other branches of the economy, politics, justice, etc. should assume an intimate tie and connection with the military power.'[10] From that time forward and until the final expulsion of the royalist Spaniards (1823), royalists and republicans invariably utilized trade, as part of the economy, for furthering their objective of military success. It should be added that the bounds of this study, June 25, 1806, and April 26, 1812, are extended to encompass a few months beyond in order to appraise the actual results, since neither commercial freedom nor the wartime economy began to operate on the very day decreed. Its limits have been shifted to January 1, 1807, and December 31, 1812, to make them coincide with calendar years.

The reason for limiting the present study to the intercourse between La Guaira and the United States also requires explanation. It cannot be simpler: this study is only one aspect of a book-length undertaking on the whole of foreign trade in Caracas province during the revolution. Of the different foreign markets, the United States has been chosen for this chapter because it was the most important.

1   Trade value during the six-year period

The total value of the merchandise handled between La Guaira and the United States during the six revolutionary years, 1807–1812, amounted to 6,595,536 pesos, 4 reales,[11] which comes to a yearly average of 1,099,256 pesos or 91,604 a month. This figure must be taken as minimal since it is based upon the *avería* (import–export levy) collected for the consulado of Caracas. Some products were duty free (almost non-existent during the colony but more numerous during the republic) and *los rezagos* (payments made *a posteriori* of the actual entrance) have also been excluded.

The first problem is to place this volume within the general framework of La Guaira's foreign markets in order to establish a clearer idea of what it presents. The following table shows the distribution of this commerce.

Table 45   Geographical distribution of La Guaira's foreign trade

Market	Value		Percentage		Grade
With the United States	6,595,536	pesos 4r	..... 35.2	....	127
With foreign colonies	6,372,818	pesos 6r	 34	....	122
With Spain	4,562,606	pesos 4½r	... 24.3	....	88
With other European countries	616,368	pesos 3r	..... 3.3	....	12
With Hispanic America	363,379	pesos 5½r	... 1.9	....	7
With other Venezuelan ports	229,139	pesos 3½r	... 1.2	....	4
Total	18,739,848	pesos 2½r	... 99.9	....	360

The chart confirms the rupture of the Spanish commercial monopoly with two other markets surpassing it, those of the United States and of the foreign colonies. The first is the more important, claiming 35.2 per cent of the total volume. The second is comprised of the English, Danish, Swedish, Dutch and French colonies in the Caribbean with whom Venezuela conducted heavy trade.

The present study has included among these the foreign colonies in Europe, such as Gibraltar and Malta, since in reality they were used to redistribute Venezuelan goods, either legally or by way of contraband. Gibraltar traded with La Guaira the exorbitant amount of 653,226 pesos, 1½ reales, and this only during 1811 and 1812, since it became a great importer of Venezuelan cacao when, owing to independence, traffic was interrupted with Spain. Obviously, the cacao was not consumed in Gibraltar but was passed on to Spain or distributed along the Mediterranean.[12]

The commerce with Spain is quite substantial considering that during this period it was conducted within the framework of free competition with foreign markets and that it was carried on during only four of the six years covered in this study. Spain imposed a naval blockage on the rebellious province of Caracas during the latter part of 1810, interrupting commercial intercourse, which did not resume until the end of 1812. The average yearly trade with Spain should therefore be based on four rather than six years and would amount to 1,140,651 pesos. The Spanish market was vital to Venezuela for two reasons: it consumed enormous quantities of cacao and provided a favorable balance of trade. Commerce with other European countries was limited to England, Ireland, Denmark and Italy (the port of Leghorn in reality).

Commerce with Hispanic America presents the same problem as Spain, since it was reduced to only four years and for the same reasons. This trade was also vital to Venezuela, especially that with Mexico, because it provided an outlet for surplus cacao and brought in the specie (Mexican silver) needed to lubricate the economy.

Commerce with other Venezuelan ports is noteworthy, for although the value is relatively low, two factors enhance its significance when taken into account. The first is that only four of the six years under study were involved since Venezuela in 1810 had split into royalist and patriot territories. The second is that merchandise traded through this avenue consisted principally of inexpensive food-stuffs (kidney-beans, corn, vegetables, cattle, etc.) which implies an enormous volume.

Returning now to trade with the United States, it should be noted that the 6,595,536 pesos, 4 reales worth of trade divided as follows: merchandise imported by La Guaira from the United States, 3,637,524 pesos, 6 reales; products exported from La Guaira to the United States, 2,958,011 pesos, 6 reales; and therefore balance against La Guaira, 679,513 pesos.

Thus, a negative balance resulted for the Venezuelans of 18.68 per cent of the total amount traded. This problem was serious for a country suffering progressive decapitalization, but the deficit did not reach the level for foreign colonies, which amounted to 19.07 per cent of the total value. In effect, the only external markets with which La Guaira had a favorable trade balance were those of Spain and Hispanic America, and both were lost in 1810. To a large extent, this situation was the cause for the failure of the First Republic since the revolutionaries suffered increasing indebtedness to British and United

States' interests, a debt which eventually destroyed the economy. This predicament was also responsible for the substitution of paper money for the circulation of silver coin in 1811. Finally, it also contributed to the conversion from a cacao to a coffee economy since neither the people of England nor the United States drank cacao. Coffee, then, became the only means to curtail the permanent deficit with foreign markets.

2   The predominance of Philadelphia and Baltimore

During this six-year period, sixteen ports in the United States vied for the commerce of La Guaira. Table 46 shows the trade volume for each of the ports as well as their trade balance with Venezuelan ports.

Table 46   Distribution of La Guaira's trade between United States' ports

Ports	Value traded	Balance
Philadelphia	2,361,499 pesos 7r	+ 174,298 pesos
Baltimore	2,264,081 pesos 1r	+ 241,170 pesos 1r
New York	662,862 pesos 4½r	+ 63,870 pesos 5½r
Salem	496,038 pesos 3½r	− 15,214 pesos 1½r
Boston	280,902 pesos ½r	+ 50,369 pesos 1½r
Beverly	187,503 pesos 6½r	+ 93,622 pesos 5½r
Norfolk	134,067 pesos 2r	+ 54,614 pesos 6r
Wilmington	83,079 pesos 2½r	+ 14,182 pesos 7½r
Marblehead	35,002 pesos 4½r	− 6,897 pesos 3½r
Alexandria	31,042 pesos 2r	+ 1,311 pesos 1r
Gloucester	25,239 pesos 1½r	− 3,823 pesos 3½r
New Haven	10,423 pesos 7r	+ 3,457 pesos 7r
Nantucket	9,202 pesos 1r	+ 7,105 pesos 5r
Portsmouth	5,976 pesos 4½r	+ 173 pesos 6½r
Charlestown	4,889 pesos 3r	+ 4,889 pesos 3r
Georgetown	3,636 pesos 1r	+ 3,636 pesos 1r

Two ports, Philadelphia and Baltimore, accounted for 70.13 per cent of the total value traded, 35.8 per cent and 34.3 per cent respectively. They were the two great colossi of this traffic. This stature derives, as will be shown later, from the privileges that the Spanish Crown bestowed on certain firms from those cities. Together, their trade surpluses come to 415,468 pesos, 1 real against Venezuela (61.4 per cent), in effect the major portion of the overall deficit. New York stood in third place with 10.5 per cent of the total trade, also with an appreciably favorable balance. Salem is surprising for its strong commerce and the largest negative balance for a United States' port. In reality, only two other ports, Marblehead and Gloucester, share the negative category in their balance with La Guaira. Boston, Beverly and Norfolk also possessed an appreciable commerce, each in excess of 100,000 pesos. The final four (Nantucket, Portsmouth, Charleston and Georgetown) did less than 10,000 pesos worth of business. Overall, the southern ports of the United States shared a tendency toward less traffic with Venezuela than the northern ports, a characteristic that the similarity of their economies to Venezuela's can probably explain, while those farther north were more complementary despite the greater distances involved. Charleston is a revealing example of this point and New Orleans had no trade at all with La Guaira.

3   The merchant fleet

Ships of different nations participated in the commercial traffic, but most came from the United States. Venezuela possessed only a tiny fleet composed of small craft limited to coastal trading. Nevertheless, some Venezuelan ships such as the schooner *Dolores* and the brig *Venezuela* did go to the United States.[13] Spaniards occasionally reached ports in the United States as part of their grand commercial voyages[14] since on their return to Spain they had to ascend to the Bahama Channel. During the years of the war with England, however, they traded very little and avoided dangerous departures from their established routes. The British and the Swedes, by contrast, did frequent ports in the United States but their major commerce centered on the Caribbean.

The United States' fleet is very difficult to reconstruct since a detailed description has not been found. In the *avería* records, there are occasional references to United States' vessels which can serve as a basis for reconstruction. These references are entered below in capital letters to identify their source. Another problem lies in the classification of the vessels since a schooner sometimes appears later as a brig (b) or as a frigate (f), or a frigate as a sloop (sl), a schooner (s), or as a brig-schooner (b-s). This problem shall be noted as the need arises. Finally, a word of caution is required owing to the possibility of errors arising from the frequent use of aliases or from identical names on British and American vessels of which the schooners *Mary, Sally, Jo Ann* and *Jane* and the brig *Betsy* are examples.

(a) SCHOONERS

In 1807: INDEPENDENCE (b), FRIENDS (perhaps the same as Three Friends), DOLPHIN, GEORGE (b), HERO, HOPE, Valona, Norfolk, Iris Ark, John Wharton, Hauke, Adela, Eagle, Jack, Federal Geroge, Lard, Deep Pull, Serpenter, Hazard, Amazon, Chesapeake, Five Brothers, and BETSY.

In 1808: none (period of the embargo).

In 1809: GEORGE, MARY, ANN (f), SALLY, JERSEY, LIBERTY, BETSY, OLIVE, EQUALITY, Richard, Pilgrim, Fishhook, and John.

In 1810: THREE FRIENDS, MARY, ANN, SALLY, POINTER, GOVERNOR KEAN, VENUS, LIBERTY, BETSY, Enterprise, Valona, Atlanta, Richard, Adventure, Whitney, Novis, Revenge, Ann Mary, Happiness, Dask, Glove, Chance, Resolution, Return of the Brothers and Pauline.

In 1811: INDEPENDENCE, THREE FRIENDS, DOLPHIN, MARY, ANN, ARRIOT, HERO, SALLY, Harmony, Hotpus, Rosamon, Enterprise.

In 1812: ELIZABETH, HORSE COLLAR, INDEPENDENCE, CONTRADICTION, THREE FRIENDS, DOLPHIN, GEORGE, RUNNEY, ATLANTIC, MARY, SPARRON, ANN, ELEONOR, ACTIVE, and Ellen.

Thus, there were twenty-seven identifiable schooners, two probable (Atlanta and Chesapeake) and thirty-eight doubtful.

(b) BRIGS

In 1807: JO ANN(s), ELISA(s), EXPECTATION, RISING SUN(s), Richmond, Midred, Anfitrit, Polly, Betsy.

In 1808: EXPECTATION.

In 1809: JANE AND JO ANN (apparently two distinct brigs), MINERVA(s), ELIZA, TREMENS, EXPECTATION, SALLY(s), BEAUTY, RISING SUN, Thomas, Agent, Female, Cincinnati, and Hunter.

In 1810: JO ANN, CASSIUS, THOMAS(s), Herman, Success, and Polly.

In 1811: JO ANN, CALLIOPE, ELISA, Thomas(s), CASSIUS, Richmond, and MINERVA.

In 1812: JANE, JO ANN, MINERVA, CALLIOPE, and CUMBERLAND.

In all, there were twelve identifiable brigs, two very probable (the Richmond and the Cincinnati) and nine doubtful.

(c) FRIGATES

MARY ELISA IN 1807, 1811, and 1812.

(d) SLOOPS

ALERT in 1807 and 1810 (s), Two Brothers and Two Friends (they both had the same captain, James Armstrong) in 1810, and Thomas Wilson in 1807 and 1808.

(e) BRIG-SCHOONERS

Rising States in 1807 and Eliza in 1809.

(f) CORVETTES

Billy in 1807.

The above data would imply that the United States' merchant fleet trading with Venezuela consisted of twenty-seven schooners, twelve brigs, one frigate and one sloop, or a total of forty-one vessels. The actual fleet probably numbered about forty-five ships or perhaps twice as many, although that is unlikely. Some of these vessels made voyages three or more times, such as the schooners *Three Friends, George, Mary, Ann, Sally* and *Betsy*, and the brigs *Jo Ann, Minerva, Eliza* and *Expectation*. The predominant vessel, of course, was the schooner, followed by the brig.

4 Consignments

The 6,596,536 pesos, 4 reales worth of trade between the United States and La Guaira correspond to 474 consignments at an average of 13,914 pesos each. These figures prove to be very high. As a point of comparison, the average consignment with foreign colonies was 7,687 pesos and that with Venezuelan ports themselves was only 351 pesos. The latter figure substantiates the idea advanced earlier that Venezuelan commerce consisted of inexpensive products whereas that from the United States involved expensive items. This pattern is logical given the expense of transport and the risks involved.

The number of consignments tends to diminish (119 in 1807, 33 in 1808, 89 in 1809, 97 in 1810 and 57 in 1812) in a manner corresponding to the value traded, but the question arises as to whether this phenomenon also appears in the averages, which would seem to be a better indicator. Table 47 elucidates this question.

The decline of this trade thus seems confirmed in all respects: the value of merchandise, the number of consignments, and the average per consignment. It is highly significant, for example, that in 1811 the average value in the Venezuelan commerce be perceptively the same as that corresponding to the period of the embargo (1808) and, of course, it is evident that the golden era of this trade was the year 1807.

The consignment averages for the different United States' ports reveal a curious hierarchy.

Table 47 Value of consignments by year

Year	Value traded	Consignments	Average
1807	2,869,178 pesos 6½ reales	119	24,110 pesos
1808	338,534 pesos 4½ reales	33	10,258 pesos
1809	993,265 pesos 7 reales	89	11,160 pesos
1810	1,068,343 pesos 2 reales	97	11,013 pesos
1811	842,006 pesos 6½ reales	79	10,658 pesos
1812	484,207 pesos 1½ reales	57	8,494 pesos

Table 48 Value of consignments by United States' ports (pesos)

Salem 18,371	New York 9,748	Gloucester 5,047
Beverly 17,045	Norfolk 7,886	Charleston 4,889
Philadelphia ... 15,849	Alexandria 7,760	Nantucket 4,601
Baltimore 15,507	Marblehead ... 7,000	Georgetown ... 3,636
Boston 10,804	New Haven ... 5,211	Portsmouth ... 2,988
Wilmington 10,284		

The ports with the highest averages are the small ones of Salem and Beverly which, together with Philadelphia and Baltimore, are the only ones to surpass the general mean of 13,914 pesos. Also confirmed is the proposition that the northern ports generally moved more costly merchandise than those of the south. The discreet averages of New York and Boston are also highly surprising. The calendar of consignments follows.

Table 49   Chronological evolution of consignments

	J	F	M	A	M	J	J	A	S	O	N	D		
1807	13	6	7	13	8	13	13	18	14	5	6	3		
1808	7	11	–	2	1	2	3	3	3	–	–	1		
1809	2	2	–	5	10	18	13	12	11	5	8	3		
1810	2	10	8	4	11	7	18	5	8	10	2	12		
1811	10	9	8	4	4	9	5	7	6	6	5	6		
1812	4	9	8	1	4	13	6	7	1	–	2	2		
Total	38	47	31	29	38	62	58	52	43	26	23	27	=	474

The highest is in June, followed next by July and August. The lowest is November, followed by October and December. Some independence appears in this trade with respect to cacao, the principal article of export for Venezuela, which is harvested in July and December. A certain relationship with the agricultural production of both countries is also visible since the highest traffic coincides with the harvest months in the two places (clearly only one of the harvest seasons in Venezuela).

5   Merchandise

Because no detailed accounts of the merchandise exchanged between the U.S. and La Guaira exist, this dimension will be treated from a qualitative perspective. In the first place, it is known that Venezuela exported mainly its crops (cacao, indigo, coffee, cotton, sugar and tobacco), its cattle (which could not endure the passage by sea), and their derivatives (hides, leathers, jerked beef, saddles, etc.), from which it can be assumed that the United States would basically import crops and hides either for its own consumption or to sell them in the world markets. A trade report for La Guaira in 1811 shows the principal items exported to friendly and neutral nations (mainly the United States and the British colonies) as shown in Table 50.[15]

Logically, it is not cacao that occupies first place as during previous years but indigo. Moveover, the value and volume for coffee are extraordinary.

Several reports by Intendant Arce help to delineate the principal items that the merchants from the United States extracted from La Guaira. In an 1806

Table 50   Exports from La Guaira, 1811

Indigo	306,380 lb. (Spanish) valued at	382,975 pesos
Cacao	36,203 *fanegas*, 60 lb valued at	332,068 pesos ½ reales
Coffee	3,186,488 lb valued at	246,650 pesos
Cowhides	49,602 units, valued at	49,602 pesos
Copper	74,359 lb valued at	14,871 pesos 6 reales

report on the cargoes picked up by ships from the firms of Craig of Phila-delphia and Luke of Baltimore, it appears that the frigate *Active* transported to Philadelphia 866 *fanegas* and 102 lb (Spanish) of raw cacao, 123 lb of second grade coffee and 5,387 lb of Guayaco wood, while the schooner *Three Fingers* took to Baltimore 675 *fanegas* and 46 lb of bulk cacao, 304 *quintales* and 81 lb of Guayaco wood, 100 *quintales* and 34 lb of first class coffee and 308 *quintales* of cotton.[16] Shortly thereafter, on May 31, 1806, the schooner *Happiness* embarked for Baltimore with 64,552 lb of first class coffee, 17,495 lb of the second class and 4,675 of the third, besides carrying 805 dressed cow-hides and some provisions.[17] The intendant expressed concern because Craig's vessels carried only indigo, provisions, hides and some cacao and affirmed that many ships carried only indigo and coffee, a situation that left cacao in storage at port without an outlet.[18]

It is also known that ten vessels originating in Venezuela and Campeche arrived in New York in 1809. Their cargo consisted of 1,373 bags of coffee, 75 bags (*zurrones*) of indigo, 9 boxes of cigars, 42 bags of medicinal bark (*quina*), 23 bags of copal, 182 flasks of Copayba balsam, 19,829 dressed cow-hides, 7,100 goat-hides, 2,345 *quintales* of log-wood from Campeche, 775 *quintales* of Nicaraguan log-wood and 460 *quintales* of yellow log-wood.[19] Undoubtedly, the coffee, indigo, cigars, hides and, perhaps, the medicinal bark were Venezuelan.

The exports of La Guaira consisted therefore of indigo, coffee, hides, cacao (for purpose of resale) and some parcels of cotton, dyewood and medicinal bark.

The exports of the United States to La Guaira are even more difficult to identify because its merchants did not limit themselves to national products, but dealt in those of other countries as well. Spanish Ambassador Luis de Onís affirmed that re-exports in 1794 reached 50 per cent of the foreign commerce of the United States, and for the period 1802–1804 he calculated them at 29,000,000 *pesos fuertes* a year. According to him, they included 'foreign articles such as woolens, linens, sugar, coffee, tea, sherry, and other liquors that they import into the country [United States], and that they re-export to foreign markets'.[20] In 1807, according to Onís, this commerce reached '103,000,000 in exports, the greater part foreign products and merchandise, and 108,000,000 in imports'.[21] Numerous historians such as Stulz,[22] Morison and Commager,[23] Max Beloff,[24] etc. have confirmed the observations of this contemporary source.

In the previously cited reports of Arce (1806), he indicated that the cargoes introduced into La Guaira by ships of the Craig Company contained French textiles, lead, needles, codfish, wines, candles, flour, knives, hats, Dutch fabrics, wax, and stockings[25] and that five ships of that company specifically carried mirrors, fine linens, muslins, light cottons, cambric, handkerchiefs, etc.[26] By contrast, a ship that reached La Guaira in 1809, coming from Alexandria, carried typical products of the United States, including 625 barrels of flour, 50 barrels of biscuits, 22 cases of soap, 16 measures (*tiersos*) of rice, 5 measures (*frequines*) of butter, 43 casks of red wine, 20 barrels of fish, 13,600 roof boards, 13 barrels containing various assortments of vegetables, and four barrels of pork.[27] Finally, in the commerce report for La Guaira of 1811, products appear that clearly originated in the United States, for example, 10,245 1/2 barrels of flour (valued at 102,455 pesos), 135,730 lb of lard and butter (valued at 18,155 pesos, 3 reales), 20,395 head of salted fish, and 12,484 *arrobas* of dried fish.[28]

The exports from the United States to La Guaira consisted, then, of national products such as flour, biscuits, salted and dried fish, butter and lard, and various vegetables, and re-exported articles such as French and Dutch fabrics, dry goods, and Spanish wines.

6   The antecedents of this historic juncture

The time frame within which the historic events of the present study unfolded corresponded to a golden age of United States' commerce. This age began with the French Revolutionary and Napoleonic Wars, which entangled all the maritime powers in an interminable series of conflicts, interrupting commercial traffic on a world-wide scale. The United States was the only neutral nation, with a powerful merchant marine, that could deal with either camp, reaping lucrative benefits from this privileged position. Luis de Onís explained this phenomenon lucidly:

This era, which ran from 1789 until 1814, was as beneficial and happy for the Anglo-North Americans as [it was] sad and disastrous for the nations of Europe. The former prodigiously expanded their merchant marine; and their flag, respected as neutral on all seas, not only carried the products of their country to the ports of the belligerent powers, but also carried products and merchandise to the other markets of Europe and America. The value of their exports in 1791 rose to 19,012,041 *pesos fuertes*, including in this sum total some two or three million [that were] the value of foreign products and merchandise that were imported into the United States and re-exported to the markets of other nations; and the value of foreign imports for domestic consumption rose to 19,082,828 *pesos fuertes*. At the same time that the war was intensifying in Europe, and that the need to maintain great armies and great fleets demanded an extraordinary, enormous level of consumption, the commerce of the United States expanded with astonishing rapidity, only suffering during the time of the embargo and of the war that its government undertook against Great Britain to placate Napoleon; nor did it decline until after the general peace of Europe.[29]

Onís' explanation is accurate, although a bit simplistic. Certainly, things were not as easy as he pictures them, because the two major belligerent powers, England and France, used all the means at their disposal to strangle the lucrative re-export business of the United States. In reality, the sale of flour and fish in Europe did not hurt either of the two in the slightest, but this was not so when the purchase of merchandise for resale in other countries accelerated the industrial growth of the enemy. They thus began to obstruct the commerce of the United States and launched what Godechot has aptly characterized as 'the war of blockades'[30] which brought the commerce of the United States to the dead-end street of the embargo. The process was long: the English activated the decree of 1756 which denied neutral countries the right to trade with enemy colonies. The United States adjusted to this obstacle, as Stulz tells us 'by means of buying the products on her account, transporting them to her ports and selling them later in Europe, as if they were goods from the United States.'[31] The subterfuge was obvious and the English ordered a blockade of all ports tied to the Parisian orbit. Napoleon reacted in 1803 by denying all manufactures of English origin entrance into France. Great Britain blockaded the mouths of the Elbe and Weser and, in 1804, 'all French ports on the North Sea and the English Channel.' On November 21, 1806, Napoleon declared the continental blockade and England responded with her Orders-in-Council by which all ships from neutral countries that went to a port subject to Napoleon were to stop first in an English port and pay duties equivalent to those for ships unloading their merchandise. Napoleon answered with the Milan Decree (December 17,1807), by which he announced that all neutral ships landing in English ports and paying the duties that the British demanded would be considered English in all respects and good prizes, consequently, for whomever might capture them.

United States' merchants patiently bore the cross of the maritime blockades, confirming that each time it became more difficult and costly to sustain the good business of re-exporting. When news of the Berlin Decree became known, they began the search for other markets, such as those of Hispanic America, and when the Milan Decree arrived, Jefferson made the sensible decision to declare an embargo, at the end of 1807. The two years 1806–1807, the beginning point of this study, marks the push of the United States into the Venezuelan market, where a series of healthy opportunities were apparent: a great demand for flour, an appreciable excess of tradeable crops such as indigo, coffee, and cacao, the absence of English merchants (owing to the war with Spain) and the lack of Spanish and French commerce because of that conflict.

7   **Periodization**

In the earlier portion of this study, where consignments were analyzed, annual trade volume during the six-year period showed great variation and the general trend was downward: 43.5 per cent in 1807; 5.13 per cent in 1808; 15.5 per cent in 1809; 16.19 per cent in 1810; 12.7 per cent in 1811; and 7.3 per cent in 1812. The proposition that the United States enjoyed better trade with Venezuela when it was an independent country than when it was a Spanish colony appears, therefore, to lack validity. Periodization by year means little, however, because political considerations of enormous consequence that do not properly coincide with calendar years affected this commerce. The beginning and end of Jefferson's embargo (from the point of view of the United States) requires consideration as does the beginning and the end of the Spanish blockade, which interrupted trade with the metropolis (from the point of view of South America). The new periodization, with these qualifications, is as follows:

i.   Period of United States' predominance: January 1, 1807 to December 31, 1807.
ii. Period of the Jefferson embargo: January 1, 1808 to March 31, 1809.
iii. Period of British predominance: April 1, 1809 to December 31, 1810.
iv. Period of independence: January 1, 1811 (Spanish blockade) to July 31, 1812.
v.   Period of the Spanish restoration: August 1, 1812 to December 31, 1812.

Trade value during these distinct periods, and above all their monthly averages permit a clearer image of the situation.

Table 51   Trade value by period

i.	2,869,178 pesos, 6½ reales	239,098 pesos
ii.	366,899 pesos, 4½ reales	24,460 pesos
iii.	2,033,244 pesos, 1 reales	96,821 pesos
iv.	1,278,296 pesos, 3 reales	67,278 pesos
v.	47,917 pesos, 5 reales	9,583 pesos

Plainly, the grand era of United States' commerce was the first period, when monthly averages reached approximately 250,000 pesos. The second period, by reason of the embargo, should have shown nothing. Consequently, the average of 24,460 pesos a month is very high. In the third period intensive trade resumed with an average of approximately 100,000 pesos. In the fourth, decline is evident, and, in the fifth, so too is the collapse of commerce with the United States, which no longer reaches even the averages during the embargo.

8 Period of United States' predominance

The new Anglo-Spanish war, following the interlude introduced by the Peace of Amiens, paralysed Venezula's commerce. Spanish merchants (the only authorized traders) ceased to frequent the port of La Guaira because of the fear of being captured by the British war fleet. Agricultural products accumulated in port waiting for buyers, and the population began to suffer shortages of certain food stuffs (flour) and manufactures. The Spanish government opened the Venezuelan market to neutral ships on May 29, 1805,[32] but only for a few days, closing it again on June 11 under pressures from peninsular merchants. The captain general of Venezuela jubilantly embraced the prohibition of neutral trade because he was convinced that United States' merchants dealt in British goods.[33] Intendant Arce, by contrast, protested the measure because the need to activate commerce was obvious, and, besides, he knew that in Spain a number of companies had been awarded, on the preceding December 24, privileges to trade with Venezuela and he feared that they would convert the Caracas market into a monopoly in the absence of competitors. Anticipating possible disorders, he urged that the matter of the concessions be kept secret as long as possible.[34]

At the end of November 1805, a United States' ship out of Baltimore, the *Comet*, arrived in La Guaira. It belonged to the Craig Company in Philadelphia and showed official documentation that authorized it to trade.[35] At that time, the port officials, the local authorities, and the public discovered the secret that the intendant had so prudently guarded: two commercial houses from the United States, Craig of Philadelphia and Luke and Tiernan of Baltimore, had secured the privilege of trading with Venezuela. During the following months, additional ships from Craig and Luke arrived[36] which in practice established a monopoly, because the English and the Spanish remained absent from La Guaira owing to the war, and neutral countries were forbidden this market. The consulado of Caracas even affirmed that these United States merchants were fixing prices in the market-place, being the sole buyers and sellers,[37] but all the protests were useless. During the first half of 1806, 26 ships of the Craig company brought in goods valued at 565,264 pesos, and extracted merchandise worth 575,438 pesos.[38] These merchants did not even bother to return to their country, merely making the voyage from La Guaira to the Danish islands of Saint Croix and St Thomas where they sold the Venezuelan goods and purchased French, Dutch and English manufactures.

The monopoly of Craig and Luke ended in June 1806 when neutral trade was re-established. This action was an unforeseen consequence of the abortive attempt by Miranda to liberate Venezuela. Captain General Guevara de Vasconcelos put all the defenses of the colony on alert because he was convinced that Miranda would return with English help, and he requested that Intendant Arce furnish him large sums of money to buy uniforms, arms and munitions. Arce informed him that royal monies were exhausted because of the commercial paralysis and that the only remedy was to authorize neutral trade which would once again permit garnering money through taxes.[39] When asked its opinion, the consulado voiced the same viewpoint,[40] and Guevara had little choice but to agree to neutral trade on June 25, 1806.[41] From this moment forward, as indicated, Venezuela enjoyed the uninterrupted rule of freedom of trade (except, naturally, with enemy nations), which brought an end to Spanish exclusionism.

Freedom of commerce broke the monopoly of Craig and of Luke, but the Venezuelan market-place remained in hands of merchants from the United States, for the English continued to be barred because of the war and the Spanish and neutrals like the Danes and Swedes operated at very low levels. Besides, the Craig company conducted a highly skilled operation that permitted it to protect its hegemony on the Venezuelan market. John Craig knew that on March 16, 1806, the King of Spain had granted to the Marqués de Branciforte (brother-in-law of the minister Godoy) the privilege of introducing 100,000 barrels of flour, with exclusive rights, into Cuba and Venezuela. The Cuban authorities refused to accede to this monopoly, but the Venezuelans honored the orders when they came. For his part, Branciforte decided to sell his privilege for 300,000 pesos and John Craig quickly bought it.[42] On December 11, 1806, the Intendant Arce received notification that Craig had obtained the monopoly to introduce flour into Venezuela and that he would begin operations within the maximum space of two months.[43] The commotion in Caracas was enormous. The consulado urged an immediate termination of the monopoly and the municipal government of Caracas filed a vigorous protest to the king, which never received an answer.[44] The Craig monopoly functioned unhindered from February 1807 until October 28, 1808, when Captain General Casas and Intendant Arce suspended it. The Crown ratified this suspension a month later, November 15, 1808.[45] The monopoly lasted, therefore, a little more than twenty months, and the consulado calculated that during that period it produced for Craig a benefit of 80,000 to 100,000 pesos. Tandron estimates that the gain was 300,000 pesos, but he erred by believing that it lasted twenty-four months.[46] The probable worth was 200,000 pesos above the 300,000 that were paid to Branciforte. On the average, 20,000 barrels of flour were imported annually. Moreover, Craig's company failed to pay the required duties to the *Caja de Consolidación*, for which a guarantee was demanded of his representative in Caracas, don Francisco Caballero Sarmiento. Sarmiento, as a result, sailed for Philadelphia with the intention of presenting the appropriate claims, but when he arrived in that city he found that John Craig had died three days earlier.[47] Craig's death was most certainly decisive in ending the privilege.

The year 1807 was, then, a time of authentic commercial domination of Venezuela by the United States. Suffice it to say that of the 4,596,866 pesos, 2½ reales worth of trade in La Guaira, 2,869,178 pesos, 6½ reales or 62.41 per cent was with ports of the United States. And to this sum total should be added the 970,133 pesos, 6½ reales of trade with St Thomas, which, as is well known, was a subsidiary traffic of the United States and of the Craig company in particular. The two commercial houses, Craig and Luke, continued with the system established in 1806, which explains the business conducted by Philadelphia and Baltimore, and the first of these enjoyed the privileged flour monopoly besides. These realities explain the large volume of nearly a 250,000 pesos worth of trade a month. Never again would the United States so dominate the Venezulan market.

9   The embargo period

The war of blockades between England and France, as indicated earlier, brought about the Jefferson embargo. The action of the President of the United States was guided by practical considerations and not by the peace-maker spirit that sometimes has been ascribed to him.[48] Jefferson did the only thing that he could: order the temporary suspension of foreign commerce to prevent the merchants of the United States from being captured by the English and the French, which inevitably would entail armed confrontation with those powers, and which therefore, could endanger the very independence of the nation.[49] He prepared the law and sent it to Congress with a brief message. The legislature approved the measure in a single day: December 22, 1807. The embargo prohibited the departure of any union ships with foreign destinations and authorized only bonded coastal shipping. When Napoleon received word of the embargo in Bayonne, now in 1808, he ordered all United States' ships found in French ports to be seized, 'because [he said ironically] these ships cannot be American; being such, they would respect the embargo; therefore only camouflaged English ships can be affected.'[50]

The embargo destroyed the privileged commercial arrangement in Venezuela, dismantling in a few days the mechanism that over the 14 years had been built so industriously. In January 1808, some movement still remained. Perhaps this came from ships that departed from the United States before the law, but later the merchant fleet of the United States disappeared from the port of La Guaira with the exception of the bergantine *Expectation*, which traded in February and August 1808, and of the bergantine *Tremens*, which entered La Guaira, coming from New York in February 1809. The rest of the commerce, which was limited to the ports of Philadelphia and Baltimore, was conducted in English ships, the Spanish *Botón de Rosa*, and the Swedish goleta *Isabel*. Despite these factors, the monthly average was high, reaching 24,460 pesos. During a number of months in 1808, such as March, October and November, trade was non-existent.[51]

The protests of the merchants of the United States, the stabilization of the Anglo-French war, and the desire of Jefferson to create a favorable climate for the inauguration of the new president, Madison, led to the revocation of the Embargo Act and the implementation in its stead of the Non-Intercourse

Act, ratified on March 1, 1809, which authorized commerce with all countries except England and France.

10   Period of British predominance

United States' merchants once again began to arrive at La Guaira in April, 1809, but they encountered a situation radically different from the one before. The port was filled with English and Spanish ships. The time of the flour monopoly as well as commercial predominance seemed Utopian, for now even free competition appeared very difficult. The Spaniards had reestablished the solid market in cacao and Mexican silver, which was vital to the Venezuelans, and the English had exploited their unusual role as a Spanish ally in the war against Napoleon to penetrate the Venezuelan market-place, enjoying, moreover, the privilege of paying only 80 per cent of the normal customs duties.[52]

The merchants of the United States accepted the challenge presented by the competition and set to work. In April 1809, they brought to La Guaira merchandise valued at 13,199 pesos, 1½ reales, and extracted products worth 29,670 pesos, ½ real. In May, their trade totaled 86,930 pesos, ½ real; in June 158,568 pesos, 6 reales; and in August it reached 189,957 pesos, 3 reales. They continued to sustain a healthy volume through the beginning of 1810 and in February their trade came to 139,503 pesos, 2½ reales.

On April 19, 1810, the revolutionary cabildo seized power. The patriots initiated contact with the United States' government to win its political support and the means to buy weapons. Madison's Florentine policy worked miracles by not aligning itself either for or against the Venezuelans, as it also did not compromise the United States to favor or oppose the Spanish, the French, etc. He encouraged the Venezuelans with words, he sold them some muskets, and he dispatched a diligent observer named Robert C. Lowry, who arrived in La Guaira on September 6, 1810. This was exactly what Madison's prudent secretary of state, Monroe, had counselled, because it would be foolhardy to jeopardize either the Spanish or the Hispanic American markets, which had provided such excellent benefits the year before,[53] nor preclude the possibility that *Fernandista* or Bonapartist Spain might agree to sell Florida or Cuba, for which great hopes had been harbored after the success enjoyed with Louisiana.

Lowry immediately grasped that his charge in Venezuela was fundamentally economic and he focused his reports on commercial realities. He reported that the Caracas market was entirely in English hands, which he explained by the fact that the revolutionaries had conceded to the English a 25 per cent reduction in tariffs on September 3, 1810.[54] He was unaware that the Spanish authorities had given them a 20 per cent reduction in 1808, which patriotic generosity had topped by only 5 per cent. Lowry also indicated that Spanish corsairs dedicated themselves to the pursuit of the United States' merchantmen, but not English, and he attributed this preference to the absence of a United States' war fleet in the Caribbean. Finally, he suggested that the demand in Caracas for armaments might be exploited to win commercial advantages similar to those that the British enjoyed.[55]

Lowry's efforts were to no avail and the commerce of the United States began to decline. In October, November, and December 1810, its trade totaled 132,729 pesos, 2 reales; 38,312 pesos, 5½ reales; and 124,962 pesos, 6 reales respectively. It appeared very difficult to beat the English.

11   The independence period

A great opportunity slipped away. The Spanish had imposed a maritime blockade on the rebel provinces since 1810 and pressured London to define its policy toward the patriots. The British continued to practice duplicity until July 5, 1811, when the Venezuelans solemely decided to proclaim their independence from Spain. At that point, they had to choose between their Spanish ally in Europe or the Venezuelan trade, and they chose the former. The patriots were enraged and Lowry punctually informed his government of the change in attitude in Caracas, which amounted to open hostility toward the English. The officious observer even pictured the possibility of English intervention in Guayana.[56] It was a great opportunity which Madison could have used to define and tighten relations with Caracas, assuring a preponderant position for the commercial interests of the United States, but he limited himself to gleefully embracing the existence of another republic on the American continent,[57] and the revolutionaries realized that they stood alone.

The commerce of the United States with La Guaira, sustained a monthly average of less that 68,000 pesos. The reason was neither British competition nor Spanish, nor that of neutral countries. What occurred was the economic collapse of the first Venezuelan Republic. Costs had risen, silver specie did not come in and harvests continued to diminish because it was necessary to mobilize the peasantry into armies. The republican government was forced to resort to issuing paper money without backing. Prices of nutritious articles exploded and inflation began to devour the revolution. In January and February 1812, the United States still traded goods worth 20,285 and 86,230 pesos respectively. On March 26, Venezuela was shaken by a powerful earthquake that principally affected the republican provinces. The loss of life, goods and real property were incalculable, and a defeatist spirit overcame the patriots, who were incapable of stopping the royalist advance. In April, Generalisimo Francisco de Miranda was named dictator and he was granted plenary powers to save the republic. He was the last hope. It was also the end of the revolution, because all the ideological principles were subordinated to the needs of war, the only immediate concern.

The United States began to react in May, when Congress voted aid totaling 50,000 dollars to help the victims of the earthquake. Commissioner Scott was sent to Caracas to administer the funds. Even Monroe began to clarify his position regarding the unstable South American Republic,[58] but it was too late. In June 1812, Puerto Cabello fell into the hands of the royalists and on July 26 they entered Caracas. When they took La Guaira, they found various United States' ships anchored in port which had arrived with succour for those injured in the earthquake: No one had forseen such a rapid collapse.

12   The period of Spanish restoration

The ambiguous policy of the United States' government regarding Venezuelan independence gained it absolutely nothing in the new period of Spanish restoration. The royalists knew full well that the real sympathies of the United States had been in complete disagreement with its official policy. Nor were they pleased that their ambassador to the United States, don Luis de Onís, still had not gained recognition despite a three-year wait, since 1809. Finally, they were allies of the British, at whose side they fought in the peninsula, and to whom they opened without reservation all Venezuelan ports. Relations between Great Britain and the United States deteriorated by the moment and it was forseeable that war might result.

The commerce of the United States with Venezuela continued to lose ground throughout the second half of 1812, finally dying without pain or glory. In August, goods worth 33,727 pesos were traded; in September only 1,587 pesos, 2 reales; in October, nothing; in November, 6,444 pesos; and in December, 6,158 pesos. Monthly averages did not reach 10,000 pesos. Only a change in the policy of the United States toward Spain could have improved this situation, but one never came. General Monteverde then decided to define positions and he gave the officious observer, Lowry, and the commissioner, Scott, forty-eight hours to leave Venezuela. Lowry communicated word of the ultimatum of January 1, 1813 to Monroe.[59] It was the end of the juncture. Madison and Monroe took no action against the insolent Spanish general, for they knew that the Venezuelan market was lost and that, on the other hand, war with England was near. Conflict with Spain would be untimely. Lowry and Scott returned to the United States leaving in La Guaira various merchantmen confiscated by the Spanish. The United States would have to await another opportunity to return to the Venezuelan market-place.

CHAPTER TEN

Commercial relations between New Orleans and the United States, 1783 – 1803

As the United States emerged from its struggle for independence and entered its early national period, it faced a delicate economic situation, owing in particular to debts accumulated during the war. Both the levying of duties on imports as a palliative for the national deficit and the expansion of commerce to secure new markets and thereby earn specie promised to alleviate this crisis. During its participation in the War of the American Revolution, Spain had opened the ports of Havana and New Orleans to trade with the rebellious colonies[1] to secure basic food-stuffs for their domestic populations as well as their garrisons.[2] Once the Treaty of Paris had been signed in 1783, however, Spain saw no reason to perpetuate this emergency measure and duly closed both ports to foreign commerce, thus causing deeply felt repercussions in the new nation.[3] Not only did the United States lose highly lucrative consumer markets but it also found itself deprived of specie from Cuba upon which it had come to rely. Not surprisingly, then, the United States, wishing to repay its war debts, to obtain specie, to bolster its economy, and to find new markets, continued to display great interest in Spain's overseas possessions, especially the Islands and Louisiana, which were ideally located and produced goods highly suitable for United States' markets. The favorable political situation that developed as a by-product of the French Revolutionary and Napoleonic Wars enhanced this interest at a time when the United States was entering a period of momentous commercial expansion. Its neutrality afforded the opportunity, albeit often a problematic one, to become a viable commercial intermediary for the European nations at war. As the colony of one such nation and the source of coveted commodities, Louisiana would be much affected by this new role of the United States in world commerce.[4]

As a result of the Royal Ordinance of July 8, 1776, and the Royal Cedula of January 22, 1782, which permitted it to trade with the French empire, Louisiana had been tied commercially to the French markets in Europe and the Caribbean.[5] Up to 1793, the treasury and administrative records show continuous comings and goings of ships between New Orleans and Martinique,

Port au Prince, Cayes de St Louis, Guarico, Bordeaux and Marseilles. The coming of war between Spain and France brought the loss of the French markets and with it the need to secure others that would supply food-stuffs and provide outlets for tobacco, sugar, cotton and hides. The United States moved into this gap, with the ports of New York, Philadelphia, Boston, Wilmington, Charleston, Salem and others becoming the new markets for Louisiana. These contacts expanded quickly, as discussed in more detail later, when perils and uncertainty on the high seas, arising from the outbreak of armed conflict between Spain and England in 1796, led the Crown to permit neutral trade, a concession that entailed an increased use of ships from the United States as carriers for Louisiana.

During the decade 1783–93, the port of New Orleans remained closed, at least in theory, to trade with the United States, although ties sustained through the Mississippi and Ohio Rivers were an exception.[6] Nevertheless, a series of tragedies, including fires and hurricanes,[7] as well as fraud such as contraband,[8] made the enforcement of the prohibition impossible. The very political authorities, governors and intendants alike, proved flexible during emergencies, even going so far as to solicit royal pardon[9] for local merchants who had imported flour from Philadelphia, New York and elsewhere without proper authorization.[10]

The clandestine trade followed two routes. The French allowed ships from both Louisiana and the United States access to their colonies, a circumstance that permitted vessels from New Orleans to secure products which merchants from the United States, or French colonists dealing with ports on the east coast, had introduced previously, while the French also had the opportunity to ship the same kind of cargo to New Orleans.[11] The other route was simply direct trade between Louisiana and the United States, the merchants using licenses issued for travel to the French islands but heading north instead. Nevertheless, very real difficulties could inhibit this kind of covert activity as agent Michael O'Connor for Nicholas Low and Company complained in 1783: '[It is] impossible to negotiate in a port where there are no products, no money, and no freedom allowed a man to dispose of his fortune as he pleases.'[12]

Although it is difficult if not impossible to quantify the value and volume of contraband goods reaching New Orleans during these ten years, a reasonably accurate calculation of the legally registered trade between the United States and New Orleans is feasible. Regarding exports between January 1, 1783, and December 31, 1792, the only port receiving Louisiana's products was Philadelphia. Four ships, one each registered for the years 1783, 1789, 1790 and 1792, sailed to that destination carrying goods valued at 35,035 silver reales, a sum accounting for only 0.24 per cent of the 14,864,067 reales worth of merchandise exported during that period. On the other hand, imports totaled 663,168 reales, or 4.13 per cent of the 16,073,679 reales at which goods arriving from non-Spanish markets were appraised, these imports originating in Rhode Island with one vessel; Carolina, one; Philadelphia, thirteen; and Baltimore, one.[13]

The abnormally high total of nine ships which arrived from the United States in 1788, all from Philadelphia, suggests a connection to the fire that had recently ravaged New Orleans. The need to rebuild burned buildings as well as a shortage of flour would explain this anomaly, especially considering that the authorities themselves chartered three ships to bring back merchandise.[14] Significantly, 192,000 reales were advanced for the purchase of 3,000 barrels of flour.[15]

As indicated earlier, the year 1793 saw a quickening of commercial inter-course between New Orleans and the United States. The outbreaks of hostilities between Spain and France created the opportunity for this advance. Only the merchant marine of the United States, neutral in a conflict that enveloped nearly all of the European powers, could hope to guarantee the Spanish the commodities that they needed while extracting their produce, a reality that provided the North Americans with the long-awaited means to penetrate Spanish markets legally. When word reached Louisiana about the imminent break and its possible consequences, several vessels laden with indigo, tobacco and cotton were moored in the port, preparing to sail for French markets, this being the season of heavy traffic. If these ships proceeded, they would run the risk of seizure at their points of destination or being intercepted at sea; if they remained in port, agriculture as well as commerce would suffer. Moreover, the additional risk loomed that the population, which for the most part was French in origin and still loyal to France, might revolt in a manner similar to 1768.[16] The governor, confronted with this delicate political situ-ation and realizing that the cargoes could not be marketed in Spanish ports, allowed the ships to set sail for the United States with the stipulation that they should pay the same export duties that they would pay if leaving for French ports.[17]

Given the outlook that faced the province, the Barón de Carondelet, Governor of Louisiana, in April 1793 authorized the export of tobacco to any port in the United States, contingent upon the payment of the required six per cent export tax and with the specification that the return cargo should be flour.[18] Nevertheless, in a different response to the international crisis, the Crown by Order of September 27, 1793, instructed the governor to work through Spain's commercial officer in the United States to secure flour if necessary.[19] Obeying this order under wartime conditions threatened un-acceptable bureaucratic entanglements and delays. In any event, the United States was really the only feasible export market for the colonies as well as an obvious source of flour. Understandably, then, the Royal Order was not enforced.[20] Months later, on July 2, 1794, for example, the authorities in Louisiana permitted the export of tobacco to markets in the United States without interference.

The potential of Louisiana's trade with the United States became evident during the period of French–Spanish hostility, as Table 52 reveals.[21]

Table 52   Louisiana trade with the United States, 1793–1796

			Exports			
Years	USA reales	Total reales	Percentage	USA ships	Total ships	Percentage
1793	1,059,933	2,851,461	37.17	30	113	26.55
1794	1,732,583	2,579,784	67.16	26	90	28.89
1795	1,495,782	2,359,788	63.39	29	95	30.53
1796	1,483,382	2,920,917	50.78	24	95	25.26
	5,771,680	10,711,950	53.88	109	393	27.73
			Imports			
Years	USA reales	Total reales	Percentage	USA ships	Total ships	Percentage
1793	1,676,834	5,487,513	30.56	21	46	45.65
1794	1,334,409	1,718,954	77.63	24	32	75.00
1795	4,183,479	5,465,638	76.54	40	51	78.43
1796	932.016	2,325,911	40.07	21	27	77.78
	8,126,738	14,998,016	54.19	106	156	67.95

The data show that Louisiana sustained vigorous commercial activity despite the closing of the traditional French markets, with more than fifty per cent of the trade conducted with the United States.

Although the Peace of Basel and the Treaty of San Ildefonso momentarily seemed to resolve the international crisis, the armed conflict with England that followed upon the settlement with France brought maritime difficulties to new levels. The disturbing impact of the new crisis became evident during 1797 when the value of Louisiana's exports slumped to a mere 1,806,836 silver reales, 38.14 per cent less than in 1796. Of this amount, the United States absorbed 54.21 per cent or 979,515 reales. Imports were affected less however, totaling 3,712,619 reales, some 59.62 per cent higher than in the previous year, owing to sources from the United States which contributed 3,391,069 reales or 91.34 per cent.[22]

In the face of the danger that this predicament entailed for Louisiana, the Crown ruled by Order of June 11, 1798, 'that for the time being and while the war lasts or His Majesty rules differently, it is resolved that entry to the river [Mississippi] as well as commerce with the capital [New Orleans] be permitted to all vessels of neutral nations, with a payment of six per cent ad valorem on all items introduced or exported.'[23] By this decision, the port of New Orleans stood open to ships from the United States. Moreover, the Treaty of San Lorenzo, which granted the United States the right of deposit, provided an additional stimulant to commerce. From this point forward, trade between the province and its neighbor nation increased rapidly. Agents Clark and Hullings in turn served as representatives of the commercial interests of the United States.[24]

Ensuing changes in the character of this commerce illustrate the significance of the new regulations. From July 1798 through the end of the year, the ships leaving New Orleans that flew the flag of the United States numbered 7 and incoming vessels, 14. In 1799, of the 64 ships of that nation leaving for home ports, 63 flew the United States' flag.

The importance that markets in the United States had for the province during the war with England, 1796–1802, is illustrated by the following data.[25]

Table 53 Louisiana trade with the United States, 1797–1802

Years	USA reales	Total reales	Exports Percentage	USA ships	Total ships	Percentage
1797	979,515	1,806,836	54.21	17	94	18.09
1798	1,103,505	1,996,432	55.27	31	106	29.25
1799	1,989,846	5,672,573	35.08	64	119	53.78
1800	1,887,247	2,847,558	66.28	77	124	62.10
1801	1,932,959	2,454,824	78.74	101	146	69.18
1802	2,685,565	7,415,322	36.22	79	209	37.80
	10,578,637	22,193,545	47.67	369	798	46.24

Years	USA reales	Total reales	Imports Percentage	USA ships	Total ships	Percentage
1797	3,391,069	3,712,619	91.34	30	37	81.08
1798	3,431,637	3,435,024	99.90	37	41	90.24
1799	8,378,063	8,814,757	95.05	70	94	74.47
1800	4,489,081	6,122,942	73.32	62	98	63.27
1801	6,874,697	8,517,980	80.71	68	111	61.26
1802	4,138,128	6,933,447	59.68	64	139	46.04
	30,702,675	37,536,769	81.79	331	520	63.65

If these markets were important to the province, as the 47.67 per cent of all exports indicates, so too was their importance as suppliers of merchandise reaching New Orleans from non-Spanish ports. During the years 1797–1802, then, the value of commercial transactions between the United States and New Orleans rose to 41,281,312 silver reales or 69.11 per cent of the 59,730,314 reales that constituted the total valuation of trade, this figure excluding products that may have come from Spanish markets.

The end of armed conflict under the Treaty of Amiens necessarily affected commercial ties with the United States. A Royal Edict of October 18, 1802, forbade further commerce with neutrals and revoked the right of deposit.[26] The end of the war and the return of security on the high seas eliminated the need to tolerate trade between Louisiana and the United States, i.e. the need to secure necessities and provide an outlet for colonial products.

The effect of the October decision is readily evident. During the months of 1803 when Spain still governed Louisiana only 1 registered ship went to Baltimore (27,600 reales), 3 to New York (180,499 reales), 1 to Philadelphia (5,366 reales), with merchandise valued as indicated in the parentheses.[27] French markets once again had replaced those of the United States.

From January of 1783 until the French government formally took possession of Louisiana in 1803, the value of transactions with the United States reached approximately 56,272,897 silver reales or 44.29 per cent of the total 127,061,569 reales. The exports to the United States rose to 16,598,817 reales or 31.19 per cent of the 53,220,539 total for sales and imports amounted to 39,674,080 reales or 53.73 per cent of the 73,841,030 total for purchases. Consequently, the Atlantic commerce between the United States and New Orleans resulted in a deficit for the province of 23,075,262 reales.

As far as individual products are concerned, a wide variety of merchandise reached New Orleans, with the greatest amount corresponding to various sorts of textiles. Most prominent among the exports were 2,625,870 pounds of cotton, 836,920 of indigo, 5,597,570 of sugar, 4,572,500 of dyewood, 1,391,465 of deer hides, 1,045,795 of leaf tobacco and 844,825 of rolled tobacco.[28]

The distribution of Louisiana's produce according to its markets in the United States was as indicated in Appendix table 54. As for the value of transactions with each port and the number of arrivals therefrom, consult Appendix table 55.[29]

The foregoing facts document unquestionably the importance of the United States for the commercial development of Louisiana during a time of adverse conditions. Yet, those very conditions, not all the will of the colonial authorities, were primarily responsible for the expansion and increased effectiveness of that relationship, although the favorable disposition of some of the local functionaries were also of marginal importance in permitting this trade.

Appendix table 54   Distribution of Louisiana's products by import destination

Cotton

Pounds	Destination
1,764,656	New York
490,453	Baltimore
206,575	Philadelphia
49,541	Salem
35,672	Wilmington
29,926	Charleston
16,456	Boston
16,401	Newburyport
16,190	Alexandria
Total 2,625,870	

Indigo

Pounds	Destination
456,486½	New York
264,660	Philadelphia
50,486	Charleston
24,740½	Baltimore
16,215	Alexandria
16,205	Wilmington
4,995	Boston
3,132	Newburyport
Total 836,920	

Sugar

Pounds	Destination
2,520,637	New York
1,165,834½	Philadelphia
1,005,621½	Baltimore
467,315	Alexandria
200,673	Salem
181,525	Charleston
26,733	Wilmington
18,581	Newburyport
10,650	Savannah
Total 5,597,570	

Appendix table 54   *continued*

Dyewood

Quintales	Destination
11,105½	Philadelphia
24,817	New York
4,768	Charleston
3,645	Baltimore
680	Alexandria
260	Wilmington
240	Boston
100	Newburyport
100	Salem
10	Savannah
Total 45,725½	

Dressed Deerskins

Pounds	Destination
623,064	New York
252,736	Philadelphia
40,274	Charleston
39,201	Salem
30,129	Wilmington
28,426	Boston
26,660	Baltimore
2,725	Savannah
Total 1,043,215	

Undressed deerskins

Pounds	Destination
171,276	New York
106,515	Philadelphia
42,029	Charleston
19,879	Salem
5,002	Wilmington
3,549	Baltimore
348,250	

Appendix table 54   *continued*

Leaf tobacco

Pounds	Destination
760,515	Philadelphia
270,474	New York
14,432	Baltimore
374	Wilmington
Total 1,045,795	

Rolled tobacco

Pounds	Destination
608,120	New York
94,571	Philadelphia
69,600	Baltimore
49,180	Wilmington
13,680	Charleston
7,500	Alexandria
2,000	Savannah
132	Boston
42	U.S.A.
Total 844,825	

Appendix table 55   Ship arrivals from United States' ports and value of imports and exports carried

New Orleans–Philadelphia commerce (1783–1803)					
Exports to Philadelphia			Imports from Philadelphia		
Year	Ships	Value (reales)	Year	Ships	Value (reales)
1783	1	4,033	1783	1	37,100
1784	–	–	1784	1	27,700
1788	–	–	1788	9	310,900
1789	1	4,800	1789	2	23,000
1790	1	25,535	1790	–	–
1792	1	667	1792	1	108,350
1793	28	1,018,750	1793	17	1,234,800
1794	14	838,233	1794	12	851,066
1795	7	534,266	1795	11	1,632,360
1796	9	509,333	1796	6	511,150
1797	1	48,750	1797	1	122,750
1798	3	43,733	1798	3	88,516
1799	5	66,350	1799	9	937,566
1800	17	195,183	1800	15	1,085,683
1801	15	395,030	1801	18	2,128,900
1802	17	446,366	1802	16	766,583
1803	–	–	1803	2	5,366
Total	160	4,131,029		124	9,871,790

New Orleans–New York commerce (1783–1803)					
Exports to New York			Imports from New York		
Year	Ships	Value (reales)	Year	Ships	Value (reales)
1793	1	5,183	1793	2	112,783
1794	9	663,633	1794	6	284,280
1795	11	669,950	1795	14	1,652,253
1796	11	718,333	1796	11	382,683
1797·	12	725,663	1797	20	2,337,572
1798	25	1,041,683	1798	25	2,648,639
1799	36	1,170,716	1799	44	4,993,266
1800	36	1,033,000	1800	26	2,394,666
1801	43	1,068,216	1801	24	2,779,066
1802	42	1,280,000	1802	23	2,388,066
1803	–	–	1803	3	175,133
Total	226	8,376,377		198	20,148,407

Appendix table 55 *continued*

New Orleans–Charleston commerce (1783–1803)

	Exports to Charleston			Imports from Charleston	
Year	Ships	Value (reales)	Year	Ships	Value (reales)
1793	1	36,000	1793	–	–
1794	1	47,433	1794	2	59,146
1795	7	153,650	1795	10	497,900
1796	3	232,383	1796	2	13,900
1797	3	157,250	1797	7	207,571
1798	1	1,374	1798	4	203,266
1799	3	11,566	1799	4	95,016
1800	4	6,666	1800	1	40,783
1801	22	207,383	1801	1	19,200
1802	5	26,850	1802	4	125,666
Total	50	880,555		35	1,262,448

New Orleans–Baltimore commerce (1783–1803)

	Exports to Baltimore			Imports from Baltimore	
Year	Ships	Value (reales)	Year	Ships	Value (reales)
1790	–	–	1790	1	65,716
1792	–	–	1792	1	51,200
1793	–	–	1793	2	125,816
1794	–	–	1794	4	139,917
1795	3	137,516	1795	5	367,766
1796	1	23,333	1796	2	24,283
1797	1	33,433	1797	1	17,750
1798	2	16,716	1798	5	385,383
1799	11	382,466	1799	7	1,033,450
1800	5	191,650	1800	7	339,700
1801	8	142,700	1801	7	787,433
1802	13	877,166	1802	8	419,383
1803	1	27,600	1803	–	–
Total	45	1,832,580		50	3,757,797

Appendix table 55   *continued*

New Orleans–Salem commerce (1783–1803)

Exports to Salem			Imports from Salem		
Year	Ships	Value (reales)	Year	Ships	Value (reales)
1799	1	72,732	1799	2	141,950
1800	2	104,650	1800	1	24,283
1801	2	42,533	1801	5	326,183
1802	1	45,900	1802	2	69,316
Total	6	265,815		10	561,732

New Orleans–Alexandria commerce (1783–1803)

Exports to Alexandria			Imports from Alexandria		
Year	Ships	Value (reales)	Year	Ships	Value (reales)
1798	–	–	1798	1	27,600
1799	3	120,350	1799	1	784,233
1800	6	279,566	1800	5	203,483
1801	1	616	1801	–	–
Total	10	400,532		7	1,015,316

New Orleans–New London commerce (1783–1803)

Exports to New London			Imports from New London		
Year	Ships	Value (reales)	Year	Ships	Value (reales)
1799	–	–	1799	1	10,433
1802	–	–	1802	2	33,083
Total	–	–		3	43,516

Appendix table 55 *continued*

New Orleans–Savannah commerce (1783–1803)

Exports to Savannah			Imports from Savannah		
Year	Ships	Value (reales)	Year	Ships	Value (reales)
1800	3	12,166	1800	2	144,050
1801	3	7,083	1801	1	124,333
1802	–	–	1802	2	16,833
Total	6	19,249		5	285,216

New Orleans–Rhode Island commerce (1783–1803)

Exports to Rhode Island			Imports from Rhode Island		
Year	Ships	Value (reales)	Year	Ships	Value (reales)
1784	–	–	1784	1	20,109
1797	–	–	1797	1	691,283
Total	–	–		2	711,392

New Orleans–Portland commerce (1783–1803)

Exports to Portland			Imports from Portland		
Year	Ships	Value (reales)	Year	Ships	Value (reales)
1800	–	–	1800	1	12,933
1802	–	–	1802	1	1,083
Total	–	–		2	14,016

New Orleans–Norfolk commerce (1783–1803)

Exports to Norfolk			Imports from Norfolk		
Year	Ships	Value (reales)	Year	Ships	Value (reales)
1795	1	400	1795	–	–
Total	1	400		–	–

Appendix table 55   *continued*

New Orleans–Wilmington commerce (1783–1803)

Exports to Wilmington			Imports from Wilmington		
Year	Ships	Value (reales)	Year	Ships	Value (reales)
1795	1	32,200	1795	–	–
1799	4	129,816	1799	4	201,016
1800	2	20,916	1800	3	136,950
1801	2	45,133	1801	3	169,633
Total	9	228,065		10	507,599

New Orleans–Boston commerce (1783–1803)

Exports to Boston			Imports from Boston		
Year	Ships	Value (reales)	Year	Ships	Value (reales)
1794	1	168,633	1794	–	–
1797	1	14,416	1797	1	14,143
1798	–	–	1798	1	7,450
1799	1	35,850	1799	2	137,300
1801	2	14,866	1801	6	332,050
1802	1	9,283	1802	4	281,916
Total	6	243,048		14	772,859

New Orleans–Newburyport commerce (1783–1803)

Exports to Newburyport			Imports from Newburyport		
Year	Ships	Value (reales)	Year	Ships	Value (reales)
1799	–	–	1799	1	43,833
1800	2	43,450	1800	1	106,550
1801	2	9,116	1801	2	168,783
1802	–	–	1802	1	35,633
Total	4	52,566		5	354,799

Appendix table 55   *continued*

New Orleans–Carolina commerce (1783–1803)

Exports to Carolina			Imports from Carolina		
Year	Ships	Value (reales)	Year	Ships	Value (reales)
1783	–	–	1783	1	19,033
Total	–	–		1	19,033

New Orleans–U.S.A. (unidentified) commerce (1783–1803)

Exports to U.S.A.			Imports from U.S.A.		
Year	Ships	Value (reales)	Year	Ships	Value (reales)
1794	1	14,651	1794	–	–
1798	–	–	1798	1	70,783
1801	1	283	1801	–	–
Total	2	14,934		1	70,783

Abbreviations

AGI	Archivo General de Indias
AGNC	Archivo General de la Nación, Caracas
AGNM	Archivo General de la Nación, Mexico
AGS	Archivo General de Simancas
AHN	Archivo Histórico Nacional (Madrid)
APC	Archives publiques du Canada
ASP, CN	*American State Papers, Commerce and Navigation*
BN	Biblioteca Nacional, Madrid
DGT	Dirección General del Tesoro
DNA	*Documentos relativos a la independencia de norteamérica existentes en archivos españoles*
GM	Guerra Moderna
HAHR	*The Hispanic American Historical Review*
HSP	Historical Society of Pennsylvania
INA	Archives of the Insurance Company of North America
Indif.	Indiferente
JALBC	*Journaux de l'assemblée legislative du Bas-Canada*
JALC	*Journaux de l'assemblée legislative des Canadas*
JLAS	*Journal of Latin American Studies*
NYHS	New York Historical Society
	Papers of the Continental Congress: National Archives of the United States, Papers of the Continental Congress, 1774–1789.
RAC	*Rapport des Archives Canadiennes*
	State Dept., American Letters: National Archives of the United States, Domestic Letters of the Department of State
TAm	*The Americas*

Notes

Chapter one

1. For an earlier version of this thesis see Jacques A. Barbier, 'Peninsular finance and colonial trade: the Dilemma of Charles IV's Spain', *JLAS*, 12 (1980), 21–37.

2. John Fisher, 'Imperial "free trade" and the Hispanic economy, 1778–1796', *JLAS*, 13 (1981), 33; and Javier Cuenca Esteban, 'Statistics of Spain's colonial trade, 1792–1820: consular duties, cargo inventories and balance of trade', *HAHR*, 61 (1981), 398–401.

3. See Fisher, 'Imperial "free trade" and the Hispanic economy', 42: and Cuenca, 'Statistics of Spain's colonial trade', 411. Both authors, using official statistics, find substantial proportions of Spanish products in exports to the colonies. None the less, it has been credibly argued that, in this matter, official sources were an exercise in self-deception. See Stanley J. Stein, 'Concepts and realities of Spanish economic growth, 1759–1789 — reality in microcosm: the debate over trade with America, 1785–1789', *Historia Ibérica*, 1 (1973), 111–19.

4. C. H. Haring, *The Spanish empire in America* (New York, 1947), 319–20, briefly describes the 1765–89 evolution of trade legislation.

5. Bibiano Torres Ramírez and Javier Ortiz de la Tabla (eds.), *Reglamento y aranceles reales para el comercio libre de España a Indias de 12 de octubre de 1778* (Seville, 1978), 4.

6. Javier Ortiz de la Tabla, *Comercio exterior de Veracruz, 1778–1821* (Seville, 1978), 167–223.

7. The problem of currency drain is treated in Jacques A. Barbier, 'Venezuelan "libranzas", 1788–1807: from economic nostrum to fiscal imperative', *TAm*, 37 (1981), 457–78.

8. For an analysis of the role of Madrid in the economy of central Spain see David R. Ringrose, 'Perspectives on the economy of eighteenth century Spain', *Historia Ibérica*, 1 (1973), 59–101.

9. During the struggle against Napoleonic France, of course, Cadiz became Spain's temporary capital and the power balance correspondingly shifted.

10. Theoretical foundations for such views may be found in John L. Phelan, 'Authority and flexibility in the Spanish imperial bureaucracy', *Administrative Sciences Quarterly*, 5 (1960), 47–65; and Frank Jay Moreno, 'The Spanish colonial system: a functional approach', *Western Political Quarterly*, 20 (1967), 308–20.

11. See John L. Phelan, *The kingdom of Quito in the seventeenth century* (Madison, 1967); and Mark A. Burkholder and D. S. Chandler, 'Creole appointments and the sale of audiencia positions in the Spanish empire under the early Bourbons', *JLAS*, 4 (1972), 187–206.

12. D. A. Brading, *Miners and merchants in Bourbon Mexico, 1763–1810* (New York, 1970), 33–92, presents the most exaggerated view of this process. See also Mark A. Burkholder, 'From creole to peninsular: the transformation of the audiencia of Lima', *HAHR*, 52 (1972), 395–415; Mark A. Burkholder and D. S. Chandler, *From impotence to authority: the Spanish Crown and the American audiencias, 1687–1808* (Columbia, Missouri, 1977); and Leon G. Campbell, 'A colonial establishment: creole domination of the audiencia of Lima in the late eighteenth century', *HAHR*, 52 (1972), 1–25.

13. Jacques A. Barbier, 'Elite and cadres in Bourbon Chile', *HAHR*, 52 (1972), 416–35; 'Tradition and reform in Bourbon Chile: Ambrosio O'Higgins and public finance', *TAm*, 34 (1978), 381–99; and *Reform and politics in Bourbon Chile, 1755–1796* (Ottawa, 1980).

14. By 'superior governments' are meant those characterized by nominal autonomy in fiscal matters.

15. The standard treatment in English remains Richard Herr, *The eighteenth century revolution in Spain* (Princeton, 1958).

16. For a critique of current interpretations of colonial policy see Jacques A. Barbier, 'The culmination of the Bourbon reforms, 1787–1792', *HAHR*, 57 (1977), 51–68.

17. Barbara H. Stein, 'Concepts and realities of Spanish economic growth, 1759–1789: growth and model and perception of achievement', *Historia Ibérica*, 1 (1973), 110.

18. Barbier, 'The culmination of the Bourbon reforms', 62–3.

19. Barbier, 'The culmination of the Bourbon reforms', 67.

20. Barbier, 'Peninsular finance and colonial trade', 27–8.

21. AGI, Indif., legs. 2466 and 2467.

22. AGI, Consulados, libro 97, letter to Urquijo, April 26, 1799.

23. R.O. of January 14, 1801, in AGI, Ultramar, leg. 733; and Viana to Vega, October 3, 1801, in AGI, Indif., leg. 1347.

24. Jacques A. Barbier and Herbert S. Klein, 'Revolutionary wars and public finances: the Madrid treasury, 1784–1807', *Journal of Economic History*, 41 (1981), 315–39.

Chapter two

1. *Papeles sobre la toma de la Habana por los Ingleses en 1762* (Havana, 1948); and David Syrett (comp.), *The siege and capture of Havana, 1762* (London, 1970).

2. Franklin W. Knight, 'Origins of wealth and the sugar revolution in Cuba, 1750–1850', *HAHR*, 57 (1977), 241–2.

3. Nancy Farriss, *Crown and clergy in colonial Mexico, 1759–1821* (London, 1968), 134.

4. 'Plan de independencia de México en 1765', in Juan Hernández y Dávalos (comp.), *Documentos para la guerra de México de 1808–1821* (6 vols., Mexico, 1877), vol. 2, 620–3; and 'Notas acerca de una pretendida conspiración ...', *Boletín del Archivo General de la Nación* (Mexico), 9 (1938), 769–79.

5. In Mariano Cuevas (ed.), *Tesoros documentales del Mexico: siglo XVIII* (Mexico, 1944), 321–33, 361–98.

6. Edith B. Couturier, 'Family economy and inheritance in eighteenth-century Puebla: a study of five families', a paper presented at the Middle Atlantic Conference on Latin American studies, Philadelphia, April 2, 1981.

7. Stanley F. Chyet, *Lopez of Newport* (Detroit, 1970); Harry Bernstein, *Origins of inter-American interest, 1700–1812* (1945; reprint edn, New York, 1965), 26.

8. Julius Goebel, *The struggle for the Falkland islands* (1927; reprint edn, New York, 1971).

9. See Ricardo Donoso, *Un letrado del siglo XVIII, el Dr. Jose Perfecto de Salas* (2 vols., Buenos Aires, 1963), vol. 1, 339–405.

10. Luis Miguel Enciso Recio (comp.), *'La Gaceta de Madrid' y 'El Mercurio Histórico y Político, 1776–1781'* (Valladolid, 1957), 66, 83–6.

11. James A. Lewis, 'Las damas de la Havana, el precursor, y Francisco de Saavedra: a note on Spanish participation in the battle of Yorktown', *TAm*, 37 (1980), 83–101.

12. See Peggy K. Liss, *Atlantic empires: the network of trade and revolution, 1713–1826* (Baltimore, 1983), chaps. 5–6.

13. Forrest McDonald, *We, the people* (Chicago, 1958), 366.

14. Eduardo Arcila Farías, 'Ideas económicas en Nueva España en el siglo XVIII', *El Trimestre Económico*, 14 (1947), 74–77; Francisco Morales Padrón, 'México y la independencia de Hispano-américa en 1781 según un comisionario regio: Francisco de Saavedra', in *Homenaje a D. Ciriaco Pérez-Bustamante* (Madrid, 1969), 335–58; and see James A. Lewis, 'Nueva España y los esfuerzos para abastecer la Habana, 1779–1783', *Anuario de Estudios Americanos*, 33 (1976), 101–26.

15. Mauro Páez-Pumar (ed.), *Los proclamas de Filadelfia de 1774 y 1775 en la Caracas de 1777* (Caracas, 1973).

16. *DNA*, vol. 1, pt. 1, 52.

17. Cited by Morales Padron, 'Mexico y la independencia ...'.

18. Alexander von Humboldt, *Political essay on the kingdom of New Spain*, tr. John Black (4 vols., London, 1811), vol. 1, 205.

19. Ella Dunbar, *La gaceta de Lima del siglo XVIII. Facsimiles ...* (Lima, 1965), October 27 – Decembêr 16, 1776.

20. Carlos E. Múñoz-Oraá, 'Pronóstico de la independencia de América y un proyecto de monarquias en 1781', *Revista de Historia de América*, 50 (1960), 439–73.

21. Vicente Palacio Atard, *Areche y Guirior*, (Seville, 1946); Eunice J. Gates, 'Don José Antonio de Areche: his own defense', *HAHR*, 8 (1928), 14–42; the quotation is from Leon G. Campbell, 'A colonial establishment: creole domination of the audiencia of Lima during the late eighteenth century', *HAHR*, 52 (1972), 15.

22. Cited in Francisco Posada, *El movimiento revolucionario de los comuneros neogranadinos en el siglo XVIII*, 2nd edn (Mexico, 1975), 24.

23. John L. Phelan, *The people and the king* (Madison, 1978), 158.

24. *Archivo del General Miranda* (24 vols., Caracas, 1929–50), vol. 8, 9.

25. Eugenio Pereira Salas, *Los primeros contactos entre Chile y los Estados Unidos, 1778–1808* (Santiago de Chile, 1971); E. Pereira Salas, *Buques norteamericanos en Chile a fines de la era colonial (1788–1810)* (Santiago de Chile, 1936); Bernstein, *Origins*.

26. Jaime Jaramillo Uribe, 'Esclavos y señores en la sociedad colombiana del siglo XVIII', *Anuario Colombiano de Historia Social y Cultura*, 1 (1963); Rolando Mellafe, *La esclavitud en Hispanoamérica* (Buenos Aires, 1964), translated as *Negro slavery in Latin America* (Berkeley, 1975); Knight, 'Origins of wealth', Miguel Acosta Saignes, *Vida de los esclavos negros en Venezuela* (Caracas, 1967); and James F. King, 'Evolution of the free slave trade principle in Spanish colonial administration', *HAHR*, 22 (1942), 36–45.

27. See *DNA*, vol. 1, pt. 1, 382; pt. 2, 659; Guillermo Céspedes del Castillo, *Lima y Buenos Aires* (Seville, 1947); 177–9; Susan M. Socolow, *The merchants of Buenos Aires, 1778–1810* (Cambridge, 1978); Jacques A. Barbier, *Reform and politics in Bourbon Chile, 1755–1796* (Ottawa, 1980), 113*ff.*; John Fisher, *Silver mines and silver miners in colonial Peru, 1776–1824* (Liverpool, 1977); David A. Brading, *Miners and merchants in Bourbon Mexico, 1763–1810* (Cambridge, 1971), 126; Brian R. Hamnett, *Politics and trade in southern Mexico, 1750–1821* (Cambridge, 1971); Charles H. Harris, 3rd, *A Mexican family empire* (Austin, 1975), 85–6; and Eduardo Arcila Farías, *Economía colonial de Venezuela*, 2nd edn (2 vols., Caracas, 1973).

28. Cited in Eduardo Arcila Farías, *El real consulado de Caracas* (Caracas, 1957), 34; see Jacques A. Barbier, 'The culmination of the Bourbon reforms, 1787–1792', *HAHR*, 57 (1977), 51–68; Barbier, *Reform*, 157–8; his exchange with John Fisher in *HAHR*, 58 (1978), 87–90; Barbier, 'Peninsular finance and colonial trade: the dilemma of Charles IV's Spain', *JLAS*, 12 (1980), 21–37; Mark A. Burkholder, 'The Council of the Indies in the late eighteenth century: a new perspective', *HAHR*,

56 (1976), 404–23; and Barbara H. and Stanley J. Stein, 'Concepts and realities of Spanish economic growth, 1759–1789', *Historia Ibérica*, 1 (1973), especially 108–17.

29. Barbier, 'Culmination', 57–58, 62.

30. Stein and Stein 'Concepts'.

31. See King 'Evolution'; and above, note 28. Free trade meant the opening of more imperial ports to trade with Spain. See Liss, *Atlantic empires*, for the evolution of policies of free trade and the meaning of the term.

32. Emilio Ravignani, 'El virreinato del Río de la Plata (1776–1810)', in Ricardo Levene (ed.), *Historia de la nación Argentina*, 2nd edn (10 vols., Buenos Aires, 1936–42), vol. 4, 197–201; Socolow *Merchants*; and German O.E. Tjarks, *El consulado de Buenos Aires y sus proyecciones en la historia del Río de la Plata* (2 vols., Buenos Aires, 1962), vol. 1, 374–85.

33. Conde de Revillagigedo, *El comercio exterior y su influjo en la economía de la Nueva España (1793)* (Mexico, 1960), 36–7.

34. José Antonio Alzate Y Ramirez, *Gacetas de literatura de Mexico* (4 vols., Puebla, 1831), vol. 3, 74–7; and see vols. 2 and 3, *passim*.

35. Pedro Fermín de Vargas, *''Pensamientos politicos' y 'Memoria sobre la población del Nuevo Reino de Granada'* (Bogota, 1966), 15, 98–9, 104; his 'Notas' and 'Diálogo' are in Rafael Gomez Hoyos, *La revolucion granadina, ideario de una generación y una época* (2 vols., Bogotá, 1962), vol. 1, 290–99.

36. Antonio Narino, 'Ensayo de un nuevo plan de administración en el Nuevo Reino de Granada, de 16 de noviembre de 1797', in José María Vergara, *Vida y escritos de General Narino* (Bogotá, 1946).

37. *Archivo del General Miranda*, vol. 4, 404.

38. Roberto María Tisnes J., *Movimientos pre-independientes gran-colombianos* (Bogota, 1962), 116–22.

39. Robert J. Shafer, *The economic societies in the Spanish world* (Syracuse, 1958), 353–4; D.S. Chandler, 'Jacobo de Villaurrutia and the audiencia of Guatemala; 1794–1804', *TAm*, 32 (1976), 402–12.

40. Francisco de Arango y Parreno, 'Discurso sobre la agricultura en la Habana y medios de fomentarla (1792)', in his *De la factoria a la colonia* (Havana, 1936).

41. Manuel Belgrano, *Estudios económicos* (Buenos Aires, 1954), 49.

42. Barbier, 'Peninsular finance'; Jacques A. Barbier, 'Venezuelan "libranzas", 1788–1807: from economic nostrum to fiscal imperative', *TAm*, 37 (1981), 457–78; and his essay below.

43. Julio LeRiverend Brusone, 'Relaciones entre Nueva Espana y Cuba (1518–1820), *Revista de Historia de América*, 37–8 (1954), 77–9; John Coatsworth, 'American trade with European colonies in the Caribbean and South America, 1790–1812', *William and Mary Quarterly*, 24 (1967), 243–65.

44. Eduardo Arcila Farías, *Economía colonial de Venezuela*, (Mexico, 1946), 360–1.

45. Humboldt, *Political essay*, vol. 4, 94, 109, 115–23, 125, 131; Brian R. Hamnett, 'Mercantile rivalry and peninsular division: the consulados of New Spain and the impact of the Bourbon reforms, 1789–1824', *Ibero-Amerikanisches Archiv*, 2 (1976), 287–8; R.S. Smith, 'Shipping in the port of Veracruz, 1790–1821', *HAHR*, 23 (1943), 5–20; R.S. Smith, 'Indigo production and trade in colonial Guatemala', *HAHR*, 39 (1959), 200–11; Chandler, 'Jacobo de Villaurrutia', 407–11; Miles Wortman, 'Government revenue and economic trends in Central America, 1787–1819', *HAHR*, 55 (1975), 259.

46. José de Cos Iriberri, 'Memoria de 1797', in Miguel Cruchaga, *Estudio sobre la organización económica y la hacienda pública de Chile* (3 vols., Madrid, 1929), vol. 3, 248.

47. Ricardo Donoso, *Antonio José de Irisarri, escritor y diplomatico*, 2nd edn

(Santiago de Chile, 1966), 13; Harry Bernstein, *Making an inter-American mind* (Gainesville, 1961), 23; Bernstein, *Origins*, 56.

48. Tjarks, *El consulado*, vol. 1, 133−4, 378, 385; Tulio Halperín Donghi, *Politics, economics, and society in Argentina in the revolutionary period* (Cambridge, 1975), 11−34, 89.

49. Gómez Hoyos, *La revolución granadina*, vol. 2, 267−8; and see vol. 2, 250−66.

50. Hamnett, 'Mercantile rivalry', 287−92; Coatsworth, 'American trade', 252, 255; *DNA*, vol. 1, pt. 2, 820−1, vol. 3, pt. 1, 77*ff.*, 91−2, 348; Arthur P. Whitaker, *The United States and the independence of Latin America, 1800−1830* (1941; reprint edn, New York, 1962), 6−9; Pereira Salas, *primeros contactos*, 26−7; Hernan Asdrubal Silva, 'The United States and the River Plate: interrelationships and influences between two revolutions', in Joseph S. Tulchin (ed.), *Hemispheric perspectives on the United States* (Westport, 1978); and so on.

51. Viscardo's *carta* appears in Miguel Batllori, *El abate Viscardo* (Caracas, 1953).

52. *Telegrafo Mercantil* (facsimile), (Buenos Aires, 1914−15); Ricardo Caillet-Bois, 'El real consulado y una tentativa para contrater maestros curtidores en los Estados Unidos en 1801', *Boletín de Instituto de Historia Argentina Americana* (2nd ser.), 1 (1956), 265−68.

53. Miguel Luis Amunátegui, *Los precursores de la independencia de Chile*, (3 vols., Santiago, 1909−10), vol. 3, 445−9.

54. Humboldt, *Political essay*, vol. 1, 154.

55. Francois R. J. DePons, *A voyage to the eastern part of Terra Firme ...*, (5 vols., New York, 1806), vol. 1.

56. The literature is extensive; I attempt a résumé of what is known to date in *Atlantic empires*, chaps. 5 and 8.

57. Humberto Tandrón, 'The consulado of Caracas and Venezuela's overseas trade, 1793−1811' (Ph.D. diss., Columbia University, 1970), 108−9, 139−40, 153−4, 165, 176−7, 180−2, 194 note 42; Harold A. Bierck, 'Tobacco marketing in Venezuela, 1798−1799: an aspect of Spanish mercantilistic revisionism', *Business History Review*, 39 (1965), 489−502; Barbier, 'Venezuelan "libranzas"'; and his essay below.

58. Gómez Hoyos, *La revolución granadina*, vol. 2, 268−72.

59. Coatsworth, 'American trade'.

60. Sergio Villalobos, 'El comercio extranjero a fines de la dominacíon española', *Journal of Inter-American Studies*, 4 (1962), 630−2.

61. Pereira Salas, *primeros contactos*, 177, 195, 216, 256, 293−4; *DNA*, as cited above, note 50.

62. Ricardo Levene (ed.), *Los sucesos de mayo contados por sus actores* (Buenos Aires, 1928), 60−71; Dorothy B. Goebel, 'British trade to the Spanish colonies, 1798−1823', *American Historical Review*, 43 (1938), 288−320.

63. Hernández y Dávalos, *Documentos*, vol. 1, 490−2; Servando Teresa de Mier, *Memorias* (2 vols., Mexico, 1946), vol. 2, 27.

64. Tandrón, 'The consulado', 108−9, and *passim*; and *cf*. the essay by Manuel Lucena S., below.

65. Camilo Torres, 'Memorial de agravios', in Gómez Hoyos, *La revolución granadina*, vol. 2, 19*ff.*; Ignacio de Herrera's 'Reflexiones' in Javier Ocampo, *El proceso ideologico de la emancipación* (Tunja, 1974), 548−62.

66. Frutos Joaquín Gutierrez de Caviedes and Camilo Torres, 'Motivos que han obligado al Nuevo Reino de Granada a resumir los derechos de la soberania ...' (Santa Fé de Bogota, September 25, 1810), in *Proceso histórico del 20 de julio de 1810 (documentos)*, (Bogota, 1960), 210−49.

Chapter three

* The author is indebted to the Department of Economics of the University of Waterloo for wide-ranging support, financial and otherwise, in the preparation of this chapter; and to the Social Sciences and Humanities Research Council of Canada for a travel grant to present a short version of this chapter to the Forty-Fourth International Congress of Americanists (Manchester, England, September 5–10, 1982). Professor John J. McCusker made a major contribution to the estimation of tonnage figures into the final version. John H. Coatsworth, Allan J. Kuethe, James A. Lewis and Linda K. and Richard J. Salvucci also made useful comments on the short version. Remaining shortcomings and errors are the author's own.

1. Timothy Pitkin, *A statistical view of the commerce of the United States of America* ..., 1st edn (Hartford, 1816), 192.
2. References to the official export values to this area of the world abound in the secondary literature, but only John H. Coatsworth has assembled and analyzed them in a systematic way: 'American trade with European colonies in the Caribbean and South America, 1790–1812', *The William and Mary Quarterly*, 3rd ser., 24 (1967), 243–266; see also Roy F. Nichols, 'Trade relations and the establishment of the United States consulates in Spanish America, 1779–1809', *HAHR*, 13 (1933), 289–313: notes 11, 21, 25, 44, 50, 67, and 74; Dorothy B. Goebel, 'British trade to the Spanish colonies, 1796–1823', *American Historical Review*, 43 (1938), 288–320, specially 301; and Arthur P. Whitaker, *The United States and the independence of Latin America, 1800–1830* (Baltimore, 1941), 23, 53, 116–17, and 130–1.
3. Import *quantities* have occasionally been quoted instead for analytical purposes; see, for example, Nichols, 'Trade relations', notes 11, 21, 25, 50 and 67.
4. Douglass C. North, 'The United States balance of payments, 1790–1860', in *Trends in the American Economy in the Nineteenth Century*, Studies in Income and Wealth of the National Bureau of Economic Research, 24 (Princeton, 1960), 573–627.
5. See Douglass C. North, *The economic growth of the United States 1790–1860* (New York, 1961), 53–4.
6. See Donald R. Adams, Jr., 'American neutrality and prosperity, 1793–1808: a reconsideration', *Journal of Economic History*, 40 (1980), 734–5, and Claudia D. Goldin and Frank D. Lewis, 'The role of exports in American economic growth during the Napoleonic wars, 1793 to 1807', *Explorations in Economic History*, 17 (1980), 23–5.
7. Coatsworth, 'American trade with European colonies'. See, especially, his economic explanation of slow growth in domestic exports to the Spanish West Indies (259–61).
8. See Antonio García-Baquero González, *Comercio colonial y guerras revolucionarias: la decadencia económica de Cádiz a raíz de la emancipación americana* (Seville, 1972); Javier Ortiz de la Tabla Ducasse, *Comercio exterior de Veracruz 1778–1821: crisis de dependencia* (Seville, 1978); John R. Fisher, 'Imperial "free trade" and the Hispanic economy, 1778–1796', *JLAS*, 13 (1981), 25–56; and Javier Cuenca Esteban, 'Statistics of Spain's colonial trade, 1792–1820: consular duties, cargo inventories, and balances of trade', *HAHR*, 61 (1981), 381–428.
9. Tax rates have also been deducted for the valuation of re-export quantities, but, for domestic exports, full wholesale prices have been used instead: see Appendix, sections A and C. James F. Shepherd and Gary M. Walton, unlike North, also drew upon official quantities and wholesale prices to estimate import and export values in 1768–72, but in no case do they appear to have allowed for tax rates. See their *Shipping, maritime trade, and the economic development of colonial North America* (Cambridge, 1972), 207.

10. The reasons for developing a new method for the estimation of tonnage, as opposed to those used by North and others, are explained in Appendix, section B. In an earlier version of the present chapter, weights and volumes were converted into cubic tons with coefficients of specific density taken from modern handbooks of chemistry and physics, packaging manuals, and other sources on the handling of bulk materials. The present conversions to cargo tons are based, for the most part, on a table of colonial stowage factors compiled by John J. McCusker: 'The tonnage of ships engaged in British colonial trade during the eighteenth century', *Research in Economic History*, 6 (1981), 91–4. The author is indebted to Professor McCusker for calling his attention to the actual methods by which cargo tons were reckoned at the time.

11. Douglass North, as a point of departure for the pricing of tonnage, used a single rate per ton on the United States to France: 'United States balance of payments', 598. The freight rate index adopted in the present paper is that developed by North, 596.

12. Earlier studies of the United States' balance of payments in this period assumed that insurance costs were a constant proportion of trade values. See North, 'United States balance of payments', 600, and Shepherd and Walton, *Shipping*, 131.

13. Shepherd and Walton set a lower bound for rates of return on the basis of percentage markups by commission agents, 133. North's estimates of brokers commissions and insurance credits are based, inevitably, on informed speculation. See North, 'United States balance of payments', 599–600.

14. Douglass North and Alan Heston, 'The estimation of shipping earnings in historical studies of the balance of payments', *Canadian Journal of Economics and Political Science*, 26 (1960), 266.

15. These include, in addition to the official export series, the estimates of import values CIF (see the comparisons with contemporary data in Appendix), the merchandise trade balances on CIF imports, the import prices and the series of gross customs revenue. Less reliable, but still highly plausible, are the breakdowns of domestic and foreign exports for 1790–1802 (which derive from official quantities of incompletely enumerated goods), and the export price indexes and related series (which are based on estimated weights): see Appendix, sections C and G.

16. These include, in addition to the series of freight and insurance costs, the FOB values of imports, which have been obtained by subtraction from CIF import values.

17. See Appendix, section E.

18. North, 'United States balance of payments', 596; James F. Shepherd and Gary M. Walton, 'Economic change after the American revolution: prewar and postwar comparisons of maritime shipping and trade', *Explorations in Economic History*, 13 (1976), 415.

19. See p. 39.

20. The importance of contraband trade in this period is beyond question, but no attempts have been made to estimate its overall extent. For examples, see among many other works, Charles C. Griffin, 'Privateering from Baltimore during the Spanish American wars of independence', *Maryland Historical Magazine*, 35 (1940), 1–25; Theodore S. Currier, *Los cruceros del 'General San Martín'* (Buenos Aires, 1944); José L. Franco, *Política continental americana de España en Cuba, 1812–1830*, 2nd edn (Havana, 1964), 117–200; and Sergio R. Villalobos, *El comercio y la crisis colonial: un mito de la Independencia* (Santiago de Chile, 1968), 145–9, and Eugenio Pereira Salas, *Los primeros contactos entre Chile y los Estados Unidos 1778–1809* (Santiago de Chile, 1971), 213–29.

21. Freight earnings from this trade can be estimated for the United States as a whole, but not for Spanish America and the Philippines. See Appendix, section B.

22. The official records of ship sales started in 1815, but no breakdowns were given by areas of the world: see United States Congress, *ASP*, Class 4, *CN* (2 vols., Washington, D.C., 1932–4) vol. 2, 42 *passim*.

23. See Appendix, section E.

24. The series of constant import values at ports of origin, given in table 12 and displayed in fig. 1, have been obtained by deflation of current values at ports of origin with prices at United States' ports; consequently, these series incorporate moderate upward biases due to fluctuations in freight and insurance costs. See Appendix, section G.

25. Breakdowns of domestic and foreign exports prior to 1803 had to be estimated from official quantities of incompletely enumerated commodities. See Appendix, section C.

26. This statement is based on estimates of Spanish colonial trade, presented in Cuenca Esteban, 'Statistics of Spain's colonial trade, 1792–1820', 381–428. The relevant data were displayed in p. 411, chart 1.

27. See Cuenca Esteban, 'Statistics of Spain's colonial trade, 1792–1820', p. 420, chart 3.

28. Exports peaked in 1809 and imports in 1810: annual data in B. R. Mitchell and P. Deane, *Abstract of British historical statistics* (Cambridge, 1971), 311. Unfortunately, the official values of British trade in this period were calculated at constant prices of the late seventeenth century; for definitive elaboration and analysis of the export and import totals, see Albert H. Imlah, *Economic elements in the Pax Britannica* (Cambridge, Mass., 1958), 20–41, and Ralph Davis, *The industrial revolution and British overseas trade* (Atlantic Highlands, New Jersey, 1979), 77–86.

29. Cited in Jeffrey A. Frankel's recent analysis of the differential impact of the embargo of the United States and Great Britain: 'The 1807–1809 embargo against Great Britain', *Journal of Economic History*, 42 (1982), 295.

30. See Whitaker's analysis in *The United States and the independence of Latin America*, 47–52, and Goebel, 'British trade to the Spanish colonies', 299, note 48.

31. The importance of this shift in Spanish policy was stressed by Nichols, 'Trade relations', 310–11.

32. Estimates of Spanish colonial trade in these years are given in Cuenca Esteban, 'Statistics of Spain's colonial trade', 399.

33. Calculated from Appendix, table 8, columns 2 and 5.

34. The official trade figures of the United States cover fiscal years ending September 30.

35. Annual British data in the first reference given in note 28.

36. Calculated from commodity values at constant prices of 1791. Current import values of sugar, molasses, coffee, and cocoa are given in Appendix, table 5.

37. See Appendix, sections G and C.

38. See Whitaker, *The United States and the independence of Latin America*, 127–30, and Coatsworth, 'American trade with European colonies', 254. Unfortunately, the official trade statistics of the United States seldom distinguish, prior to 1821, between the Spanish West Indies and 'other [Spanish] American colonies'.

39. See Appendix, section B.

40. 226.7 dollars per ton for sugar and 82.2 dollars per ton for molasses: calculated from official quantities, modified wholesale prices, and stowage factors (sources given in *infra*, Appendix, sections A and B). The difference between these values per ton seems large enough to warrant the analysis that follows. It should be borne in mind that the present freight rates, unlike the tonnage figures, are based on global estimates rather than an actual quotations for individual commodities: see Appendix, section B.

41. See references in note 18.

42. See Appendix, section B and table 7, colum 1.
43. See Adams, 'American neutrality and prosperity', 723.
44. See Adams' index of shipbuilding costs for 1790–1807, 725.
45. See table 3, columns 1 and 2.
46. See sources in note 140.
47. This statement is based on Adams' index of shipbuilding costs (see note 44), extended to 1819 from the same sources, and, as far as possible, with similar methods.
48. Ralph Davis, *The rise of the English shipping industry in the seventeenth and eighteenth centuries* (Newton Abbot, Devon, 1962), 364.
49. Adams, 'American neutrality and prosperity', 726.
50. See data of wages for seamen out of Philadelphia in Donald R. Adams, 'Wage rates in the early national period: Philadelphia, 1785–1830', *Journal of Economic History*, 27 (1968), 422.
51. See North, 'United States balance of payments', 596.
52. Official data of shipbuilding activity reproduced in Adams, 'American neutrality and prosperity', 727. The evidence on costs is that referred to in note 47.
53. 25 dollars per month in 1809 compared with 20 dollars in 1806 and 8 dollars in 1808: Adams, 'Wage rates', 422.
54. Source referred to in notes 47 and 52.
55. A one-tail test based on Fisher's Z transformation shows that the correlation of freight costs with tonnage (0.983) is significantly greater, at the ninety-nine per cent level of probability, than that with freight rates (0.8) in the period 1795–1807.
56. Calculated from Appendix, table 7, columns 1, 2, and 7.
57. Sources and procedures in Appendix, section B.
58. See Vernon G. Setser, *The commercial reciprocity policy of the United States 1774–1829* (Philadelphia, 1937), 161–9, and Anna C. Clauder, *Commerce as affected by the wars of the French Revolution and Napoleon 1793–1812* (A. M. Kelley, New Jersey, 1972 reprint of the 1932 ed), *passim*.
59. Numbers of insurance companies in the years 1790–1807 reproduced from a contemporary printed source in North, *The economic growth of the United States*, 50.
60. These associations competed successfully with insurance companies up to 1824: see Isaac Smith Homans, (jt. ed.), *A cyclopedia of commerce and commercial navigation* (2 vols., New York, 1858), vol. 2, 1042.
61. See Stevens and Benecke [*sic*], *Treatises on average, and adjustments of losses in marine insurance, with notes by Willard Phillipe*, 2 edn (Boston, 1833), 2, 12–15; and Homans, *Cyclopedia*, vol. 2, 1042.
62. See Appendix, table 8.
63. See, for example, John Back McMaster, *Life and times of Stephen Girard, mariner and merchant* (2 vols., Philadelphia, 1818), vol. 2, 47.
64. See Appendix, section A and table 6.
65. 'Report to the Senate of the Committee of Commerce and Manufactures of 20 December 1819', *ASP, CN*, vol. 2, 395.
66. Data for the United States as a whole in Pitkin, *A statistical view*, 1835 edn, 334.
67. Estimates in North, 'United States balance of payments', 592.
68. Calculated from table 1, columns 4 and 1.
69. Trade on the shorter route from Cuba was by then far more important than that with the rest of Spanish America; in 1821, the first year when figures for Cuba were given separately, imports from the island were valued at 75.4% of total: calculated from Pitkin, *A statistical view*, 1835 edn, 222 and 225.
70. W. P. Sterns, 'The beginnings of American financial independence', *Journal of Political Economy*, 6 (1898), 191.
71. See North, 'United States balance of payments', 594.

72. Re-exports belong in the balance of services, but those of Spanish American and Philippine goods to the rest of the world can only be roughly estimated from the official sources. (See note 99, and table 1, column 1.)

73. No official figures for the former appear to have been given until 1821 (on this point see North, 'United States balance of payments', 599); data of imports of gold and silver from the Indies in 1821−32 are given in Pitkin, *A statistical view*, 1835 edn, 153−4.

74. As noted in the Appendix, the official figures of exports to the Indies are probably undervalued, while the present allowances for duty-free imports from this area may be insufficient (p. 60 and note 119).

75. Shorter distances to the Indies also account for the relatively small shares of freight earnings in the totals for the United States as a whole. On the other hand, the shares of United States' ships in the trade with the Indies were probably greater than average, thus making for larger freight earnings accrueing to United States' citizens.

76. United States' merchants occasionally accumulated balances abroad, and Stephen Girard of Philadelphia did charge interest of 6 per cent on sums retained by his agents in Havana. On the whole, however, the size of such foreign lending and borrowing does not appear to have been significant at this time. See Walter B. Smith and A. H. Cole, *Fluctuations in American business, 1790−1860* (Cambridge, Mass. 1935), 24 and American Philosophical Society, *Stephen Girard collection*, series 2, reel 47, frame 430: Yriarte y Lasa to Stephen Girard, Havana, 23 June 1810.

77. Re-exports to the Indies sharply declined in 1808−11. See Appendix, table 10, column 6. So did, perhaps, re-exports of Spanish American goods to the rest of the world. See table 1, column 1. Imports, by contrast, declined only marginally. See table 3, column 2.

78. See table 2, column 3.

79. See chart 3, middle panel.

80. See Appendix, section B.

81. As noted in the Appendix, North's total import figures are probably CIF values at United States' ports, like those arrived at in the present paper. See Appendix, section A. The freight rate adopted here as a point of departure for pricing the tonnage figures is that used by North, 42, as is the freight rate index, 45.

82. Calculated from North, 'United States balance of payments', 600, table A-4, annual data for 1790−91 and 1795−1819. North's export and import values add up, respectively, in millions of dollars, to 154.3 and 208.5 (1790−96, 1792−94 excluded), 362.2 and 435.8 (1797−1801), 206.0 and 232.0 (1802−04), 305.4 and 406.8 (1805−07), 202.7 and 266.1 (1808−11), 125.9 and 199.5 (1812−15), 333.0 and 474.2 (1816−19), and 1689.5 and 2222.9 (1790−1819, 1792−94 excluded).

83. The trade deficit in 1790−91 and 1795−1819 adds up to 533.4 million dollars and freight earnings to 594.1 million dollars: calculated from North, 'United States balance of payments', 600, table A-4.

84. The reader is reminded that the present estimates of freight earnings exclude those on trade not carried through United States' ports.

85. See North, 'United States balance of payments', 599−600. North's insurance debits in 1790−91 and 1795−1819 add up to 77 million dollars.

86. North's estimates of debt service costs for 1792−94 have been excluded at all stages for lack of official records of trade with the Indies. North's overall balances in these three years turn a net debit of 3 million dollars: calculated from North's 'United States balance of payments', 600, table A-4.

87. Sources in North, 'United States balance of payments', 601. Estimates of default range from 70 to 100 million dollars.

88. In his 'United States balance of payments', North apportioned a total

payment to Barbary pirates of 2 million dollars to the years 1794–96 in equal shares; the debit for 1794 is not included in the totals given in table 3, column 10. The United States' government paid a regular tribute to Algiers until 1810: Peter Earle, *Corsairs of Malta and Barbary* (London, 1970), 257.

89. North's estimates of specie flows are not included in column 10 because he could not trace the original sources. See North, 'United States balance of payments', 599, note 35. North's annual estimates are relatively small, tend to cancel one another, and add up to a net credit of 6.5 million dollars in 1790–91 and 1795–1819.

99. North assumed that the total foreign debt of the United States was 60 million dollars in 1789; he accumulated subsequent annual balances over the 1789 base: 'United States balance of payments', 588 and 600, table A-4.

91. Net freight earnings are here defined as gross freight earnings (table 3, column 3) minus charges at Spanish American and Philippine ports (table 7, column 6).

92. Reference in note 182. Shepherd and Walton allowed for minimum profits of 10% of both imports and exports, while the present estimates (table 3, column 6) add up to a mere 3.4%.

93. Pitkin, *A statistical view*, 1st edn, 192.

94. See note 74.

95. A total foreign debt of 60 million dollars in 1789 (see note 90) would have increased by 60% without the net balances with the Indies estimated in the preceding paragraph; overall, total net indebtedness would have more than doubled by 1819.

96. See Coatsworth, 'American trade with European colonies', 259 and note 43. Coatsworth linked supply rigidities to rising export prices; the present index of domestic export prices peaks in 1795 and declines later in the decade. See fig. 2.

97. Coatsworth, 'American trade', 259–61.

98. Calculated from Appendix, table 10, column 6 and North, 'United States balance of payments', 591–2, table A-2 (column 2 plus column 4 on p. 592). The shares of re-exports to the Indies in total re-exports are 3% (1790–96), 17% (1797–1801), 7% (1802–04), 14% (1805–07), 19% (1808–11), 13% (1812–15), and 16% (1816–19).

99. Figures of exports of Spanish American and Philippine goods to the rest of the world have not been found. The total for 1795–1819 has been roughly estimated as current imports CIF from the Indies times the ratios of drawbacks returned upon re-export (of the principal Spanish American commodities imported) over gross customs revenue on the same commodities. Sources in Appendix, section F. Shares of re-exports in imports CIF from the Indies are given in table 1, column 1.

100. The importance of re-exports and carrying earnings for north-eastern sub-sectors of merchants and industrialists now seems beyond question, but the controversy on a wide range of related issues is far from settled: see Adams, 'American neutrality and prosperity, 1793–1808, a reconsideration', *passim*.

101. See Goldin and Lewis' analysis of the short-term impact on income of improvements in the net barter terms of trade in the 1790s ('The role of exports', 8–10). The net barter terms of trade with the Indies appear to have increased strongly in most years when trade volumes were the largest: see *supra*, fig. 2 (bottom panel), and fig. 1.

102. See above, p. 29.

103. Table 4, columns 2 and 3 must be interpreted with caution, because drawbacks have been estimated from revenue shares returned for *total* exports of the principal commodities imported from the Indies. See Appendix, section F.

104. The basic government source on United States' trade by foreign countries and their dependencies is *ASP, CN*, vol. 1 for 1789–1815 and vol. 2 for 1815–23. Official trade figures were also given in contemporary printed sources, the most useful of which are Pitkin, *A statistical view*, 1st and 1835 edns, and Adam Seybert, *Statistical annals ... of the United States of America founded on official documents ...* (Philadelphia, 1818).

105. See 'Report 1819', *ASP, CN*, vol. 2, 391–2.

106. See 'Report 1819', *ASP, CN*, vol. 2, 393.

107. 'Report 1819', *ASP, CN*, vol. 2, 394. The estimates presented in this paper place goods subject to specific duties at 97% of total imports from Spanish America and the Philippines.

108. See North, 'United States balance of payments', 590–1.

109. See North, 'United States balance of payments', 594 and 597 (port costs). See also p. 52 above and note 126.

110. See North, 'United States balance of payments', 594–8 and North and Heston, 'The estimation of shipping earnings in historical studies of the balance of payments', 265–76.

111. The layout of the official accounts was discussed critically in the 'Report 1819', *ASP, CN*, vol. 2, 391–403.

112. This sample was compiled from *ASP, CN*, vols. 1 and 2, *passim*. It comprises fruits (almonds, currants, raisins, plums, prunes, figs, and other fruits), salt, spices (cloves, mace, nutmegs, pepper, pimento), chocolate, cocoa, coffee, tea (Bohea, Hyson, Souchong), tobacco, snuff and cigars, sugar (Havana brown, Havana white, loaf, lump, other sugars), molasses, wines and sherries (Tenerife, Madeira, Sherry, St. Lucar, Lisbon, Port, other wines), spirits from grain, from other materials, beer, ale and porter, cotton, cordage, duck ravens, indigo, iron, lead, soap, Spanish brown and other paints, and tallow and tallow candles.

113. Anne Bezanson, R.D. Gray, and M. Hussey, *Wholesale prices in Philadelphia, 1784–1861* (2 vols., Philadelphia, 1936), part 2, *passim*.

114. Exceptions were few and easily bridged with closely related price series. 'Other sugars' were valued with the average prices for Havana white and loaf; and 'other wines' with the averages for Tenerife cargo and Lisbon. Only rarely was it necessary to convert import weights and measures to the units given for the respective prices. See sources in note 154.

115. Conversion factors from relative to actual prices are given for most commodities. The conversion procedure is explained in Benzanson *et al.*, *Wholesale prices*, vol. 2, xxxviii.

116. Most of these rates were compiled from five sources: the annual tables of customs revenue given by Seybert for 1801–13 in *Statistical annals*, 398–424; the U.S. Tariff of 1794, text given in Tench Coxe, *A view of the United States of America ...* (New York, 1965), 459–69; U.S. Congress, *American State Papers, Finance* (3 vols.), vol. 1, 15, 107, 158, 276, 494, 642, 655–6; vol. 3, 36–8, 85–99 (Tariff of 12 February 1816); *ASP, CN*, vol. 1, 35–43; and Pitkin, *A statistical view*, 1835 edn, 499. Other rates had to be interpolated.

117. This range is given from contemporary evidence in Norman Sydney Buck, *The development of the organisation of Anglo-American trade, 1800–1850* (New Haven, Conn., 1925), 15; and in Fred Mitchell Jones, *Middlemen in the domestic trade of the United States, 1800–1860* (Urbana, 1937), 23.

118. A number of commodities had to be excluded from the sample for lack of parallel price series; but, judging from random valuations with related prices, these goods amount to less than two per cent of the total estimated import values.

119. Very rough estimates of total duty-free imports into the United States as a whole were given in the 'Report 1819', *ASP, CN*, vol. 2, 394. Douglass North's improved estimates amount, on the average, to a mere 2.95% of his total ('accepted') import values in the period 1790–1819 (calculated from 'United States balance of payments', 591–2, table A-2). The value of duty-free imports from Spanish America and the Philippines may well be greater, for such goods as dye woods, barilla, and raw hides and skins were exempted. A list of tax free imports is given in Seybert, *Statistical annals*, 389–90. The present allowances for duty-free imports would thus

be insufficient but resulting errors in the balance of merchandise trade would tend to be offset by a probable undervaluation of the official export figures. See p. 60.

120. A higher levy of 20% was applied to goods coming from beyond the Cape of Good Hope: 'Report 1819', *ASP, CN*, vol. 2, 393.

121. The 1819 report placed the true excess of CIF over FOB values at more than 35%, but this estimation included import duties (p. 395). For an analysis of the report's estimate see above, p. 39.

122. Sources and procedures in Appendix, section B.

123. Calculated from Pitkin, *A statistical view*, 1st edn, 214–17.

124. Seybert, *Statistical annals*, 266–73. Seybert, unlike Pitkin, stated that imports had been valued 'at the places of importation' (p. 266).

125. See North, 'United States balance of payments', 590–91.

126. See North, 'United States balance of payments', 593. One implication is that North's estimates of United States' indebtedness would be biased upwards, for his import debits seem too large; furthermore, he did not credit charges on foreign ships at United States' ports and made further adjustments elsewhere because he felt it necessary to counterbalance the debits implicit in the presumed 'at sea' valuation of imports. See 597 and 601.

127. For a critical survey of indirect estimations, see North and Heston, 'The estimation of shipping earnings', *passim*.

128. See McCusker, 'The tonnage of ships', 89–91.

129. Only five specific commodities are covered by the freight rates for the period 1790–1815 given by Douglass North, and they refer to British routes and are quoted in British currency: see *The economic growth of the United States*, Appendix I and references in note 18.

130. See McCusker, 'The tonnage of ships', 89–94.

131. See McCusker, 'The tonnage of ships', 89–90 and 98–9 (note 32).

132. The changes amount to 9% (pounds of sugar) and 21% (gallons, wine measure): stowage factors in McCusker, 'The tonnage of ships', 92 (for New York in 1771–2); and in Robert White Stevens, *On the stowage of ships and their cargoes, freights, charter parties, & &*, 2nd edn (London, 1859), 36–7 (factors given for New York and Baltimore). By contrast, the ton equivalent of flour (a major export to Spanish America and the Philippines) appears to have changed significantly in the intervening period of 87 years.

133. Cotton was reckoned at seven cwt. per ton on the assumption that this commodity was still inefficiently packed at low density (see McCusker, 'The tonnage of ships', 93, note g). Stowage factors for lesser commodities not covered by McCusker's list (fruit, spices, cordage, duck ravens, lead, and Spanish brown) have been reckoned at 2464 pounds per ton (the most common rate by far for goods measured in pounds).

134. Cited by Sterns, 'The beginnings of American financial independence', 194. Sterns' find was also used by North in his estimation of freight costs. See 'United States balance of payments', 598.

135. All mileage figures were compiled and calculated from George Goodall (ed.), *The mercantile marine atlas: specially designed for merchant shippers, exporters, and ocean travellers*, 14th edn (London, 1952), *passim*.

136. See J. Wade Caruthers, *American Pacific Ocean trade: its impact on foreign policy and continental expansion, 1784–1860* (New York, 1973), 73–4.

137. See Thomas R. and Mary C. McHale (eds.), *Early American–Philippine trade: the journal of Nathaniel Bowditch in Manila, 1796* (New Haven, Conn., 1962), Introduction, 7–8.

138. In the five years 1798–1802 at least, New York was by far the principal destination of ships leaving New Orleans for United States' ports. Data from Spanish customs records in Arthur Preston Whitaker, *The Mississippi question 1795–1803:*

a study in trade, politics, and diplomacy (1934, reprint edn, Gloucester, Mass., 1962), 137.

139. In 1806–07 at least, Baltimore appears to have developed close commercial ties with this area. Data of shipping from Baltimore to Veracruz in Robert S. Smith, 'Shipping in the port of Veracruz, 1790–1821', *HAHR*, 23 (1941), 13.

140. Data in Eugenio Pereira Salas, *Los primeros contactos entre Chile y los Estados Unidos 1778–1809, 347–53; C. L. Chandler*, 'United States merchant ships in the Río de la Plata (1801–1808), as shown by early newspapers', *HAHR*, 2 (1919), 26–8; and Nichols, 'Trade relations', 297, note 25.

141. Calculated from data supplied by Nichols, 'Trade relations', 297n, 303n, 311n, 313n.

142. One such instance is documented in C. L. Chandler, 'United States shipping in the La Plata region, 1809–1810', *HAHR*, 3 (1920), 167.

143. In later years at least, the greatest proportion of tonnage employed in the trade with Cuba belonged to New England. See Whitaker, *The United States and the independence of Latin America*, 129.

144. The import shares were calculated from Pitkin, *A statistical view*, 1835 edn, 222 and 225. The import share of the Spanish West Indies in 1821 (86.6%) is considerably greater than that estimated from ship data for 1809 (65.8%). Contemporaries were aware of Cuba's growing importance for the United States in the 1810s, but they appear to have underestimated that of other parts of Spanish America. See Whitaker, *The United States and the independence of Latin America*, 130–9.

145. These proportions are very rough estimates from data of ship numbers given in the sources mentioned in notes 122 and 124.

146. North drew on three sets of freight rates for routes centered in Britain and on scattered United States' rates, largely for the post 1814 period. See 'United States balance of payments', 596.

147. Data in North, 'United States balance of payments', 595, table A-3, column 3. The rate for 1818 was chosen as a base because those for 1817 and 1819 are interpolations. Import freight rates appear to have been identical in 1820 and 1821. See p. 607, table B-2, column 8.

148. American Philosophical Society, Stephen Girard Collection, Series 2, rolls 362–4. Annual ranges for six alternative routes in 1783–1807 are given in Adams, 'American neutrality and prosperity', 729.

149. Most quotations were taken from *Hope's new Philadelphia price current* (1805–14) and *Grotjan's Philadelphia public sale report and general price current*, vols. 4–8 (1815–19). Rates for 1791–2 are given in *Pennsylvania Mercury and Universal Advertiser*; that for March 3, 1791 was adopted for 1790. The rate for 1796 was calculated from three quotations in *Boston Price Current and Marine Intelligencer*. Rates for 1793 and 1795 were taken from scattered insurance policies (source in the preceding note), and that for 1794 was interpolated. The author is indebted to Professor McCusker for calling his attention to the availability of insurance rate quotations in contemporary price currents.

150. See above, pp. 56–7.

151. This deficiency was noted in 'Report 1819', 393.

152. See Pitkin, *A statistical view*, 1st edn, 192. Some evidence for such unspecified clearances can be found in source cited in note 148.

153. Source first mentioned in note 104. The totals for 1793 and 1794 include weights and volumes given in *Supplements* for those two years.

154. Sources and procedures in notes 113, 115, 116. The units of measurement for prices and quantities do not always match. The following manuals and sources proved most useful for conversion: Stephen Dresner, *Units of measurement* (Aylesbury, Bucks., 1971), Appendix 4 ('Obsolete and old-fashioned units'); Ronald Edward

Zupko, *A dictionary of English weights and measures: from Anglo-Saxon times to the nineteenth century* (Madison, 1968); F. G. Skinner, *Weights and measures: their ancient origins and their development in Great Britain up to A.D. 1855* (London, 1967); Arthur Harrison Cole, *Wholesale commodity prices in the United States, 1700–1861* (Cambridge, Mass., 1938), p. x; Homans, *Cyclopedia*, vol. 2, 1952; and McCusker, 'The tonnage of ships', 93–4.

155. Calculated from table 9.

156. Pitkin, *A statistical view*, 1835 edn, 86–8, 90–2, 98, 119–25, 127; 1st edn, 125.

157. These values had to be estimated from comparable breakdowns in other years, because the sample figures for 1800–02 cover only 14% of the official totals (calculated from table 9, columns 8 and 10).

158. Evidence and analysis in Cuenca Esteban, 'Statistics of Spain's colonial trade', 406, 409–10 and 419–20.

159. Summary of sample data in table 9. Column 7 includes wheat, cotton, Indian corn, whale oil, lard, hams and bacon, cheese, salt, soap and pepper. All these commodities but wines, spirits, salt, soap and pepper were assumed to be of domestic origin. On the average, the total value of these goods amounts to 44.9% of official domestic exports from 1790–1816. If only the years 1790–99 are included, the proportion rises to 76.8% (official sub-totals and estimates in table 10, column 5). The stowage factors used to calculate cargo tons for several of these commodities appear to have changed significantly from 1771–2 to 1859. See note 132.

160. Ratios in current values would have introduced an additional bias, for price movements differed widely across commodities. The sample quantities were valued at 1791 prices for this purpose. Deflation procedures are explained in Appendix, section G.

161. This sample includes wines, spirits, salt, soap and pepper, all of which were assumed to have been of Spanish or foreign origin. On the average, the total value amounts to 17.1% of estimated official re-exports in 1790–9 (estimates in table 10, column 6).

162. Estimated tons = sample tons + [sample tons × (official re-exports − sample re-exports) × 60% ÷ sample re-exports].

163. Calculated from Pitkin, *A statistical view*, 1835 edn, 364–5; data for 1815–19 include lesser amounts of Mexican and Colombian tonnage, which are given separately.

164. The estimates of export tonnage to Spain, as opposed to those to the Indies, are based on much wider coverage of commodities in the official sources (rates of sample coverage for the latter estimates are given in notes 159 and 161). The freight rate per ton in the base year 1818 was derived from the nautical mileage from New York to Cádiz as compared to that from Philadelphia to Bordeaux. Cf. p. 56.

165. Column 7 was calculated from Pitkin, *A statistical view*, 1835 edn, 364–5.

166. Calculated from table 10, columns 6 and 7.

167. See Eduardo Arcila Farías, *Comercio entre Venezuela y México en los Siglos XVI y XVII* (Mexico, 1950), 245–8. According to a contemporary traveller, the 54 insurance companies established in Cadiz were ruined at the turn of the nineteenth century. Cited in Antonio García-Baquero González, *Comercio colonial y guerras revolucionarias*, 155.

168. See references in notes 59 and 60. Adams has recently argued, from very rough estimates by Douglass North, that the resulting gain in the proportion of domestic insurers was short-lived. See 'American neutrality and prosperity', 727–8.

169. Robert Giffin, *Essays in finance*, 2nd series (London, 1886), 183 (cited and used for the same purpose in North, 'United States balance of payments', 597).

170. See the Dispatch of Henry Hill, Jr., published with an introduction by Roy F. Nichols: 'Cuban commercial regulations in 1805', *HAHR*, 16 (1936), 213−19.

171. See Richard Pares, *Yankees and creoles: the trade between North America and the West Indies before the American revolution* (London, 1956), 139−46.

172. American Philosophical Society, Stephen Girard Collection, Series 2, rolls 42−49. Access to this correspondence is provided in the microfilmed index to the collection under the heading *Havana, Trade Conditions*.

173. The cargo of Stephen Girard's ship *Helvetius* appears to have turned a net loss late in 1811 as a result of a sudden and unexpected collapse of prices in Havana; however, losses were regarded as most unusual (Girard, roll 49, frames 474, 484 and 524, Yriarte y Lasa to Stephen Girard, Havana, 7 and 12 November 1811 and 1 January 1812). As pointed out by Richard Pares, agents reported losses more often than profits, 'for very few people feel the need to calculate or explain where all seems to be going well'. See *Yankees and creoles*, 140.

174. American Philosophical Society, Girard, roll 47, frame 470: Yriarte y Lasa to Stephen Girard, Havana, 20 July 1810.

175. Girard, roll 46, frame 85: Yriarte y Lasa to Stephen Girard, Havana, 30 January 1810.

176. This line of approach was suggested but not pursued in Shepherd and Walton's estimation of mercantile profits for 1768−72: see *Shipping*, 133−34.

177. American Philosophical Society, Stephen Girard Collection, Series 2, roll 44, frame 250, Yriarte y Lasa to Stephen Girard, Havana, 20 June 1809; and roll 46, frame 247, Yriarte y Lasa to Stephen Girard, Havana, 27 March 1810.

178. Nichols, 'Cuban commercial regulations in 1805', 216.

179. Pares, *Yankees and creoles*, 73.

180. Pares, *Yankees and creoles*, 81.

181. Buck, *The development and organisation of Anglo-American trade*, 14−15.

182. See Shepherd and Walton, *Shipping*, 134.

183. Reference in note 1.

184. See American Philosophical Society, Stephen Girard Collection, Series 2, roll 43, frames 415 and 443: letters dated 3 and 31 October, 1808, respectively.

185. Albert H. Imlah, *Economic elements*, 47−8.

186. These values were estimated as the shares of the United States in total freight earnings on exports to the Indies (column 9 over column 3 in table 11) × total exports FOB (in table 10, column 7).

187. See Appendix, section A (sources in notes 112 and 116).

188. Sugar, molasses, coffee, cocoa, indigo, cotton, spirits and goods subject to ad valorem duties. Current values of the first four commodities are given in table 5; those of the first seven averaged 95.2% of total import values in the years 1791−2 and 1796−1819.

189. Official data of drawback payable and duties received, by commodities and ad valorem rates, given in Seybert, *Statistical annals*, 439−53.

190. Calculated from data in Pitkin, *A statistical view*, 1835 edn, 334.

191. Totals for the United States as a whole taken from Seybert, *Statistical annals*, 454 (1794−1814, calendar years), and calculated from Pitkin, *A statistical view*, 1835 edn, 334, table 2, columns 1 and 4 (1815−19 calendar years).

192. See 'Report 1819', *ASP, CN*, vol. 2, 394. A comprehensive list of imports subject to ad valorem duties as of 27 April 1816, is given in Seybert, *Statistical annals*, 385−9.

193. Monthly data in Bezanson *et al, Wholesale prices*, vol. 1, 360. All monthly data were converted, as before, into averages for fiscal years (October−September).

194. See Appendix, section C.

195. Data summarized in table 9 and table 10 (columns 5 and 6).

196. Out of 100%. For lack of sample data, weights of 100% had to be given to the secondary index for domestic exports in 1817–19 and to that for re-exports in 1800–19.

197. Monthly data in Bezanson *et al, Wholesale prices*, vol. 2, 352.

198. Monthly data in Bezanson *et al, Wholesale prices*, vol. 2, 353.

199. For this purpose, quantities and prices of imports from Spain were separately compiled and processed with similar methods to those described in Appendix, section A.

200. Monthly data in Bezanson *et al, Wholesale prices*, vol. 2, 384.

201. Averages for spirits and four types of wines were obtained for this purpose from the individual price series used in the estimation of import values (see note 112).

Chapter four

1. H.A. Innis, *The fur trade in Canada: an introduction to Canadian economic history* (New Haven, 1930); *The cod fisheries: the history of an international economy* (New Haven, 1940).

2. J.B. Brebner, *North Atlantic triangle: the interplay of Canada, the United States and Great Britain* (New Haven, 1945).

3. F. Ouellet, *Histoire économique et sociale du Québec, 1760–1850: structures et conjoncture* (Montréal, 1966). The graphs on pp. 599–620 are only a small part of the statistical series assembled for this work.

4. F. Ouellet, *Histoire économique et sociale du Québec*, 39.

5. F. Ouellet, J. Hamelin and R. Chabot, 'Les prix agricoles dans les villes et les campagnes du Québec avant 1850: aperçus quantitatifs', *Histoire Sociale/Social History*, 15 (1982), 83–127.

6. F. Ouellet, *Histoire économique et sociale du Québec*, 28.

7. G. Paquet and J.-P. Wallot, 'Aperçu sur le commerce international et les prix domestiques dans le Bas-Canada (1793–1812)', *Revue d'histoire de l'Amérique française*, 21 (1967), 447–73.

8. C. Moore, 'The other Louisbourg: trade and merchant enterprise in Ile Royale, 1713–58', *Histoire Sociale/Social History*, 12 (1979), 79–97.

9. F. Ouellet, 'La formation d'une société dans la vallée du Saint-Laurent: d'une société sans classes à une société de classes', *Canadian Historical Review*, 62 (1981), 443–449.

10. F. Ouellet, 'Dualité économique et changement technologique dans la vallée du Saint-Laurent, 1760–1790', *Histoire Sociale/Social History*, 9 (1976), 256–296.

11. APC, MG. 23, G.I., 10.

12. For a resumé of the controversy over agriculture, see F. Ouellet, 'Le mythe de l'habitant sensible au marché', *Recherches sociographiques*, (1976), 115–132.

13. *RAC*, 1888, B. 201.

14. C. Moore, 'Merchant trade in Louisbourg, Ile Royale' (M.A. thesis, University of Ottawa, 1977); J. Mathieu, *Le commerce entre la Nouvelle-France et les Antilles au XVIIIe siècle* (Québec, 1981), 238–243.

15. See in particular, *JALBC*, 1822–23, app. W.

16. APC, RG. 4, B. 28: the report of the year in progress.

17. See the appendixes to the *JALBC* and *JALC*, for the years in question.

18. Imperial Blue Books, vol. 1 and 2.

19. APC, RG. 4, B. 32.

20. *RAC*, 1888, B. 201.

21. APC, MG. 11, Q. 109.

22. See the appendixes to the *JALBC* for the years in question.

23. *JALBC*, 1832–33 and 1835–36. See the appendixes.

24. *JALBC*, 1828–29, app. Aa, Hh; and 1830, app. Q.

Chapter five

1. 'Testimonio de Luis Joseph de Vilate', Pensacola, December 16, 1761, AGNM, Marina, tomo 17, fols. 215–270v; Esteban Geronio to Gerónimo Enrile Guersi, Cap Français, October 2, 1776, AGI, Santo Domingo, leg. 1598A, exp. 1355; 'Extracto que manifiesta los géneros comestibles ... [que] se han conducido de las colonias estrangeras a la ciudad de Santo Domingo ... desde 1754 a 1769', BN, ms. 17616, fol. 57; J. Edward Marrero, 'El impacto de la revolución americana en el desarrollo de Puerto Rico: 1776–1854', *Revista Interamericana Review*, 5 (Winter, 1975–6), 611; Harry Bernstein, *Origins of inter-American interest: 1700–1812* (Philadelphia, 1945), 20; Arturo Morales Carrión, *Puerto Rico and the non-Hispanic Caribbean: a study in the decline of Spanish exclusivism* (San Juan, 1971), 90.

2. Appendix table 40 gives some idea of how extensive the maritime traffic in Havana was.

3. The daily ration for Spanish soldiers consisted of 24 ounces of fresh bread, 12 ounces of meat, and 4 ounces of vegetables. See 'Noticia de los oficios pasados al ... dn. Juan Barrutia ...', José de Ezpeleta, Guarico, 1782, AGI, Indif., leg. 1581. Leví Marrero explains succinctly what the Europeans ate, or tried to eat, in the tropical climate of Cuba. See Leví Marrero, *Cuba, economía y sociedad*, vol. 3 (Madrid, 1975), 240. Havana and its environs numbered some 75,000 inhabitants. See Kenneth F. Kiple, *Blacks in colonial Cuba* (Gainesville, 1976), 84.

4. Conde de Macuriges to José de Gálvez, Havana, October 17, 1777, BN, ms. 17616, fols. 211–26; Antonio María de Bucareli to Diego José Navarro, Mexico, December 30, 1777, AGI, Cuba, leg. 1275, num. 14.

5. For the problem with Mexican flour in Havana, see James A. Lewis, 'Nueva España y los esfuerzos para abastecer la Habana, 1779–1783', *Anuario de Estudios Americanos*, 33 (1976), 501–26.

6. One of the casualties of the war will be the *gremio*, which the Crown blamed for many of the economic problems plaguing Havana. See Bernardo de Troncoso to Gálvez, Havana, August 5, 1785, AGI, Estado, leg. 9, num. 8; Macuriges to Gálvez, Havana, October 17, 1777, BN, ms. 17616, fols. 211–26; and 'auto' of Luis de Unzaga, Havana, July 21, 1784, AGI, Santo Domingo, leg. 1240, exp. 451. For an interesting view of the *gremio de panaderos* elsewhere in the empire, see Lyman L. Johnson, 'The entrepreneurial reorganization of an artisan trade: the takers of Buenos Aires, 1770–1820', *TAm*, 37 (1980), 139–60.

7. It is a mistake to make too clear a distinction between commercial and military ships in the eighteenth century. Spanish naval officers had the right in the 1780s to use their men-of-war to transport private merchandise. This, or course, could cause some serious problems with unscrupulous officers. Appendix table 41 illustrates the amount of commerce carried by military ships from Veracruz to Havana.

8. For scattered ship registries containing flour shipped to Havana from 1765 to 1779, see 'Registros de buques para La Habana', AGI, Contratación, legs. 1457 and 1472B. See also 'Relaciones de la carga de embarcaciones del comercio libre, 1767–1780', AGI, Indif., legs. 2410–18. Some precise data, however, exists for 1778 and 1779 and is presented in Appendix table 42.

9. In 1777, the Conde de Macuriges estimated that the *asiento* shipped 6,200 barrels of flour annually to Havana from Spanish ports. Macuriges to Gálvez, Havana, October 17, 1777, BN, ms. 17616, fols. 211–26.

10. R.O. to Pascual de Cisneros, n.p., October 19, 1765, AGI, Santo Domingo, leg. 1220. *Pan de casaba* suffered from a social stigma in Cuba much the way that tortillas do in modern Mexico. *Casaba* bread was 'pan de pobre'. See Marrero, *Cuba*, vol. 3, 239.

11. Until 1776, Havana tried to keep supplies on hand sufficient enough to

withstand a six month siege. This proved to be so expensive that the King approved a recommendation to reduce Havana's stores by half, enough to endure a three month siege. Marqués de la Torre to Gálvez, Havana, May 8, 1776, AGI, Santo Domingo, leg. 1224, num. 1077.

12. Appendix table 43 shows the increasing level of flour exports from Veracruz to Havana just before the Spanish entry into the war.

13. In 1778, for example, the *asiento* shipped only 1,703 barrels of flour to Havana, well below its average of 6,200 barrels: 'Entradas y salidas', AGI, Santo Domingo, leg. 1217.

14. A fleet and expeditionary army under José de Solano reinforced Havana in 1780. See Navarro to Mayorga, Havana, August 8, 1780, AGNM, Intendencia, tomo 56. No historian has yet described all the Spanish military activities in the New World during the war. For the campaign against Pensacola, the most recent study is William S. Coker and Hazel P. Coker, *The siege of Pensacola in maps* (Pensacola, 1981). Also excellent are John Walton Caughey, *Bernardo de Gálvez in Louisiana: 1776–1783* (Berkeley, 1934) and Francisco de Borja Medina Rojas, *José de Ezpeleta: gobernador de la Mobila: 1780–1781* (Seville, 1980). For the expedition against Jamaica, see Guillermo Porras Muñoz, 'El fracaso de Guarico', *Anuario de Estudios Americanos*, 24 (1969), 569–609.

15. Juan Ignacio de Urriza to Gálvez, Havana, February 15, 1781, AGI, Santo Domingo, leg. 1658, num. 56; Navarro to Gálvez, Havana, January 27, 1781, AGI, Santo Domingo leg. 1233, num. 935; Governor of Havana to Gálvez, Havana, October 20, 1780, AGI, Cuba, leg. 1299.

16. Governor of Havana to Gálvez, Havana, October 20, 1780, AGI, Cuba, leg. 1299. To make sure that the Americans would return, the Intendant Urriza reduced the import and export taxes that foreigners would have to pay by underevaluating their goods. See Urriza to Gálvez, Havana, October 4, 1780, AGI, Indif., leg. 1582, num. 690.

17. Robert Morris to Robert Smith, Philadelphia, July 17, 1781, in E. James Ferguson (comp.), *The papers of Robert Morris: 1781–1784*, vol. 1 (Pittsburgh, 1973), 318–22; Navarro to Francisco Rendón, Havana, September 27, 1789, AGI, Cuba, leg. 1282; Urriza to Gálvez, Havana, October 5, 1780, AGI, Indif., leg. 1582, num. 692.

18. Business records, of course, are very hard to find. Account books for the general exchequer and the navy, however, are surprisingly detailed and give an excellent view of the flour merchants in Havana. For those of the general exchequer see AGI, Santo Domingo, legs. 1846–50; and for the navy equivalent, see AGI, Santo Domingo, legs. 1864–5.

19. Lázaro Chávez to Gálvez, Havana, April 20, 1784, AGI, Indif., leg. 2477; 'representación' of Cornelio Coppinger, Havana, May 22, 1784, AGI, Indif., leg. 2821; petition of Joseph Laserre, Santiago de Cuba, January 27, 1789, AGI, Ultramar, leg. 83, num. 16; 'instancia' of José Gato, Havana, February 28, 1793, AGI, Santo Domingo, leg. 2192. Even Spanish men-of-war brought flour from the Thirteen Colonies. See Urriza to Gálvez, Havana, September 6, 1785, AGI, Santo Domingo, leg. 1665, num. 1650.

20. Custom records show that the United States took 29% of Cuba's sugar exports in 1780, 11% in 1781, and 32% in 1782. See 'Extracto de los frutos [de Cuba]', Astigarreta, Havana, January 2, 1781, AGI, Santo Domingo, leg. 1658, num. 792; 'Extracto de los caudales y frutos de … Cubá, Raymundo de Onís, Havana, December 31, 1782, AGI, Santo Domingo, leg. 1973; 'Estado que demuestra el dinero y frutos … de 1781', Onís, Havana, January 2, 1782, AGI, Santo Domingo, leg. 1659, num. 905. Anglo-American merchants also shipped liquor and hides back to the Thirteen Colonies.

21. Both Ramón de Posada (*fiscal* of the exchequer in New Spain) and Francisco

Saavedra (an influential official in the Ministry of the Indies during the war) give this figure. Since these two men personally discussed the problem of flour for Havana, one undoubtedly obtained the estimate of 3,000,000 pesos from the other, most likely Posada from Saavedra. See the 'dictamen' of Ramón de Posada, Mexico, November 30, 1781, AGNM, Industria, tomo 14, exp. 5, fols. 66–81, and Manuel Ignacio Pérez-Alonso, S. J., 'War mission in the Caribbean: the diary of Don Francisco de Saavedra (1780–1783)' (4 vols., Ph.D. diss., Georgetown University, 1954), vol. 1, 152–3.

22. 'Certificatión' of Vicente Joseph Nuñez, Guarico, December 23, 1782, AGI, Santo Domingo, leg. 946. Custom records show only 80,000 pesos shipped to the Thirteen Colonies in 1780, 91,905 pesos in 1781, and 35,410 pesos in 1782. As will be discussed later, smuggling money out of Cuba was very common during the war. The general exchequer records show massive amounts of money paid directly to Anglo-American merchants. How much they received indirectly cannot be determined. See the sources listed in notes 18 and 20.

23. 'Relación que manifiesta los comerciantes yngleses americanos que se hallan en esta ciudad ...', Manuel Cabello, Havana, May 23, 1784, AHN, Estado, leg. 3885 bis, exp. 4, num. 14.

24. See note 19.

25. English men-of-war appeared off the port of Havana only once during the war, in August, 1782, when war ships escorting a convoy from Jamaica blockaded the harbor for a few days. See Urriza to Gálvez, Havana, October 25, 1782, AGI, Santo Domingo, leg. 2088B, num. 1023.

26. Juan Cologan and sons to [Gálvez?], [1784?], AGI, Indif., leg. 2427.

27. Urriza to Bernardo de Gálvez, Havana, October 11, 1782, AGI, Indif., leg. 1579.

28. See note 5.

29. 'Representación' of Juan Nepomuceno de Victoria, Madrid, August 6, 1782, AGI, Indiv., leg. 2421; Urriza to J. de Gálvez, Havana, October 17, 1783, AGI, Santo Domingo, leg. 2188, num. 1218.

30. Cisneros to Marqués de Esquilache, Havana, July 23, 1765, AGS, Secretaría y Superintendencia de Hacienda, leg. 2343.

31. See 'Relación que manifiesta ...'.

32. Memorial of Da. Beveridge to the Honorable the United States of North America in General Congress Assembled, 1785, State Dept., American Letters, 1: 237. Table 39 shows about 25% more ships entering than leaving Havana in 1782 and 1783.

33. One of these slave shipments from the newly independent English colonies resulted in a tragic attempt by the slaves to seize control of their ship. These individuals may well have been part of the spoils of war taken by one side from the other during the American Revolution. See 'certificación' of José Alvarez, Havana, May 22, 1784, AGI, Indif., leg. 2821.

34. It was Urriza, for example, who pushed the famous contraband case against Francisco de Miranda during the war. Although the full story of Miranda's activities in Cuba is yet to be told, Urriza effectively ended Miranda's promising military career in the Spanish army as well as that of Miranda's superior, Juan Manuel de Cagigal, Governor of Havana (1781–2). See the 'residencia' of Juan Manuel de Cagigal, AHN, Consejos Suprimidos, leg. 20878. By the 1790s, Urriza was a supernumerary member of the Council of the Indies. See Gildas Bernard, *Le secrétariat d'état et le conseil espagnol des Indes (1700–1805)* (Geneva, 1972), 222.

35. Urriza to J. de Gálvez, Havana, November 27, 1783, AGI, Santo Domingo, leg. 2188, num. 131 reservada. At times, the Anglo-Americans simply tried to take advantage of the busy harbor and evening darkness in Havana to smuggle goods over the city walls. See Urriza to J. de Gálvez, Havana, January 26, 1785, AGI, Santo Domingo, leg. 1665, num. 1532; Cagigal to J. de Gálvez, Havana, June 16, 1782, AGI, Santo Domingo, leg. 1234, num. 35 reservada.

36. Urriza to J. de Gálvez, Havana, October 4, 1784, AGI, Santo Domingo, leg. 1663, num. 1436; Urriza to J. de Gálvez, Havana, December 21, 1784, AGI, Santo Domingo, leg. 1663, num. 1504. Oliver Pollock estimated that merchants smuggled out of Havana as much as one-third of all specie leaving that port in order to avoid paying export taxes. See Exports for Havana [Oliver Pollock, 1785], State Dept., American Lettes, 1: 355−6. Anglo-Americans also smuggled fugitives out of Havana, the most famous being Francisco de Miranda. See John S. Ezell (ed.), *The new democracy in America: travels of Francisco de Miranda in the United States, 1783−1784*, tr. Judson P. Wood (Norman, 1963), 3.

37. Still useful on Pollock are James A. James, *Oliver Pollock* (New York, 1937) and Roy F. Nichols, *Advance agents of American destiny* (Philadelphia, 1956), 18.

38. A list of the Officers in the Department of Foreign Affairs, 1785, State Dept., American Letters, 2: 108.

39. Bribery is one of those intriguing crimes that seemed to swirl around the Anglo-American entrepreneurs in Havana. It may well be the natural companion of smuggling, but Spanish officials and American merchants blamed the national character of each other for its presence. See Certification of Oliver Pollock, Havana, June 30, 1784, Papers of the Continental Congress, 64: 461−7; Memorial of Da. Beveridge to the Honorable the United States of North America in General Congress Assembled, 1785, State Dept., American Letters, 1: 235−9; Urriza to J. de Gálvez, Havana, November 27, 1783, AGI, Santo Domingo, leg. 2188, num. 131 reservada.

40. The best description of Pollock's attempted smuggling is in 'Consulta del Consejo de las Indias', June 26, 1788, AGI, Santo Domingo, leg. 1142, exp. 23; Urriza to J. de Gálvez, Havana, October 2, 1784, AGI, Santo Domingo, leg. 1663, num. 1432.

41. R.O. to the Governor of Havana, San Ildefonso, August 29, 1782, AGI, Cuba, leg. 1367, exp. 22.

42. 'Certificatión' of Miguel Antonio Eduardo, Havana, May 3, 1783, AGI, Cuba, leg. 1364.

43. Rendón to Unzaga, Philadelphia, August 15, 1783, AGI, Cuba, leg. 1354, num. 33. Rendón, Spanish envoy in Philadelphia, noted that the American public reacted with 'general disgust' to the news that Havana was closed to foreigners since no other port offered the Americans such opportunities to earn specie.

44. Urriza to J. de Gálvez, Havana, October 17, 1783, AGI, Santo Domingo, leg. 2188, num. 1218; Urriza to Unzaga, Havana, October 2, 1783, AGI, Santo Domingo, leg. 2188, num. 1218−5.

45. R.O. to the Intendant, El Pardo, January 23, 1784, AGI, Santo Domingo, leg. 2188, num. 1218; R.O. to the Governor of Havana, El Pardo, February 18, 1784, AGI, Santo Domingo, leg. 2188.

46. The expelled American merchants complained loudly about Governor Unzaga's conduct, not realizing that it was the Intendant Urriza who had far more to do with their expulsion. See Beveridge to John Jay, Philadelphia, January 29, 1785, State Dept., American Letters, 1: 232−4; Robert Totten to Pollock, Havana, February 27, 1784, Papers of the Continental Congress, 150: 861−3.

47. Urriza to J. de Gálvez, Havana, November 27, 1783, AGI, Santo Domingo, leg. 2188, num. 131; R.O. to the Governor of Havana, El Pardo, February 18, 1784, AGI, Santo Domingo, leg. 2188; R.O. to the interim Governor of Havana, El Pardo, March 10, 1785, AGI, Estado, leg. 9, num. 78.

48. The expulsion of this group of Americans is best told in J. de Gálvez to Conde de Floridablanca, San Ildefonso, October 5, 1785, AHN, Estado, leg. 3885 bis, exp. 4, num. 12; 'Relación que manifiesta ...'; Urriza to J. de Gálvez, Havana, July 1, 1785, AGI, Santo Domingo, leg. 1665, num. 1612. See also note 46.

49. Diego de Gardoqui to Jay, New York, September 10, 1785, Papers of the Continental Congress, 107: 375−8.

50. Appendix table 44 gives some idea of the American involvement in the Havana flour market after the war.

51. See 'Relación que manifiesta ...'.

52. This was Thomas Plunkett, an Irish-American merchant from Philadelphia. Plunkett's complaint in the 'residencia' of Unzaga provoked a later governor to protest bitterly that the only opposition to Unzaga's rule had been Plunkett, a prostitute, and a 'pardo libre'. Ezpeleta to Antonio Valdés, Havana, May 28, 1788, AHN, Consejos Suprimidos, leg. 20917, exp. 69, num. 187. Plunkett was able to return to Havana because he was a personal friend of Bernardo de Gálvez. He remained on the island at least until 1788, if not longer. See Beveridge to Jay, Philadelphia, April 12, 1786, State Dept., American Lettes, 2: 270–5; Troncoso to J. de Gálvez, Havana, August 1, 1785, AGI, Santo Domingo, leg. 1242, num. 70.

53. Pérez-Alonso, 'War Mission', vol. 2, 153.

54. See note 19.

Chapter six

* The author is indebted to the Lincoln Educational Foundation for research assistance, and to the Executive Committee of the Forty-Fourth International Congress of Americanists for a travel grant to present a short version of this chapter to that body (Manchester, England, September 5–10, 1982). She would also like to thank James Kettner, Michael Meranze and John Coatsworth for criticizing earlier drafts of this essay, and Jules Boymel for graciously making available the results of his detailed research in the Boone Papers at the Historical Society of Pennsylvania.

1. Josiah Blakeley to James Madison, Santiago de Cuba, November 1, 1801, Despatches from United States Consuls in Santiago de Cuba, 1799–1906, National Archives and Records Service, Microcopy No. T-55, Washington, D.C., 1959, roll 1, vol. 1. Blakeley was writing from prison, having been arrested the previous month by order of the intendant of Havana on suspicion of an illegal private business transaction.

2. Jacob Price, 'Economic function and growth of American port towns in the eighteenth century', *Perspectives in American History*, 8 (1974), 123–85; Gordon C. Bjork, 'Stagnation and growth in the American economy, 1784–1792' (Ph.D. diss., University of Washington, 1963); David T. Gilchrist (ed.), *The growth of seaport cities, 1790–1825* (Charlottesville, 1967); Joseph A. Pratt, 'Regional development in the context of national economic growth' in Glenn Porter (ed.), *Regional economic history: the mid-Atlantic area since 1700* (Greenville, Del., 1976), 25–40; Robert G. Albion, *The rise of New York port, 1815–1860* (Hamden, Ct., 1961); Diane Lindstrom, *Economic development in the Philadelphia region, 1810–1850* (New York, 1978); Linda Kerrigan Salvucci, 'Development and decline: the port of Philadelphia and Spanish imperial markets, 1783–1823' (Ph.D. diss., Princeton University, in progress); James W. Livingood, *The Philadelphia-Baltimore trade rivalry, 1780–1860* (Harrisburg, 1947); and Geoffrey N. Gilbert, 'Baltimore's flour trade to the Caribbean, 1750–1815' (Ph.D. diss., The Johns Hopkins University, 1975).

3. Roy F. Nichols, 'Trade relations and the establishment of United States consulates in Spanish America, 1799–1809', *HAHR*, 8 (1933), 289–313; James A. Lewis, 'Nueva España y los esfuerzos para abastecer La Habana, 1779–1803', *Anuario de Estudios Americanos*, 33 (1976), 501–26.

4. Anna C. Clauder, *American commerce as affected by the wars of the French revolution and Napoleon, 1793–1812* (Philadelphia, 1932); John H. Coatsworth, 'American trade with European colonies in the Caribbean and South America, 1790–1812', *The William and Mary Quarterly*, 3rd. ser., 24 (1967), 243–66. Also see

Donald R. Adams, Jr., 'American neutrality and prosperity, 1793–1808: a reconsideration', *Journal of Economic History*, 40 (1980), 713–37; and Claudia Goldin and Frank D. Lewis, 'The role of exports in American economic growth during the Napoleonic wars, 1793 to 1807', *Explorations in Economic History*, 17 (1980), 6–25.

5. Thomas M. Doerflinger, 'Enterprise on the Delaware: merchants and economic development in Philadelphia, 1750–1791' (Ph.D. diss., Harvard University, 1980); Stuart Bruchey, 'Success and failure factors: American merchants in foreign trade in the eighteenth and early nineteenth centuries', *Business History Review*, 32 (1958), 272–92. For defining entrepreneurship, see Hugh G. J. Aitken, 'The future of entrepreneurial research', *Explorations in Entrepreneurial History*, 1 (1963), 3–9; the essay on entrepreneurship by J. R. T. Hughes in Glenn Porter (ed.), *Encyclopedia of American economic history: studies of the principal movements and ideas* (3 vols., New York, 1980), vol. 1, 214–28; Israel M. Kirzner, *Perception, opportunity, and profit: studies in the theory of entrepreneurship* (Chicago, 1979); Peter Kilby (ed.), *Entrepreneurship and economic development* (New York, 1971); and Sidney M. Greenfield, Arnold Strickon, and Robert T. Aubey (eds.), *Entrepreneurs in cultural context* (Albuquerque, 1979).

6. Charles Lyon Chandler, 'The River Plate voyages, 1798–1800', *American Historical Review*, 23 (1918), 816–24.

7. Stuart Weems Bruchey, *Robert Oliver, merchant of Baltimore, 1783–1819* (Baltimore, 1956).

8. Nichols, 'Trade relations'; James A. Lewis, 'New Spain during the American revolution, 1779–1783: a viceroyalty at war' (Ph.D. diss., Duke University, 1975).

9. Light T. Cummins, 'Spanish agents in North America during the revolution, 1775–1779' (Ph.D. diss., Tulane University, 1977), 290–92. When the merchant John Barry, not to be confused with the commodore, died in 1813, John Leamy and Patrick Hayes, a ship captain often employed by Leamy, served as excutors of the Barry estate. Bond for 7200 dollars to Sarah Barry, Patrick Hayes and John Leamy, executors ..., Philadelphia, January 12, 1813, Arthur C. Bining Collection, HSP.

10. Francisco Rendón to Antonio Ramón del Valle, Philadelphia, June 11, 1781, AGI, Cuba, leg. 1283. Diego Gardoqui to Esteban Miró, New York, October 5 and December 3, 1788, AGI, Cuba, leg. 104A.

11. Jáudenes and Viar to Floridablanca, Philadelphia, October 18, 1791, AHN, Estado, leg. 3894 bis; Policy No. 2611, Fire Blotter, III, INA, for Jáudenes' residence; Duque de Frías to Evaristo Pérez de Castro, London, September 26 and October 24, 1820, AGS, Estado (Inglaterra), leg. 8180 for Leamy's secret efforts. John Stoughton, Spanish consul at Boston, Account Book of Fees Received, July 24, 1802 – September 1, 1809 NYHS. Stoughton was still consul in 1820, when his son James, a lawyer who sometimes defended Spanish shipping interests in U.S. courts, was killed by an irate Baltimore merchant who had been accused of commercial fraud in New York: Mateo de la Serna to Duque de San Carlos, Washington, January 2, 1820, AGS, Estado (Inglaterra), leg. 8223.

12. To Charles Howard, New York, September 24, 1792, Lynch and Stoughton Letterbook, 1791–1794, NYHS.

13. For Jáudenes' and Viar's activities in Philadelphia, see José Antonio Armillas, 'Viar y Jáudenes', in *Suma de Estudios homenaje al Dr. Canellas* (Zaragoza, 1969), 51–76; Carmelo Richard Arena, 'Philadelphia–Spanish New Orleans trade: 1789–1803' (Ph.D. diss., University of Pennsylvania, 1959). AGI, Cuba, leg. 1469 contains some of the trading permits; a portion of this particular legajo is available as photocopies from microfilm at the Library of Congress. Also see Eric Beerman, 'Spanish envoy to the United States (1796–1809): Marqués de Casa Irujo and his Philadelphia wife Sally McKean,' *TAm*, 37 (1981), 445–56. For John Craig's in-laws,

who included Sarmientos, Olivers, and Biddles, see Bruchey, *Robert Oliver*, and Marten
G. Buist, *At Spes Non Fracta: Hope and co., 1770–1815, merchant bankers and
diplomats at work* (The Hague, 1974), 312–16. Virtually all of the ships that left
Philadelphia for Venezuela in 1805 had been loaded by John Craig for his and the
Olivers' accounts: AGI, Ultramar, leg. 839.

14. Jáudenes and Viar to Floridablanca, Philadelphia, August 2, 1791, AHN,
Estado, leg. 3894 bis, for Carroll's introduction; Miguel Gómez del Campillo, *Relaciones diplomáticas entre España y los Estados Unidos*, vol. 1 (Madrid, 1944), xx–xxiii,
for Rendón's engagement. For Jáudenes' drinking with Jefferson, see Arena,
'Philadelphia', 24–7; also Jáudenes and Viar to Floridablanca, Philadelphia, November
6, 1791, AHN, Estado, leg. 3894 bis. Leamy's patronage of City Tavern is discussed
in Marquis James, *Biography of a business, 1792–1942* (New York, 1942), 21. James,
p. 116, also relates how Leamy tried — unsuccessfully — to use his connections in Spain
to try to collect the claims of the Insurance Company of North America against Spain
after 1795.

15. To Pedro Juan de Erice, New York, October 3, October 7, and November
23, 1793; February 4, June 27, July 16, and August 28, 1794, Lynch and Stoughton
Letterbook, 1791–1794, NYHS. Also see John Stoughton Letterbook, July
1794 – February 1795, NYHS, for a record of his travels throughout the Caribbean.

16. José Pablo Valiente to Gardoqui, Havana, December 3, 1793, AGI, Santo
Domingo, leg. 1672. During his voyage to Cuba in 1794–95, John Stoughton was quite
anxious to establish contact with James Leamy, whom he had not yet met personally.

17. For an overview of the consular situation, see Despatches from the United
States Consuls in Havana, 1783–1806, National Archives and Records Service,
Microcopy No. T-20, Washington, D.C., 1956, rolls 1–3.

18. To John Leamy, New York, August 14 and August 28, 1793, Lynch and
Stoughton Letterbook, 1791–94, NYHS; Marine Blotters, INA.

19. Bruchey, 'Success and failure factors', 292.

20. John Stoughton Letterbook, July 1794 – February 1795, NYHS.

21. 'The memorial and petition of the owners, supercargoes, and masters of
American vessels now embargoed in the port of Havana to the Captain-General ...',
Havana, June 19, 1797, AGI, Cuba, leg. 1518A.

22. Arena, 'Philadelphia'; Bruchey, *Robert Oliver*, 126. For evidence of indirect
routing for other Spanish imperial markets, see Pablo Tornero Tinajero, *Relaciones
de dependencia entre Florida y los Estados Unidos (1783–1820)* (Madrid, 1979);
Demetrios Ramos Pérez, 'El problema de los embarques de harinas en los registros
para América', in *Il Coloquio de Historia Canario-Americana – 1977*, vol. 2 (n.p.,
1979), 35–44; Fernando Barreda, *Comercio marítimo entre los Estados Unidos y
Santander (1778–1829)* (Santander, 1950).

23. Nichols, 'Trade relations', 292; lists of ships carrying slaves into Cuba are
found in AGI, Santo Domingo, legs. 1673, 1675–77, and 1687. These lists cover parts
of months from 1793, 1795–99, 1805, and 1806. For the following months, 100% of
all foreign ships arriving in Havana were Anglo-American, and 100% of the slaves
delivered to that port came in Anglo-American ships: January and May 1797; October
and November 1798; June 1799; December 1805; and March, August, September,
October, November, and December 1806.

24. George C. Morton, Havana, May 27, 1801, Despatches from U.S. Consuls
in Havana, National Archives and Records Service, Microcopy T-20.

25. To Cantera y Zavalata, New York, September 24, 1792, Lynch and Stoughton
Letterbook, 1791–1794, NYHS, shows that the Stoughtons were involved in the sale
of sixteen slaves. While John Leamy took out over 200 insurance policies for himself
and his associates between 1792 and 1805, not one was written on slaves. Marine
Blotters, INA. Along with Daniel Clark, who traded frequently to New Orleans,

the son-in-law of Charles Carroll, a Mr. Keating of Baltimore, was involved in supplying blacks to Spanish colonies: Clement Biddle to General Wilkinson, Philadelphia, April 10, 1789, Am 9180, HSP.

26. Jules Boymel, unpublished and untitled biography of Jeremiah Boone and his businesses, 1981. Mr. Boymel graciously made available the results of his detailed research, based on materials in the Boone Papers, HSP.

27. Phineas Bond, British consul at Philadelphia, estimated that over 500,000 dollars arrived at that port alone from Spanish America in 1787. Arthur P. Whitaker, 'Reed and Forde: merchant adventurers of Philadelphia', *Pennsylvania Magazine of History and Biography*, 61 (1937), 244–5. Also see Jonathan Goldstein, *Philadelphia and the China trade, 1682–1846: commercial, cultural, and attitudinal effects* (University Park, 1978).

28. Bernard Bailyn, *The New England merchant in the seventeenth century* (New York, 1964). See also the works cited in note 5.

29. James, *Biography of a business*, 36. Leamy left the Insurance Company of North America late in 1806 and formed his own Marine and Fire Insurance Company at 121 South Third Street in Philadelphia: advertisement in *Aurora – General Advertiser*, Philadelphia, December 4, 1806.

Chapter seven

* The author wishes to acknowledge the support of his research by grants of the Social Sciences and Humanities Research Council of Canada.

1. R.C., August 31, 1752, AGI, Mexico, leg. 1948.

2. For a late regulation explaining the scope of the operation, see *Reglamento e instrucción del real giro* ... (Madrid, 1802), in AGS, DGT, Inv^o 23, leg. 9.

3. See AGI, Contaduría, leg. 647A, for such examples.

4. Jacques A. Barbier and Herbert S. Klein, 'Revolutionary wars and public finances: the Madrid treasury, 1784–1807', *Journal of Economic History*, 41 (1981), 331.

5. AGI, Indif., leg. 2333.

6. See María Lourdes Díaz-Trechuelos Spinola, *La Real Compañía de Filipinas* (Seville, 1965), 18–19.

7. There is, indeed, some confusion as to the meaning of the word *libranza*. In Hapsburg and early Bourbon times, it seems to have meant no more than a payment order on a particular treasury, thus, the *Real Cédula de Libranza*. In this usage, the word was largely replaced by *libramiento*, and all late eighteenth century *libranzas* which I have examined were undoubtedly negotiable instruments. One cannot exclude the possibility, however, that the word was occasionally used in its older sense.

8. Troncoso to Lerena, March 2, 1791, AGI, Guatemala, leg. 669.

9. Valiente to Saavedra, May 25, 1798, AGI, Santo Domingo, leg. 1676.

10. Zambrano and Montes to Gardoqui, September 19, 1792, AGS, Secretaría y Superintendencia de Hacienda, leg. 284.

11. Marquina to Valdés, December 18, 22, and 29, 1788, and July 31, 1799, AGI, Filipinas, legs. 787 and 794.

12. Gil to Lerena or Gardoqui, April 20, May 26, June 5, July 5, and July 20, 1792, and October 20, 1792, AGI, Lima, legs. 701 and 702.

13. Guarda to Floridablanca, January 3, 1780, AGI, Indif., leg. 1565.

14. Jacques A. Barbier, 'Venezuelan "libranzas", 1788–1807: from economic nostrum to fiscal imperative', 37 (1981), 457–78.

15. The system was also applicable to Maracaibo. See *acuerdo* of the *junta de gobierno* of the Philippines Company, February 2, 1792, AGI, Filipinas, leg. 981.

16. In addition to its Philippines and Venezuela dealings, the company was in these years receiving 150,000 *pesos fuertes* yearly in Peru, which it shipped off to the islands in coin. In return it provided *recibos* to the viceroys of Peru, which do not seem to have been true *letras*. See Gil to Gardoqui, February 8, 1796, AGI, Filipinas, leg. 989, and Osorno to Varela, May 22, 1797, AGI, Lima, leg. 716.

17. R.O., December 7, 1795, AGI, Mexico, leg. 2468.

18. R.O., January 14, 1797, AGI, Mexico, leg. 2468.

19. Valiente to Gardoqui, February 1, 1797, and Valiente to Saavedra, May 24, 1798, AGI, Santo Domingo, leg. 1676.

20. Valiente to Saavedra, December 31, 1798, AGI, Santo Domingo, leg. 1677.

21. See AGI, Indif., leg. 1704.

22. Valiente to Saavedra, December 31, 1798, AGI, Santo Domingo, leg. 1677; Azanza to Soler, March 30, 1799, AGI, Mexico, leg. 1590; R.O., August 27, 1799, AGI, Mexico, leg. 2367.

23. Valiente to Saavedra, September 7, 1798, AGI, Santo Domingo, leg. 1676.

24. Viguri to Soler, April 18, 1802, AGI, Santo Domingo, leg. 1682; and AGI, Santo Domingo, leg. 1680.

25. Castaño to Rodríguez, February 15, 1799, AGS, DGT, Inv^{O} 31, leg. 40; R.O., February 26, 1799, AGI, Indif., leg. 1563–2^{O}.

26. AGS, DGT, Inv^{O} 31, leg. 40.

27. AGI, Indif., leg. 1563–2^{O}.

28. Viguri to Soler, August 22, 1800, AGI, Santo Domingo, leg. 1679.

29. See AGI, Indif., leg. 1563–2^{O}.

30. AGI, Estado, leg. 29, num. 23a; the 'mesa' to the minister of finance, September 30, 1801, AGI, Indif., leg. 1347; ministerial expediente on *giro*, AGI, Indif., leg. 2469.

31. Viguri to Soler, AGI, Santo Domingo, legs. 1681 (num. 191), 1682 (num. 212 and 274), and 1684 (num. 291, 305 and 331); Arce to Soler, AGI, Santo Domingo, leg. 1684 (num. 343); Hoz to Soler, AGI, Santo Domingo, leg. 1685 (num. 389); and Gómez Roubaud to Soler, AGI, Santo Domingo, leg. 1685 (num. 477). This does not include the nearly 300,000 *pesos fuertes* spent on the forces which were evacuated to Cuba from the Haitian debacle, or the over 70,000 *pesos fuertes* in outstanding bills.

32. Viguri to Soler, April 8, 1803 (which includes a bill for 51,178 *pesos fuertes* on Juan Morfí of Cadiz), AGI, Santo Domingo, leg. 1684.

33. Gómez Roubaud to Soler, January 22, 1807, AGI, Santo Domingo, leg. 1688.

34. Gómez Roubaud to Soler, January 22, 1807, AGI, Santo Domingo, leg. 1688.

35. Gómez Roubaud to Soler, December 9, 1806, AGI, Santo Domingo, leg. 1687. Gómez Raubaud tells of a transfer of 200,000 *pesos fuertes* by this means.

36. Gómez Roubaud to Soler, October 26, 1807, AGI, Santo Domingo, leg. 1688.

37. Someruelos to Gómez Roubaud, December 30, 1806, AGI, Santo Domingo, leg. 1687.

38. See Jacques A. Barbier, 'Peninsular finance and colonial trade: the dilemma of Charles IV's Spain', *JLAS*, 12 (1980), 35; John Rydjord, 'Napoleon and Mexican silver', *South-West Social Sciences Quarterly*, 19 (1938), 171–82; and Philip G. and Raymond Walters, 'The American career of David Parish', *Journal of Economic History* (1944), 149–66.

Chapter eight

* Part of the research for this chapter was conducted with the financial assistance of the American Philosophical Society.

1. Quoted in Pablo Tornero, 'Hacendados y desarrollo azucarero cubano (1763–1818)', *Revista de Indias*, 153–4 (1978), 724.

2. See Peter James Lampros, 'Merchant–planter cooperation and conflict: the Havana consulado, 1794–1832', unpublished dissertation (Tulane University, 1980), chaps. 7–8.

3. I have dealt more fully with this subject in 'The development of the Cuban military as a sociopolitical elite, 1763–1783', *HAHR*, 61 (1981), 695–7.

4. Allan J. Kuethe, 'La introducción del sistema de milicias disciplinadas en América', *Revista de Historia Militar*, 47 (1979), 95–112.

5. Kuethe, 'La introducción', 101–8.

6. Rafael Nieto y Cortadellas, *Dignidades nobiliarias en Cuba* (Madrid, 1954), 71–2, 98–9, 113–15, 250–1, 294–5, 308–10, 411–13, 420–1, 480–2, 495–6, 609–11.

7. Leví Marrero, *Cuba: economía y sociedad*, 7 (Madrid, 1978), chap. 1; Hugh Thomas, *Cuba: the pursuit of freedom* (New York, 1971), 32.

8. Francisco Xavier de Santa Cruz y Mallen, *Historia de familias cubanas* (6 vols., Havana, 1940–50), vol. 3, 334–7; vol. 4, 265.

9. Marrero, *Cuba*, vol. 7, 126.

10. Franklin W. Knight, 'Origins of wealth and the sugar revolution in Cuba, 1750–1850', *HAHR*, 57 (1977), 234–8, 243–9.

11. Service records, Regiment of White Volunteers of Havana, Volunteer Cavalry Regiment of Havana, and the Volunteer Dragoon Regiment of Matanzas, 1765, AGI, Santo Domingo, leg. 2093; Santa Cruz, *Historia de familias cubanas*, vol. 2, 81–2, 228; vol. 3, 335–6; Nieto, *Dignidades nobiliarias*, 308–10, 411–14, 420–1, 495–9.

12. R.O., June 18, 1779, Archivo Nacional de Colombia, Milicia y Marina, vol. 17, fols. 532–4.

13. Kuethe, 'The development of the Cuban military', 698. Although import duties on slaves were abolished, the Crown attempted to regain some of its financial loss by implementing the *captación*, a head tax on slaves who had been imported duty free. R.O., October 16, 1765, AGS, Hacienda, leg. 2342.

14. *Real declaración sobre puntos esenciales de la ordenanza de milicias provinciales de España* ... (Madrid, 1767), tit. 7; 'expediente', R.C., April 15, 1771, AGI, Santo Domingo, leg. 2142; Lyle N. McAlister, *The 'fuero militar' in New Spain, 1764–1800* (Gainesville, 1957), 5–8. In Spain, only officers and sergeants enjoyed the *fuero* in civil suits.

15. The service records for the Havana–Matanzas militia in 1792 can be found in AGS, GM, leg. 7261. See also leg. 7263 for the 1797 service records of the Matanzas dragoons. For the geneology, see Santa Cruz, *Historia de familias cubanas*, vol. 3, 335–41, and Nieto, *Dignidades nobiliarias*.

16. Allan J. Kuethe, *Military reform and society in New Granada, 1773–1808* (Gainesville, 1978), chap. 5; Leon G. Campbell, *The military and society in colonial Peru, 1750–1810* (Philadelphia, 1978), 158–9. In the upland provinces of Río de la Plata, which had been affected by the Túpac Amaru rebellion, the authorities also worked to limit creole influence in the military. See Juan Beverina, *El virreinato de las provincias del Río de la Plata: su organización militar* (Buenos Aires, 1935), 288–91. Official anti-Americanism did not emerge in New Spain until the end of the decade. See Christon I. Archer, *The army in Bourbon Mexico, 1760–1810* (Albuquerque, 1977), 29–30.

17. Kuethe, 'The development of the Cuban military', 701–4.

18. James A. Lewis, 'Las damas de la Havana, el Precursor, and Francisco

Saavedra: a note on Spanish participation in the battle of Yorktown', *TAm*, 37 (1980), 90−7. The list of creditors did not contain the names of many planter families. Presumably, they were merchant-bankers.

19. Jacques A. Barbier and Herbert S. Klein, 'Revolutionary wars and public finances: the Madrid treasury, 1784−1807', *Journal of Economic History*, 41 (1981), 341−4; 'instrucción reservada', Palace, July 8, 1787, AHN, Estado, vol. 1, fols. 182−5.

20. The ministerial reorganization and policy adjustments are treated in Jacques A. Barbier, 'The culmination of the bourbon reforms, 1787−1792', *HAHR*, 57 (1977), 51−68.

21. Archer, *The army in Bourbon Mexico*, 31−2; Campbell, *The military and society*, 210−12; Kuethe, *Military reform and society*, chap. 7.

22. 'Expediente', R.O., January 12, AGS, GM, leg. 6844.

23. 'Expediente', uniform and armament fund, AGI, Santo Domingo, leg. 2160. See also Kuethe, 'The development of the Cuban military', 701−2.

24. The first serious challenge to the *fuero militar* did not come until later.

25. Proceedings, *Junta de Estado*, February 19, 1789, AHN, Estado, vol. 3. A copy of the order can be found in Ricardo Levene (ed.), *Documentos para la historia argentina*, vol. 5 (Buenos Aires, 1915), 394−9. The order extended the same privilege to Santo Domingo, Puerto Rico, and Caracas.

26. Franklin W. Knight, *Slave society in Cuba during the nineteenth century* (Madison, 1970), 11.

27. Titles since 1770 included the Marqueses del Real Socorro, Guiza, Vallellano, Casa Calvo, Prado Ameno, Arcos, and Casa Peñalver and the Condes de Lagunillas, Casa Montalvo, Casa Barreto, Santa María de Loreto, Santa Cruz de Mopox, and Zaldívar. See Nieto, *Dignidades nobiliarias*. For Las Casas' relationship to the O'Reilly family, see Las Casas to Valdés, Madrid, March 17, 1790, AGS, GM, leg. 6844.

28. 'Expediente', petition of the Conde de Buena Vista, 1792, AGS, GM, leg. 6847. Regarding proposals to expand the army, see the petition of the Conde de Casa Montalvo, 1792, AGS, GM, leg. 6848; the petition of Domingo Sánchez, 1794, AGS, GM, leg. 6852; the petition of Juan Vaillant, 1794, and the petition of Martín de Ugarte, 1795, AGS, GM, leg. 6860.

29. Service records, Havana militia, 1795, AGS, GM, leg. 7262.

30. Service records, Havana militia, 1805, AGI, Cuba, leg. 1771B.

31. See, for example, the 'expedientes' of the Conde de Lagunillas, 1789, and of Miguel Antonio de Herrera, 1791, AGS, GM, legs. 6870 and 6871.

32. 'Expediente', Lieutenant Colonel José Francisco Beitia, 1797, AGS, GM, leg. 6876.

33. 'Expediente', retirement of José Joaquín Zayas, 1787−88, and the petition of the Conde de Casa Montalvo, June 30, 1790, AGS, GM, leg. 6869 and 6844.

34. For biographical data on Gonzalo O'Farrill, see Jacobo de la Pezuela, *Diccionario geográfico, estadístico, histórico de la Isla de Cuba*, 4 (Madrid, 1863), 159−62.

35. *Reglamento para las milicias de infantería y caballería de la Isla de Cuba* ... (Madrid, 1769), chap. 2, art. 1.

36. 'Expediente', formation of the Infantry Regiment of Cuba, AGS, GM, leg. 6880.

37. Captain General Domingo Cabello to Valdés, Havana, October 13, 1789, and review report, third battalion, Infantry Regiment of Havana, 1790, AGS, GM, leg. 6881 and 6872.

38. See, for example, the petition of Tomás Morales, 1799, AGS, GM, leg. 6863.

39. Petitions of Juan Valdéz y Navarrete, 1799, and Adriano José de Armas, 1800, AGS, GM, legs. 6863 and 6867.

40. 'Expediente' on the captaincy of Manual José de la Cruz, 1800, AGI, Cuba, leg. 1587.

41. 'Expediente', petition of Joaquín de Orta y Ozeguera, 1799, AGS, GM, leg. 6863.

42. 'Expediente', 1799, AGS, GM, leg. 6863; 'expediente', petition of the Conde de Casa Bayona, 1799, AGS, GM, leg. 6878.

43. 'Expediente', petition of Anastasio Francisco de Armenteros y Zaldívar, 1797, AGS, GM, leg. 6876.

44. 'Expediente', petition of the Conde de Casa Barreto, 1799, AGS, GM, leg. 6863.

45. 'Expediente', petition of Agustín de Sotolongo, 1795, AGS, GM, leg. 6874.

46. *Reglamento para la guarnición de la Habana* ... (Madrid, 1719); *Reglamento para la guarnición de la Habana* ... (Madrid, 1754). As late as the formation of the Infantry Regiment of Cuba, the Crown attempted to restrict creoles to positions of lieutenant and below, except, of course, when considerations of purchase intervened.

47. 11 of the 102 creoles were from other colonies, mainly Florida, Mexico, and Santo Domingo.

48. Service records, army of Cuba, December 1799, AGS, GM, leg. 7264.

49. Biographical data on the Conde de Santa Cruz de Mopox can be found in Nieto, *Dignidades nobiliarias*, 496–9, 520–1, and in Santa Cruz, *Historia de familias cubanas*, vol. 1, 336–45. His early service record is with those of the Volunteer Infantry Regiment of Havana, December, 1789, AGS, GM, leg. 7260. For his early attempts to gain promotion and his appointment as inspector general, see AGS, GM, leg. 6874. For his commercial exploits, see Lampros, 'Merchant-planter cooperation', 292–9, 327–35. The best documentation on the conde's development project is in the Museo Naval, Madrid, under his name.

50. The documents do not provide fully satisfactory data because the second battalion of the Havana infantry was normally deployed in Santiago and during much of the mid-to-late 1790s a substantial portion of the infantry was deployed in Santo Domingo. Complete inspection reports are, therefore, rare. See the troop inspection reports for November, 1792 and November, 1794, AGS, GM, leg. 6882; for October, 1797, AGS, GM, leg. 6859; for August, 1805 and May, 1810, AGI, Cuba, legs. 1580 and 1583. For the troop transfers to Louisiana, see the R.O. of September 7, 1792, San Ildefonso, AGS, GM, leg. 6850 and Las Casas to the Ministry of War, March 1, 1793, AGI, Cuba, leg. 1487.

51. Kuethe, 'The development of the Cuban military', 702–03.

52. The correspondence on the fate of the two Mexican regiments can be found in AGI, Cuba, legs. 1664, 1711, and 1712.

53. Troop Reviews, Havana, May 3, 1803 and R.O., October 16, 1810, AGI, Cuba, legs. 1590 and 1730.

54. Troops were also sent to Hispaniola to prevent a possible slave uprising in Santo Domingo and for a time helped garrison Louisiana. For troop deployments and militia mobilization, see Las Casas to Minister of War Conde de Campo Alange, Havana, March 11, 1793, July 30, 1793, and November 5, 1793, AGI, Cuba, leg. 1487; Las Casas to Campo Alange, Havana, May 31, 1794, AGI, Cuba, leg. 1488; Cabello to Campo Alange, Havana, November 17, 1794, AGI, Cuba, leg. 1449; Cabello to Las Casas, Havana, September 25, 1795, AGI, Cuba, leg. 1449; Las Casas to Azanza, Havana, November 3, 1796, AGS, GM, leg. 6857; Las Casas to Conde de Campo Alange, May 7, 1793, AGS, GM, leg. 6850; Troop Report, Havana, November 10, 1794, AGS, GM, leg. 6882; and Las Casas to Campo Alange, Havana, January 17, 1795, AGS, GM, leg. 6852.

55. Las Casas to Campo Alange, Havana, January 17, 1795, and March 3, 1796, AGS, GM, legs. 6853 and 6855.

56. Cabello to Las Casas, Havana, February 21, 1794, AGI, Cuba, leg. 1449.
57. The service records for militia mobilization during the French War can be found in AGI, Cuba, legs. 1487–88, 1449; the First British War, AGI, Cuba, legs. 1526, 1576–79, 1587–89, and 1711; for the Second British War, AGI, Cuba, legs. 1580–82 and 1667.
58. New Spain, where cooperation was rare and chaos reigned offers a contrasting example, See Archer, *The army in bourbon Mexico*.
59. R.O., Aranjuez, May 23, 1791, AGS, GM. leg. 6845.
60. Ylincheta to the Marqués de Bajamar, Havana, November 11, 1791, AGI, Santo Domingo, leg. 2142. Ylincheta also advanced jurisdictional challenges at the local level. AGI, Cuba, leg. 1460.
61. 'Expediente', statement of Brigadier Domingo Cabello, 1794–5, AGS, GM, leg. 6854.
62. The 'expediente' for this case can be found in AGI, Santo Domingo, leg. 2142 and AGS, GM, leg. 6865.
63. Kuethe, *Military reform and society*, 162.
64. The militia response may be found in AGI, Cuba, leg. 1486.
65. 'Expediente', the Marqués del Real Socorro, 1789–96, AGS, GM, leg. 6856.
66. See the previously cited 'expediente' in AGI, Santo Domingo, leg. 2142.
67. See 'expediente', AGI, Santo Domingo, leg. 2142.
68. A copy can be found in José María Zamora y Coronado (comp.), *Biblioteca de legislación ultramarina* ... (Madrid, 1845), vol. 3, 326.
69. 'Expediente', marriage authorization for José Ylincheta and Gabriela O'Farrill, 1803, AGI, Ultramar, leg. 12. Ylincheta was eventually promoted to *oidor* of the Guatemalan audiencia. See also, Santa Cruz, *Historia de familias cubanas*, vol. 3, 341.
70. Although merchants and the sugoracracy shared much common ground, especially those merchants connected to planter families, Cádiz-oriented interests were not always inclined toward the pursuit of neutral trade. Lampros, 'Merchant-planter cooperation', chaps. 2, 7–8.
71. Lampros, 'Merchant-planter cooperation', 58–68.

Chapter nine

1. Despite the importance of trade in Venezuelan history, monographic works on the subject are scarce. The only one is by Eduardo Arcila Farías, *Comercio entre Venezuela y México en los siglos XVII y XVIII* (Mexico, 1950). Important aspects of foreign commerce are analyzed in general works on the Venezuelan economy. The outstanding include Eduardo Arcila Farías, *Economía colonial de Venezuela*, 2nd edn, (2 vols., Caracas, 1973); Tomás Polanco Martínez, *Esbozo sobre historia económica venezolana* (2 vols., Madrid, 1960); Antonio Arellano Moreno, *Orígenes de la economía venezolana* (Caracas, 1973). Important information on the subject of trade also exists in the studies on the consulado of Caracas, including the following: Eduardo Arcila Farías, *El Real Consulado de Caracas* (Caracas, 1957); Mercedes M. Alvarez F., *El tribunal del Real Consulado de Caracas* (2 vols., Caracas, 1967); Manuel Nunes Díaz, *El Real Consulado de Caracas (1793–1810)*, Fuentes para la historia colonial de Venezuela, 106 (Caracas, 1971); Humberto Tandron, *El Real Consulado de Caracas y el comercio exterior de Venezuela* (Caracas, 1976).
2. Arcila Farías clearly defines this aspect in his *Comercio entre Venezuela y México*, 166: 'Only the cacao trade with New Spain, after 1622, brought Venezuela sufficient specie to permit her monetary system to function, elevating her from the characteristically primitive economy'.

3. This theme has been treated recently in Salvador Arregui, 'El Real Consulado de la Habana, 1794–1830' (Ph.D. diss., Universidad de Murcia, 1982).

4. Lombardi's census for the ecclesiastical province of Caracas shows 427,205 inhabitants. See John Lombardi, *People and places in colonial Venezuela* (Bloomington, 1976). Humboldt calculated the total population of Venezuela at 900,000 and DePons at 728,000.

5. Trade volume by port in Venezuela at the end of the eighteenth century was as follows: La Guaira 87%, Cumaná 5%, Maracaibo 4%, and Guayana 4%. See Núnes Díaz, *El Real Consulado*, 340.

6. The percentages for La Guaira and Cabello come from the *avería accounts in the two ports, which can be found in the Caracas, leg. 637C for 1807, leg. 637 for 1808, leg. 638 for 1809 and 1811, leg. 638B for 1810, leg. 639 for 1812, and in the AGNC, Intendencia de Ejército y Real Hacienda, January 1813.*

7. It is curious that on the same dates Miranda likewise negotiated Venezuelan free trade with Cochrane on board the *Northumberland*. In addition, the precursor conceded a 10% reduction of duties to England as a most favored nation. See Jules Mancini, *Bolívar* (Bogotá, 1970), 212.

8. Report of Intendant Juan Vicente de Arce, November 29, 1808, AGI, Caracas, leg. 804.

9. This documentation is published in *Materiales para el estudio de la cuestión agraria en Venezuela (1800–1830)* (Caracas, 1964), vol. 1.

10. *Epistolario de la I República*, Biblioteca de la Academia Nacional de la Historia, vol. 35, sesquicentennial of Independence (Caracas, 1960), tomo 1, 242.

11. This figure comes from the ledgers of the port of La Guaira and the legajos of the AGI cited in note 6.

12. Manuel Lucena Salmoral, 'Características del comercio entre La Guaira y los puertos andaluces durante la revolución caraqueña', in *Primeras Jornadas de Andalucía y América* (La Rábida, 1981), vol. 1, 149–66.

13. The *Dolores* left La Guaira in November 1809 for Philadelphia, captained by Domingo Brito, and the brig *Venezuela* sailed in the same month and year for Norfolk under the command of Captain Jaime Juanico y Sans. The latter made various voyages to the United States.

14. Among these ships were the schooner *Botón de Rosa*, which arrived at La Guaira coming from Spain, after effecting a stopover in Philadelphia (May 1808); the brig *Nuestra Señora del Pilar*, captained by José Martínez Bandujo, which arrived at La Guaira (July 1810) coming from Norfolk; and the brig *General Monteverde*, which sailed from La Guaira for New York (December 1812) captained by Francisco Pérez.

15. AGNC, Intendencia de Ejército y Real Hacienda, march 1812.

16. AGI, Caracas, leg. 899.

17. AGI, Caracas, leg. 899.

18. AGI, Caracas, leg. 899.

19. AGI, Indif., leg. 2463.

20. Luis de Onís, *Memoria sobre las negociaciones entre los Estados Unidos de América, que dieron motivo al tratado de 1819* (Madrid, 1820), 42.

21. Onís, *Memoria*.

22. Stulz wrote: 'The Americans had managed to channel toward their country the traffic between Europe, the States, and the West Indies and serve as intermediaries in the inter-European trade, given the fact that the European nations that had remained out of the struggle could not view favorably a powerful belligerent meddling in their commercial affairs. In North America, farmers, merchants, and ship owners realized fat profits ...' Josef Stulz, *Historia de los Estados Unidos de América* (Barcelona, 1944), 195.

23. Morison y Comager affirmed: 'But the British courts became aware that

Americans were landing French colonial produce in their own ports in bond, reloading it in time to escape customs duty, and then taking it to a European port under Napoleon's control'. Samuel Eliot Morison and Henry Steele Commager, *Historia de los Estados Unidos de Norteamérica* (Mexico, 1951), 391–2.

24. Max Beloff indicated that when the Anglo-French war resumed in 1803, United States merchants enjoyed a time of prosperity 'and especially their re-exports of colonial produce, rapidly grew', Beloff, *Thomas Jefferson and American democracy* (New York, 1965), 177.

25. AGI, Caracas, leg. 899.

26. AGI, Caracas, leg. 899.

27. AGI, Indif., leg. 2463.

28. AGNC, Intendencia de Ejército y Real Hacienda, March 1812.

29. Onís, *Memoria*, 41–2.

30. Jacques Godechot, *Europa y América en la época napoleónica* (Barcelona, 1969), 94.

31. Stulz, *Historia*, 195.

32. José de Limonta, *Libro de la razón general de la Real Hacienda del Departamento de Caracas*, Fuentes para la historia colonial de Venezuela, 61 (Caracas, 1962), 328.

33. In his report to the Crown of June 25, 1808, he explained 'We are at war with the English. They have many possessions nearby that are the repository for contraband and for projects and subversive maxims against our government. The North Americans have harmonious connections and interests with them in their conduct and commerce; the Danish and Dutch possessions are the only purely mercantile establishments, populated by all sorts of people ...', concluding that 'the major portion of the funds either are English or are linked to them'. AGNC, Gobierno y Capitanía General, tomo 168, fol. 108.

34. Tandron, *El Real Consulado*, 179–80.

35. The ship, according to Arce, did not possess certification for its cargo from the Spanish consul in Baltimore, for which cause it was required to deposit a bond. The same problem and reaction also arose with later ships, which did not retrieve their bonds until the situation was rectified. AGI, Caracas, leg. 519.

36. The cargoes of the ships of Craig and Luke were highly valuable. For example, the United States frigate *Olive* (of Craig) carried merchandise worth 559,812 pesos; the frigate *Margaret* (Craig), 623,412 pesos; the brig *Endymion* (Craig) 8,000 ounces of gold braid; the frigate *Active* (Craig) 83,857 pesos; and the schooner *Hope* (Luke) 187,197 pesos, AGI, Caracas, leg. 519.

37. Tandron, *El Real Consulado*, 184.

38. AGI, Caracas, leg. 899.

39. Tandron, *El Real Consulado*, 182.

40. Tandron, *El Real Consulado*, 183.

41. On June 15, 1806, ten days before the decision taken in Caracas by the Spanish authorities, the Crown also authorized trade with ships from neutral nations for the duration of the war with Great Britain. AGI, Indif., leg. 2463.

42. Tandron, *El Real Consulado*, 187.

43. Consulado report, February 19, 1807, AGI, Caracas, leg. 921.

44. In the protest, the *síndico's* report was submitted in which he commented that 'so as not to endure the terms that Sarmiento (representative of Craig) would impose on them, neutrals stayed away from the ports, leaving in his hands all the commerce that would result if our produce fell into the same morass that it was in before freedom of commerce, and we would have to cover our necessities at the price that he would wish to exact, especially for bread, just when the harvest of corn, which is the sustenance of the poor, has failed ...' AGI, Caracas, leg. 921.

45. Report of Arce, March 14, 1809, AGI, Caracas, leg. 489.

46. Tandron, *El Real Consulado*, 191.

47. Report of Arce, November 29, 1808, AGI, Caracas, leg. 804.

48. Richard Hofstadter, for example, wrote: 'Jefferson himself was both a fierce patriot and a sincere pacifist. During the Napoleonic Wars, when England and France began to prey upon American commerce, he tried to retaliate by a pacifistic policy of economic coercion. In December 1807 Congress passed his drastic Embargo Act which simply confined American ships to port. His aim was to bring both sides to terms by withholding food and other supplies'. See Hofstadter, *La tradición política americana* (Barcelona, 1969), 54−5.

49. Manuel Lucena Salmoral, 'El comercio de los Estados Unidos con España e Hispanoamérica a comienzos de la presidencia de Madison: 1809', in *Actas del Congreso de Historia de los Estados Unidos* (Madrid, 1978), 179.

50. Henry William Elson, *Estados Unidos de América* (Barcelona, 1956), 265.

51. AGI, Caracas, leg. 637−8.

52. Report of Intendant Basadre, August 17, 1809, AGI, Caracas, leg. 917.

53. See Lucena Salmoral, 'El comercio'.

54. Benjamin A. Frankel, *Venezuela y los Estados Unidos: 1810−1888* (Caracas, 1977), 17.

55. Frankel, *Venezuela*.

56. His report was dated August 21, 1811. Frankel, *Venezuela*, 22.

57. President Madison and his wife invited Orea to a dinner on November 15, 1811, during the course of which Madison stated that '... the government and the people look with sympathy on the cause of the Hispanic American patriots. But the international situation is unfavorable! The war between Napoleon and the allies is at this moment coming to a head. And incidents between English and American vessels are becoming more frequent and serious'. Frankel, *Venezuela*, 21.

58. In the instructions of the State Department to Commissioner Scott, it was specified on May 14, 1812, that 'The United States is inclined to favor independence and instructions have been given in Paris, St. Petersburgh and London to make known that the United States takes an interest in their independence'. Frankel, *Venezuela*, 23.

59. Frankel, *Venezuela*, 24.

Chapter ten

1. R.O. to Martín Navarro, San Lorenzo, October 29, 1781, AGI, Cuba, leg. 83.

2. Francisco Rendón to José de Gálvez, Philadelphia, June 15, 1783, AGI, Santo Domingo, leg. 2597.

3. Navarro to Gálvez, New Orleans, March 12, 1784, AGI, Cuba, leg. 633, and AHN, Estado, leg. 3885.

4. A. González Enciso, 'España y USA en el siglo XVIII: crecimiento industrial comparado y relaciones comerciales', University of Vallodolid, *Estudios y documentos*, 39 (Valladolid, 1979).

5. For the trade with French markets during these years, see my unpublished dissertation, 'El comercio exterior de Luisiana, 1775−1783' (University of Zaragoza, 1977).

6. For commerce through the Ohio, 1783−93, the noteworthy works include Arthur P. Whitaker, *The Spanish American frontier, 1783−1795* (Boston, 1927) and Lawrence Kinnaird (ed.), *Spain in the Mississippi Valley, 1765−1794* (3 pts., Washington, 1946).

7. Miró to Antonio de Valdés, New Orleans, April 1, 1788, AGI, Cuba, leg. 2368 and Santo Domingo, leg. 2667.

8. Gardoqui to Miró, Philadelphia, 1787, AGI, Cuba, leg. 104A.

9. Miró to Valdés, New Orleans, October 25, 1787, AGI, Santo Domingo, leg. 2657.

10. Memorial of the deputy *síndico*, August 31, 1787, AGI, Santo Domingo, leg. 2667.

11. By R.O. November 15, 1786, the Crown instructed the intendant to prevent the entrance of flour from the French islands that Anglo-Americans had clandestinely brought to them. AGI, Cuba, leg. 2317A.

12. Michael O'Connor to Nicholas Low and Company, October 31, and November 24, 1783, in the Robert Smith and Nicholas Low Papers, 1782–1811 (Tulane University Library, Manuscript Division, 1857).

13. This data was compiled from the treasury account books found in AGI, Cuba, legs. 498, 499, 500, 637, 667, and 2320.

14. Treasury account book, 1788, AGI, Cuba, leg. 498.

15. See note 7.

16. For the revolution of 1768, see Vicente Rodríguez Casado, *Primeros años de dominación española en la Luisiana* (Madrid, 1942); Villiers du Terrage, *Les dernieres annés de La Louisiane francaise* (Paris, 1906); John Preston Moore, *Revolt in Louisiana: the Hispanic occupation, 1766–1770* (Baton Rouge, 1976).

17. Barón de Carondelet to Gardoqui, New Orleans, May 16, 1793, AGI, Santo Domingo, leg. 2669. On April 30, he gave instructions to this effect to Antonio de Hoa. AGI, Cuba, leg. 2343.

18. Carondelet to Jaudenes y Viar, New Orleans, August 13, 1793, AGI, Cuba, leg. 104A.

19. R.O., September 27, 1793, AGI, Santo Domingo, leg. 2634.

20. Carondelet to Gardoqui, New Orleans, March 27, 1794, AGI, Santo Domingo, leg. 2634.

21. Treasury account books, AGI, Cuba, legs. 513, 620 and 2318A. The number of ships that arrived in New Orleans from the United States during 1796 differs in the sources consulted. According to the treasury account book, AGI, Cuba, leg. 620, there were 21 ships (Philadelphia 6, New York 11, Charleston 2, Baltimore 2), but according to the book for registered merchandise, AGI Cuba, leg. 620, there were 28 (Philadelphia 6, New York 15, Charleston 5, and Baltimore 2).

22. Treasury account book, 1797, AGI, Cuba, leg. 654.

23. On this question, see my article 'New Orleans: el derecho de depósito y su problemática' (Zaragoza, 1978).

24. Morales to Antonio de Hoa, New Orleans, June 25, 1798, AGI, Cuba, leg. 635.

25. Treasury account books, AGI, Cuba, legs. 503, 654 and 676. The data recorded on the number of ships entering and leaving New Orleans during these years do not tally with those contained in John Garretson Clark, *New Orleans, 1718–1812: an economic history* (Baton Rouge, 1970), 228*ff.* and in Arthur P. Whitaker, *The Mississippi question* (New York, 1934), 135*ff.*

26. See note 23.

27. Treasury account book, 1803, AGI, Cuba, leg. 503.

28. These data come from the registry books for merchandise entering and leaving New Orleans. AGI, Cuba, legs. 519B, 540, 651, 654, 662, 667, 2318A, 2319 and 2310.

Index